"President Thomas-Felix has been able to combine her extensive practical and rich experience at the Industrial Court for so many years, and her well-known legal expertise, to produce a book that is so much needed, not just for Trinidad and Tobago but the entire region. This is a truly timely and treasured text. It's of immense practical value to all involved in the field of industrial relations, including lawyers, trade unionists, employers, teachers, researchers...right across the region. A must read!"

RUGGLES FERGUSON
President
Organisation of Commonwealth Caribbean Bar Associations

"President Deborah Thomas-Felix, in her relatively short time at the helm of the Industrial Court, has led the way in bringing about much needed innovation and modernisation to an institution that is so critical to ensuring industrial relations stability in Trinidad and Tobago. Her Honour has applied her impressive combination of knowledge, skills and experience to breathe new life into the Court and to enhance its reputation and relevance to industrial relations practitioners on all sides of civil society. Her book will undoubtedly serve as an essential guide for all in the field for years to come."

GERARD EMILE PINARD
CEO
Zatopek Solutions Inc., Management Consultants

"President Thomas-Felix has elevated the science of Industrial Relations to a level of commonsense, simplicity and practicality. This book is a "must read" by all who are practitioners in the field of industrial relations, conciliation, dispute resolution, labour leaders, HR and IR practitioners and students of labour studies. Books like these are of value and, may I say, come around once in a lifetime. The book is developed around specific concepts and principles related to Management Prerogative, Layoff, Dismissals, Retrenchment, Labour Supply Contracts, among others. The Honourable President, in her usual style, has simplified the law on many of the complicated IR and HR issues that have baffled some of the best practitioners in industrial relations. She has demonstrated that experience is truly a quality without limits in any real sense. I therefore wish to publicly thank the Honourable President for conceptualising the need for such a relevant and timely book. It is a breath of fresh air in this COVID-19 pandemic period. Honourable President, thank you for sharing your Intellectual Capacity and labour of love to the Caribbean and beyond. I fully endorse this book as a must to all who seek to understand industrial relations. Thank you! Thank you! Your Honour for this treasure and timely work of art."

Michael Annisette
General Secretary
The Caribbean Congress of Labour

Labour Law in the Commonwealth Caribbean

Labour Law in the Commonwealth Caribbean

The Practice of Good Industrial Relations in the 21st Century

Deborah Thomas-Felix

Labour Law in the Commonwealth Caribbean

Written and Published by Deborah Thomas-Felix
8 Flamboyant Avenue
Paxvale, Santa Cruz
Trinidad and Tobago, West Indies
dtfceo2021@gmail.com
www.trendsinlabourlaw.com
Tel.: 1-868-467-8309

ISBN: 978-976-96584-0-0
FIRST EDITION

Cover image by Monil Andharia for Unsplash
Cover design by Lyle Rodriguez for Studio7 Graphics
Author photograph by Garth Murrell for PIPS-Personal Image Photo Studio
Layout by Paria Publishing Co. Ltd.
Printed and bound by Trinidad and Tobago Printing Works Ltd, Port of Spain, Trinidad and Tobago

Dedicated to my parents

Charles Thomas (deceased)
and
Bernadette Thomas

CONTENTS

Table of Cases

Alleyne, Arthur and Hunte Ltd v Griffith (1992) WIR 53.

Allison v Bega Valley Council 1995 63 IR 68.

Antigua Village Condo Corporation v Watt AG 1994 CA 2.

Application No. 2 of 1998 Steel Workers' Union of Trinidad and Tobago and Caribbean Ispat Limited / Civil Appeal No. 211 of 2009 ArcelorMittal Point Lisas Limited (formerly Caribbean Ispat Limited) and Steel Workers' Union of Trinidad and Tobago / Privy Council Appeal No. 0087 of 2013 ArcelorMittal Point Lisas Limited v Steel Workers' Union of Trinidad and Tobago [2015] UKPC 36.

Bailey v BP Oil (Kent Refinery) Ltd [1980] ICR 642.

BBC v Ioannou [1975] 2 All ER 999.

Bentley Engineering Co. v Mistry [1979] ICR 47.

BL Cars Ltd. vs. Lewis an Employment Appeal Tribunal of England [1983] IRLR 58.

Braganza v BP Shipping Ltd [2015] UKSC 17, [2015] IRLR 487.

British Home Stores Ltd v Burchell [1978] [IRLR] 379.

Bryden & Co. v C. Thomas IRLA Vol.5 No. 6.

Cable & Wireless (WI) Ltd v Hill and Others (1982) WIR 30.

Cable and Wireless plc v Muscat (2006) IRLR 354.

Cantor Fitzgerald International v Callaghan and ORS, [1999] IRLR 234.

Caroni (1975) Limited v Association of Technical Administrative Supervisory Staff (2002) 67 WIR 223 / TD No. 351 of 1997 Application A6 of 1997 Association of Technical Administrative Supervisory Staff and Caroni (1975) Limited.

Catamaran Cruisers Ltd v Williams [1994] IRLR 386 EAT.

Ceccol v Ontario Gymnastic Federation 2001 CANLII 8589 (ON, CA).

Charles Lett & Co. Ltd v A.E.C.T Howard [1976] IRLR 248.

Civil Appeal No. 4 of 2003 The Epicurean Ltd v Medeline Taylor.

Civil Appeal No. 9 of 1995 Bank Employees Union v Republic Bank Ltd. / I.C.A. No. 8 of 1995 Bank Employees Union and Republic Bank Ltd.

Civil Appeal No. 13 of 1997 Duncan v Attorney General decided 8th December, 1977 (unreported).

Civil Appeal No. 23 of 1990 Charles Hunte and Life of Barbados.

Civil Appeal No. 29 of 2004 Jewellers Warehouse v Cecile Norde.

Civil Appeal No. 37 of 2000 Claude Albert and Alstons Building Enterprise Limited.

Civil Appeal No. 53 of 1966 Trinidad Bakeries Limited and Union of Foods, Hotels, Beverages and Allied Workers.

Civil Appeal No. 81 of 1978 Flavourite Foods Ltd. and Oilfields Workers' Trade Union.

Civil Appeal No. 83 of 2002 Caribbean Development Company Limited and National Union of Government and Federated Workers.

Claim No. BVIHCV2010/0049 Ian Charles and The Board of Governors of the H. Lavity Stoutt Community College.

Commercial Finance Co Ltd (in liquidation) v Ramsingh Mahabir (1994) 45 WIR 447, Privy Council Appeal No. 27 of 1993 [1994] UKPC 30.

Complaint No. GSD – IRO 031 of 2015 Steel Workers' Union of Trinidad and Tobago and ArcelorMittal Point Lisas Limited.

Complaint No. GSD-IRO 36 of 2018 Oilfields Workers' Trade Union and Trinidad Cement Limited.

Courtaulds Northern Textile Ltd. v Andrew [1979] IRLR 84.

Dacas v Brooks Street Bureau [2004] ICR 1437.

Derby City Council v Marshall [1979] IRLR 261.

Dixon v BBC [1979] QB 546, [1979] ICR 281, [1979] IRLR 114, CA

ESD No. 371 of 2011 Oilfields Workers' Trade Union and Nestle Trinidad and Tobago Limited.

GSD-MPD No. 003 of 2012 Oilfields Workers' Trade Union and Ministry of Education and the Chief Personnel Officer.

Grundy (Teddington) Ltd v Plumier (1983) ICR 367.

Heatons Transport (St Helens) Limited v Transport and General Workers' Union and other (1973) A.C. 15.

I.C.A. No. 9 of 1986 Transport and Industrial Workers' Union and Consolidated Appliances Limited.

I.I.A. No. 25 of 1978 John Dickinson & Co. Ltd and Transport and Industrial Workers' Union.

IRO Nos. 23 & 24 of 1987 between Transport and Industrial Workers' Union and Bata Trinidad and Tobago Limited.

Lewis v Motorworld Garages Ltd (1985) IRLR 465.

John v Rees 1969 2 All ER 274.

Malik v Bank of Credit and Commerce International SA [1997] 3 All ER 1.

Market Investigation Limited v Minister of Social Security (1969) 3 All ER 732.

Neely v Credit Suisse Trust Ltd BS 2009 SC 12.

Norwest Holst Group Administration Ltd. v Harrison [1984] IRLR 419 EAT.

Omilaju v Waltham Forest London Borough Counsel (2004) EWCA Civ 1493.

Patterson vs Messrs. Bracketts (1977) IRLR 137.

Performing Right Society v Mitchell and Booker Ltd [1924] 1 KB 762.

Pillinger v Manchester Area Health Authority [1979] IRLR 430 EAT.

Privy Council Appeal No. 69 of 2003 Jamaica Flour Mills Ltd v The Industrial Disputes Tribunal and National Workers Union [2005] UKPC 16.

Privy Council Appeal No. 0081 of 2015 between Chief Personnel Officer v Amalgamated Workers Union [2020] UKPC 17 / Civil Appeal No. P 285 of 2012 between Chief Personnel Officer and the National Union of Government and Federated Workers / TD No. 25

of 2008 The Amalgamated Workers Union and the Chief Personnel Officer.

Privy Council in Jupiter General Insurance Co. Ltd. v Ardeships Bomanji 1937 3 All ER 67, Privy Council Appeal No. 44 of 1936 [1937] UKPC 51.

Ready Mixed Concrete (South East) Limited v Minister of Pensions and National Insurance (1968) 1 All ER.

Reference No. 1 of 2009: Donna Christopher and Geotech Company Limited.

Reference No. 4 of 2004: Jennifer Geran and Dream Company Ltd (K-Club Barbuda).

Reference No. 7 of 2009: Edwin Brown and Kings Casino Limited the Hon. Philip A. Pilgrim.

Reference No. 9 of 2007: Colet Acham and Caribbean Star Airlines Ltd.

Reference No. 9 of 2008: Hyacinth Pestaina and Dickenson Bay Management Ltd (DBA Sandals Antigua).

Reference No. 11 of 2005: Caryle Anthony and BBR Sportive Ltd Antigua and Barbuda Industrial Court.

Reference No. 25 of 2005: Eural Baptiste and Bank of Nova Scotia.

Reference Nos. 27 and 40 of 1996 Carlene Vigo and David Jarvis v Swiss American National.

Reference No. 35 of 2002 Alexander Hughes v Antigua Brewery Limited.

RF Hill Limited v Mooney [1981] IRLR 258.

RSBD No. 04 of 2017 Government Industrial and General Workers Union and Laughlin & De Gannes Limited.

RSBD No. 10 of 2008 Seamen and Waterfront Workers Trade Union and West Indian Tobacco Company Limited.

RSBD No. 22 of 2009 National Workers Union and Kee- Chanona Limited.

Sadler v Henlock (1) 4 E & B, 570.

Security and Facilities Division v Hayes (2001) IRLR 81 C.A.

Sheffield v Oxford Controls Company Limited [1979] IRLR 133.

Sheet Metal Components Ltd. v Plumridge & ors. (1974) I.C.R. 373.

Shield's Furniture Ltd. v Goff (1973) ICR 187.

Sillifant v Powell Duffryn Timber Ltd. (1983) IRLR 91.

Simmonds v Dowty Seals Ltd [1978] IRLR 211 EAT.

Stevenson Jordan and Harrison Ltd v Macdonald and Evans [1952] 1 T.L.R. 101.

TD No. 2 of 1965 The Marketing Board and the Civil Service Association.

TD No. 2 of 1992 Caroni (1975) Limited and All Trinidad Sugar and General Workers' Trade Union.

TD No. 2 of 2001 Banking, Insurance and General Workers Union and Hindu Credit Union Co-operative Society Limited.

TD No. 3 of 2001 Oilfields Workers' Trade Union and Trinidad and Tobago National Petroleum Company Limited.

TD No. 4 of 1991 Transport and Industrial Workers' Union and Trinidad Distributors Limited.

TD No. 12 of 1994 Oilfields Workers' Trade Union and Trinmar Limited.

TD No. 15 of 2000 Bank and General Workers' Union and Public Service Association of Trinidad and Tobago.

TD Nos. 15-19 of 2009 (S) Oilfields Workers' Trade Union and Offshore Atlantic Limited.

TD 15A of 1982 and TD 15B of 1982 Trinidad & Tobago Electricity Commission and Oilfields Workers' Trade Union.

TD No. 20 of 1990 American Stores Limited and Union of Commercial and Industrial Workers.

TD No. 21 of 2008 Banking, Insurance and General Workers Union and Fibis Wireless Limited trading as Wireless and Mobility Solutions (WAMS).

TD No. 21 of 2015 Banking, Insurance and General Workers Union and Tobago House of Assembly.

TD Nos. 23 and 24 of 1990 Transport and Industrial Workers' Union and Public Transport Service Corporation.

ESD TD No. 24 of 2005 Oilfields Workers' Trade Union and Trinidad and Tobago Electricity Commission.

TD No. 27 of 2011 Oilfields Workers' Trade Union and Caribbean Packaging Industries.

TD No. 43 of 2001 Oilfields Workers' Trade Union and Trinidad and Tobago National Petroleum Company Limited.

TD No. 47 of 2003 The Association of Technical, Administrative and Supervisory Staff and Grace Kennedy (Trinidad and Tobago) Limited.

TD Nos. 48 and 188 of 2015 Oilfields Workers' Trade Union and University of Trinidad and Tobago Limited.

TD No. 50 of 1978 Sissons Paints (W.I.) Limited and Transport and Industrial Workers' Union.

ESD TD No. 52 of 2013 Banking, Insurance and General Workers Union and North- West Regional Health Authority.

ESD TD No. 55 of 2006 Communication Workers' Union and Telecommunications Services of Trinidad and Tobago.

TD No. 72 of 2000 Union of Commercial and Industrial Workers and El Dorado Consumers Co-operative Society Limited.

TD No. 74 of 1997 Bank and General Workers' Union and Trinidad Express Newspaper Limited.

TD 98 of 1997 Barclays Bank and Barclays Employees Union.

TD No. 90 of 1995 All Trinidad Sugar and General Workers' Trade Union and Seereeram Brothers Limited.

TD No. 90 of 2001 Banking, Insurance and General Workers Union and Air Canada.

TD No. 90 of 2004 All Trinidad Sugar and General Workers' Trade Union and Fen Mohammed Stores Limited.

TD No. 93 of 2002 Oilfields Workers' Trade Union and PCS Nitrogen.

TD No. 93 of 2008 Banking, Insurance and General Workers Union and Kemicals Worldwide (T&T) Limited.

TD No. 94 of 1982 and I.I.A. No. 22 of 1982 Beatrix Limited and Union of Commercial and Industrial Workers.

TD No. 97 of 2003 Transport and Industrial Workers' Union and National Maintenance Training and Security Company Limited.

TD No. 101 of 1992 Communication Workers' Union v. Busy Business Systems and Equipment Limited.

TD No. 105A of 1969 Halliburton Tucker Limited and Oilfields Workers' Trade Union.

TD No. 106 of 2014(S) All Trinidad General Workers' Trade Union and Ace Contractors Limited.

TD No. 108 of 2009 National Union of Domestic Employees and Courts (Trinidad) Limited.

TD No. 110 of 2003 Oilfields Workers' Trade Union and Schlumberger Trinidad Incorporated.

TD No. 114 and 115 of 2004 Communication Workers' Union and Mega Brite Industries Limited.

TD No. 116 of 1998 Communication Workers' Union and Snooker World Recreation Club.

TD No. 119 of 1993 Seamen and Waterfront Workers Trade Union and Port Authority of Trinidad and Tobago.

TD No. 125 of 1979 Prison Officers Association of Trinidad and Tobago and Ship Builders, Ship Repairers and Allied Workers Trade Union.

TD No. 131 of 2005 Transport and Industrial Workers' Union and Public Transport Service Corporation.

TD. No. 140 of 1997 Bank and General Workers' Union and Home Mortgage Bank.

TD No. 148 of 2003 Transport and Industrial Workers' Union and National Maintenance Training and Security Limited.

TD No. 163 of 2005 Communication Workers' Union and Front Row Limited.

TD No. 181 of 2004 Banking, Insurance and General Workers Union and Maraj and Sons Limited.

TD No. 182 of 2007 National Union of Domestic Employees and Columbia Marketing and Contracting Company (Caribbean) Ltd.

TD No. 187 of 2002, Transport and Industrial Workers' Union and Public Transport Service Corporation.

TD No. 196 of 1967 Southern Drilling Contractors Limited and Oilfields Workers' Trade Union.

TD No. 203 of 2004 National Union of Government and Federated Workers and Half Moon Belle and La Belle Creole Limited.

TD No. 204 of 2004 Westend Sawmill and Lumber Yard and National Union of Government and Federated Workers.

TD No. 205 of 2007 Transport and Industrial Workers' Union and Furness Employment Limited.

TD No. 216 of 2001 Banking, Insurance and General Workers Union and Royal Bank of Trinidad and Tobago.

TD No. 226 of 1976 Trinidad Lake Asphalt Company Ltd and Contractors and General Workers Trade Union.

TD No. 227 of 2001 National Union of Government and Federated Workers and Caribbean Development Company Limited.

TD No. 227 of 2012 between Communication Workers' Union and Mr. Cooper, Permanent Secretary to the Prime Minister, Office of the Prime Minister.

TD Nos. 244 & 245 of 2004 Banking, Insurance and General Workers Union and Public Services Association.

TD No. 250 of 2012 Public Services Association of Trinidad and Tobago and Housing Development Corporation.

TD No. 252 of 2007 Communication Workers' Union and Varona Limited trading as Club de Vegas.

TD No. 262 of 2004 Toucan Inn & Bonkers Restaurant and Bar and Oilfields Workers' Trade Union.

TD No. 267 of 2010 Communication Workers' Union and Home Construction Limited.

TD No. 275 of 2009 Transport & Industrial Workers' Union and Penta Paints Caribbean Limited.

TD No. 277 of 2004 National Union of Government and Federated Workers and N.P. Service Station.

TD No. 303 of 2002 Banking, Insurance and General Workers Union and Cariflex Limited.

TD No. 309 of 2004 National Union of Government and Federated Workers and Battimamzelle Restaurant.

TD No. 314 of 2004 Communication Workers' Union and Maibrol Insurance Brokers Limited.

TD No. 315 of 2002 Contractors and General Workers Trade Union and National Quarries Company Limited.

TD No. 331 of 2013 and TD No. 57 of 2008 (consolidated) Contractor and General Workers Trade Union and Tucker Energy Services Limited.

TD Nos. 345 and 346 of 2013 Communication Workers' Union and Servisair Trinidad and Tobago Limited.

TD No. 348 of 2014 Banking, Insurance and General Workers Union and Royal Bank Trinidad and Tobago Limited.

TD No. 353 of 2009 Government Industrial and General Workers Union and Island Club Casino Limited.

TD No. 365 of 2014 National Union of Domestic Employees and Superstore Limited.

TD No. 377 of 2010 National Workers Union and Servisair of Trinidad and Tobago.

TD No. 384 of 2010 Oilfields Workers' Trade Union and Chief Personnel Officer and Ministry of Education.

TD No. 509 of 2017 Banking, Insurance and General Workers Union and Smith Robertson and Company Limited.

TD No. 717 of 2013 and IRO 23 of 2013 (Consolidated) Trinidad and Tobago National Petroleum Marketing Company Limited and Oilfields Workers' Trade Union / Civil Appeal No. P 306 of 2014 between Trinidad and Tobago National Petroleum Marketing Co. Ltd. and Oilfields Workers' Trade Union.

Terry v East Sussex County Council [1976] ICR 536.

UCATT v Brain (1981) IRLR 225.

Wadham Stringer Commercials (London) Ltd and Wadham Stringer Vehicles Ltd. v Brown [1983] IRLR 46.EAT.

Walker v Josiah Wedgwood & Sons Ltd. [1978] ICR 744 EAT.

Waithe v Caribbean Confection Co. (2004) 67 WIR 41.

Western Excavating (ECC) Limited v Sharp [1978] QB 761, [1978] IRLR 27.

WHPT Housing Association Ltd. v Secretary of State for Social Services (1981) ICR 737.

Woods v W. M. Car Services (Peterborough) Ltd. [1981] IRLR 347.

Young and Woods Limited v West [1980] IRLR 201 CA.

Foreword

This publication deals with subjects that are inherently germane to industrial relations. They are also critical for developing public policies to address the labour-related aspects of national development agendas as well as the labour market impacts of current and future crises that may emerge from various sources.

The author, Her Honour Mrs Deborah Thomas-Felix, President of the Industrial Court of Trinidad and Tobago, was in the early stages of developing the outline for a publication on Industrial Relations when the Coronavirus disease (COVID-19) pandemic was declared by the World Health Organization on 11th March, 2020. Around the world, and locally, public health regulations and related policies instituted with the aim of stemming the spread of infection, were giving rise to concern and questions about their impacts on the operations and survival of enterprises, jobs and incomes.

In the light of those developments, the author decided to revisit the topics, structure and timeframe for completing the planned publication. She retained 'layoffs', 'redundancies' and 'employment contracts', which were already in the original plan and given their heightened salience in the context of the pandemic. Other topics of widespread interest were selected to complement them.

This publication focuses on seven subjects. After the Introduction, there is a paper by Dr Leighton Jackson on the history of the Industrial Court of Trinidad and Tobago - the first Industrial Court in the English-speaking Caribbean, set up in March 1965. The background and changing environment in which the institution has operated over the decades are examined, providing the context in which case material relating to the different subjects in the text, can be appreciated. Thereafter, the following topics are analysed: 'Management Prerogative', 'Fixed-term Contracts', 'Layoff', 'Retrenchment', 'Dismissal/Termination', 'Reinstatement' and 'Labour-supply Contracts' (also called, 'Labour-only Contracts').

These issues are among the many that are handled by the Industrial Court, including in its well-known public outreach series entitled 'Meet with the Court Symposium' that brings together experts and practitioners from various fields to share knowledge on industrial relations and relevant public policy.

The publication brings under one 'umbrella' for examination, subjects that are critical for dealing with policies affecting the world of work, national development as well as long-term recovery and transformation following a crisis.

The author brings to this work her wealth of knowledge and professional experience, including from years of engagement in the International Labour Organization's supervisory system on international labour standards. As a member of the Committee of Experts on the Application of Conventions and Recommendations, HH Mrs Deborah Thomas-Felix contributes to the examination of all instruments under review. Her main focus however, is on instruments dealing with the maritime sector, including the Maritime Labour Convention 2006 (MLC) which applies to more than 91 per cent of the world's shipping fleet; and occupational safety and health (OSH) standards, which she handles jointly with another Committee Expert.

This publication comprehensively explores the history, principles and application of international labour standards in different subject areas. It analyses the national laws of different sovereign states: Antigua and Barbuda, The Bahamas, Barbados, Guyana, Jamaica, Trinidad and Tobago and the United Kingdom. Cases of the Industrial Court of Trinidad and Tobago, some of which date from 1965, as well as cases of the Industrial Court of Antigua and Barbuda, are examined; so too are several Privy Council Cases. Comparative case studies make it possible to distil similarities, specificities, positive developments with respect to coverage and implementation as well as issues that are still to be addressed. The additional references on different topics that are provided, enriches this resource for users.

This is a trove of information that is meticulously analysed and well-structured. It is a welcome resource for tripartite constituents (i.e. governments, employers, workers and their representative organisations), advisors, educators, students and other stakeholders with an interest in Industrial Relations and Labour Standards. It is also useful for anyone addressing 'world or work' issues through the broader 'lens' of 'Sustainable Development'.

One of the goals of the *2030 Agenda for Sustainable Development* that was adopted by the international community in 2015 is to "... Promote sustained, inclusive and sustainable economic growth, full and productive employment and decent work for all." With 'rights at work' (together with 'employment creation', 'social protection' and 'social dialogue') being one of the four pillars of 'decent work', the relevance of this timely publication for those planning initiatives under this Goal, is unquestionable.

Ana Teresa Romero, PhD

Former Senior Official, International Labour Organization, Offices in Geneva, Switzerland; New York, United States of America; and Port of Spain, Trinidad and Tobago

Part-time Senior Lecturer and Member of the Board, Institute of International Relations, University of the West Indies, St Augustine

ACKNOWLEDGEMENTS

My deep appreciation and thanks to all those who helped to make this book possible.

I must also express my sincere and profound gratitude to the following persons:-

- Charmaine Cooper
- Phyllis Inniss
- Dr. Leighton M. Jackson
- Jamilah Juman-Babwah
- Yvienne Lawrence
- Dr. Ana Teresa Romero and
- Terneille Samuel Herbert

for their great assistance and their general interest in this project.

Sincerest thanks also to

- His Honour Mr. Lawrence Achong
- Shane Boodoosingh
- Chad Felix
- Her Honour Mrs. Kathleen George-Marcelle
- Dr. André Vincent Henry
- The Honourable Mr. Justice Norton Jack and
- Simone Young

for their invaluable advice and encouragement.

Special thanks to my friends and family, especially

- Cari Chandler
- Steve Chandler
- Araya Felix
- Makiri Felix
- Kurt Quashie and
- Paula Vankummer

for their continued love and support.

Abbreviations

CA	Court of Appeal
CPO	Chief Personnel Officer
EAT	Employment Appeal Tribunal
ESD	Essential Service Division (Trinidad and Tobago)
EU	European Union
GSD	General Services Division (Trinidad and Tobago)
H H	His/Her Honour
ICA	Interpretation of a Collective Agreement
ILO	International Labour Organisation
Industrial Court	Industrial Court of Trinidad and Tobago (except where otherwise stated)
IRA	Industrial Relations Act, Chapter 88:01
IRO	Industrial Relations Offence
ISA	Industrial Stabilisation Act
J.	Justice
J.A.	Justice of Appeal
LJ	Lord Justice
MR	Master of the Rolls
PC	Privy Council/Judicial Council of the Privy Council
RMU	Recognised Majority Union
RSBD	Retrenchment and Severance Benefits Act, Chapter 88:13
ST	Special Tribunal (Trinidad and Tobago)
TD	Trade Dispute (Trinidad and Tobago)
THA	Tobago House of Assembly
UTT	University of Trinidad and Tobago

INTRODUCTION

Labour Law, and Industrial Relations Law are embodiments of the law, rules and practice of the relationship in the world of work between workers, trade unions, employers, employing entities and the government. Some theorists say that Labour Law and Industrial Relations Law deal with the collective rights of many workers while Employment Law deals with individual employment relationship that is, applying to individuals and their employers.

The Industrial Court of the Republic of Trinidad and Tobago, a Superior Court of record, is empowered by law to adjudicate on cases related to labour and employment law. On 19th March, 1965, the Industrial Stabilisation Act[1] (ISA) was passed by the Parliament of Trinidad and Tobago and on the next day, 20th March, 1965, it was assented to by the then Governor General. This paved the way for the Industrial Court to commence its operations on 29th April 1965 with a complement of five Judges. The ISA was amended twice in 1967 and it was subsequently repealed and replaced by the Industrial Relations Act Chapter 88:01 of 1972 (IRA).

Today, at the beginning of the third decade of the 21st century, the Industrial Court continues to derive its power from the IRA and has a stated legal mandate "*to make better provision for the stabilisation, improvement and promotion of industrial relations in Trinidad and Tobago.*"

In Trinidad and Tobago, the legal framework for labour law and industrial relations includes a system of compulsory arbitration with the registration of collective agreements at the Industrial Court, which upon their registration, become legally enforceable between the parties. Moreover, the Industrial Court has jurisdiction conferred by various pieces of legislation, to hear and determine workplace related disputes; including individual disputes between workers

1 Industrial Stabilisation Act No. 8 of 1965 of the Laws of Trinidad and Tobago.

and employers, disputes between employers and trade unions such as those related to strikes, lockouts, industrial action, discipline in the workplace, collective bargaining, occupational safety and health, minimum wage, maternity protection, promotion, transfers, layoff, retrenchment, redundancy, freedom of association, negotiations, the interpretation of collective agreements; among other disputes.

The Court is comprised of two divisions, the Essential Services Division which exercises the jurisdiction of the Court as set out in section 7 of the IRA with respect to essential services and essential industries. There is also the General Services Division which exercises the jurisdiction of the Court with respect to services other than essential services and essential industries. Within the Essential Services Division there is a Special Tribunal which hears and determines disputes in the Civil Service, the Police Service, the Fire Service, the Prison Service, the Teaching Service, the Supplemental Police and the Central Bank.

Since 1972, by virtue of the provisions of the IRA, the Industrial Court provides Conciliation Services to its stakeholders. These Conciliation Services are facilitated by the Judges of the Court, and as a result, a significant number of disputes are resolved by this process.

In a recent decision (13th July, 2020) of the Judicial Committee of the Privy Council, the Board in its dicta on the jurisdiction of the Industrial Court of Trinidad and Tobago stated that it:-

> "Readily accepts that the Industrial Court has been established as a new superior court of record with its own broad jurisdiction to deal with disputes between employers and their workers and between employers and unions which represent those workers. The court's procedures are flexible and may be informal, and wide powers are conferred on the court to make orders which are fair and just having regard to all the circumstances including the interests of the parties, others who are immediately concerned in the dispute and the community as a whole. The judges of the court are no doubt appointed on the basis of, among other things, their knowledge and

expertise and their understanding of local communities and labour relations, and so they are well equipped to achieve the objective of resolving disputes speedily and, in most cases, finally.

It is therefore no surprise that the 1972 Act limits the right of any party to a dispute before the Industrial Court to appeal against its decisions. These limitations are contained in, among other provisions, sections 10(6) and 18(1). They render it very difficult for any party to appeal against findings of fact or to challenge evaluative decisions that necessarily involve the assessment of a number of different matters which the Industrial Court is, in light of its experience and expertise, particularly well placed to make. But these provisions are, implicitly in the case of section 10(6) and expressly in the case of section 18(1), subject to section 18(2) which provides a right of appeal to the Court of Appeal on any one of the five specified grounds. These grounds, including as they do such matters as want of jurisdiction, or that the order was obtained by fraud or error of law, provide a valuable safeguard and are eminently suitable for consideration by the Court of Appeal." [2]

Moreover, the words of Sir John Donaldson of the Court of Appeal in England encapsulate the work and function of the Industrial Court of Trinidad and Tobago, when he stated that:-

"The National Industrial Relations Court is a court, but a court with a difference. All courts exist to uphold the rule of law. So does this court. All courts are concerned with people. So is this Court...Why, then, is this court different? It is different in its composition, in its objects and in its procedures. It is a court of law, but not a court of lawyers...The Industrial Court is more than a court of law, it is a court of industrial common sense. The Court's

2 Privy Council Appeal No. 0081 of 2015 Chief Personnel Officer v Amalgamated Workers Union [2020] UKPC 17.

> procedure is different. It is designed to be quick, informal and suited to the needs of those who are not lawyers." [3]

This comment about the National Industrial Relations Court of England is indeed an apt description of the work and function of the Industrial Court of Trinidad and Tobago. The Judges of the Industrial Court of Trinidad and Tobago comprise not only of Lawyers but also of Industrial Relations Experts, Accountants, and Economists; and the Court uses the "industrial commonsense" approach, to resolve Disputes.

The Future of Work

Although the world is currently experiencing what has been described, in some quarters, as one of the worst global health and economic crisis, we should think ahead and prepare for life after this crisis. In my view, policy makers should embrace the ideals and the guiding principles of the ILO (for the past 101 years) which promote decent work for all, in conditions of *"freedom, security and dignity"* particularly in this crisis.

Labour is at the heart of a society's human, social and economic development, therefore the adoption and application of international labour standards are fundamental to any society's sustainable development and to the achievement of the United Nations' Sustainable Development Goals by 2030. I cannot overstate the value and importance of the adherence to these standards to minimise instability in our societies now and in the future (after the pandemic).

According to the International Labour Organisation (ILO),

> "International labour standards are first and foremost about the development of people as human beings. In the Declaration of Philadelphia (1944), the international community recognized that labour is not a commodity. Labour is not an inanimate product, like an apple or a

3 Heatons Transport (St. Helens) Limited v Transport and General Workers' Union [1973] A.C. 15.

television set that can be negotiated for the highest profit or the lowest price. Work is part of everyone's daily life and is crucial to a person's dignity, well-being and development as a human being. Economic development should include the creation of jobs and working conditions in which people can work in freedom, safety and dignity. In short, economic development is not undertaken for its own sake, but to improve the lives of human beings. International labour standards are there to ensure that it remains focused on improving the life and dignity of men and women.

Decent work resumes the aspirations of humans in relation to work. It brings together access to productive and suitably remunerated work, safety at the workplace and social protection for families, better prospects for personal development and social integration, freedom for individuals to set out their claims, to organize and to participate in decisions that affect their lives, and equality of opportunity and treatment for all men and women.

Decent work is not merely an objective, it is a means of achieving the specific targets of the new international programme of sustainable development. At the United Nations General Assembly in September 2015, decent work and the four pillars of the Decent Work Agenda – employment creation, social protection, rights at work and social dialogue – became the central elements of the new Sustainable Development Agenda 2030 . Goal 8 of the 2030 Agenda calls for the promotion of sustained, inclusive and sustainable economic growth, full and productive employment and decent work for all." [4]

4 www.ilo.org, last visited on 7th December, 2020.

The primary objective of this book is to share my perspective on the principles and the practice of good industrial relations with the use of cases as they relate to: -

(a) Management Prerogative

(b) Fixed-Term Contracts

(c) Layoff

(d) Retrenchment

(e) Dismissal/Termination

(f) Reinstatement and

(g) Labour Supply Contracts/Labour Only Contracts

To this end, I have examined case law from Trinidad and Tobago, Bahamas, England, Antigua and Barbuda (which has an Industrial Court similar to that of Trinidad and Tobago and a Labour Code). In addition, I have also examined legislation with respect to layoff from Guyana, Barbados, Jamaica, Bahamas and Antigua and Barbuda.

My aim is to add to the discussion on the application of the law and the labour standards which govern the labour market in the Commonwealth Caribbean and the wider global context. Mindful that discussions of relevant laws and principles can easily descend into the weeds, to avoid such a hapless journey, the Chapters of this book will focus, for the most part, on the fundamental tenets of good industrial relations and the jurisprudence which have emerged from the Industrial Court of the Republic of Trinidad and Tobago, from England and some Commonwealth jurisdictions.

Chapter I

A Historical Perspective Of The Industrial Court Of Trinidad And Tobago

In 2015, the Industrial Court of the Republic of Trinidad and Tobago commemorated its 50th Anniversary as an institution.

As part of the celebration of this historical event, the Court invited distinguished jurist Dr. Leighton Jackson to share his perspective on the history and jurisprudence of the Industrial Court at the Court's Symposium. Dr. Jackson's presentation, has stood the test of time as a seminal piece of work regarding the development of the jurisprudence of the Industrial Court which I think is important to share with you, the readers. The following is Dr. Jackson's presentation:-

"The Jurisprudence of the Industrial Court of Trinidad and Tobago: 50 Years Delivering Social Justice [5]

Introduction

In his very significant work entitled "The Evolution of Labour Relations Legislation in Trinidad and Tobago", Chucks Okpaluba stated the following:-

> "The experience of Trinidad & Tobago in the sphere of labour relations legislation is not only unique; it is also a chequered one. It is an experience that preceded the development of trade unionism and the practice of labour relations in Trinidad & Tobago. ***The crucial date for the commencement of the study of the evolution of labour relations legislation in that territory is 1920*** for the simple reason that it was in that year that such an enactment made its first appearance." [6]

The difficulty with the highlighted sentence in this statement is the author's use of the adjective 'crucial' to describe the date for commencement of the study of the evolution of labour relations legislation in Trinidad and Tobago. The author may have meant 'official' in relation to 'modern' legislation but could certainly not have meant 'crucial'. Because to accept 1920 as the 'crucial' date for the commencement of the study of the evolution of labour relations legislation in these former plantation colonies would totally erase from consideration the significant, systematic and complex body of laws which regulated the labour relations between slaves, indentured servants and their masters. These plantation economy laws regulating slavery and indentured servitude are the 'crucible' within

5 Leighton M. Jackson at the Industrial Court's Meet with the Court Symposium May 16, 2015.

6 C. Okpaluba *The Evolution of Labour Relations Legislation in Trinidad and Tobago* (ISER St. Augustine Trinidad 1980) 1. (emphasis added).

which those societies were forged and from which the modern labour relations legislation and the institutions were spawned. It is interesting that 'crucial' and 'crucible' share the same etymology and the use of the word crucial by the author is a classic Freudian slip, as many would want to erase this history as never having existed.

The definition of the word 'crucible' from the Oxford English Dictionary is:-

> "A ceramic or metal container in which metals or other substances may be melted or subjected to very high temperatures."

This leads to the metaphorical extension of the word to mean:-

> "A situation of severe trial, or in which different elements interact, leading to the creation of something new."

The word 'crucial', as in 'crucial date', shares the same root as crucible and was originally the adjectival description of the form of a cross. Crucial has come to mean, according to Oxford Advanced American Dictionary, *extremely important, not because of itself, but because it will affect other things – that is, vital to the determination of an outcome.* [7] With this background, in assessing the achievement of the Industrial Court over the 50 years of its existence, we can only do so if we know the crucible within which it was forged and if we accurately identify what were crucial the questions.

Putting these together it is clear that the 'crucial' date for the study of the evolution of labour relations legislation in Trinidad and Tobago, *ergo* the achievement of the Industrial Court, cannot be 1920. It begins with the

7 The etymology of crucible is late Middle English from Medieval Latin *crucibulum* night lamp, crucible (perhaps originally a lamp hanging in front of a crucifix), from Latin *crux, cruc-* 'cross'.

very reason for the creation of these 'societies' in the West Indies. Simply put, they were constructed for the exploitation of labour. The very personhood of those whose labour was exploited was singularly for the benefit of the economy and the best social life and development of Europe and Europeans. They were not participants in the institutions of social or political governance – they were mere factors of production. This history is the crucial point in any discussion of the evolution of labour legislation in Trinidad and Tobago and consequently of the Industrial Court. It is the *experimentum crucis*, the "guidepost that gives directions at a place where one road becomes two", or more. Many roads met at the time of the creation of the Industrial Court and the Court is the guidepost that gives direction.

Chucks Okpaluba taught at the new Faculty of Law of UWI in the early 70's and contributed significantly to its intellectual development, but like many of us today, we forget the crucible of our existence which accounts for the development of our social, political and economic institutions by which our societies are constituted and reconstituted. George Santayana wrote: "Those who cannot remember the past are condemned to repeat it." [8] This was not a call to live and remain in history but to learn from its lessons in order to advance. In fact the full context of this well-known statement is within the context of achieving progress.

> "Progress, far from consisting in change, depends on retentiveness. When change is absolute there remains no being to improve and no direction to set for possible improvement and when experience is not retained, as among savages, infancy is perpetual. ***Those who cannot remember the past are condemned to repeat it.***"

8 *The Life of Reason*, 1905.

This squares very well with the concept of the role of law stated by Oliver Wendell Holmes Jr., American jurist and Justice of its Supreme Court for 30 years, when he famously said:-

> "The life of the law has not been logic; it has been experience... The law embodies the story of a nation's development through many centuries, and it cannot be dealt with as if it contained only the axioms and corollaries of a book of mathematics." [9]

Thus the laws regulating slavery, indentured servants, the Emancipation Act 1834, and the battery of other colonial laws which were meant to subordinate labour into its role as a factor of production are part of the construct. Included as well are the struggles, rebellion and resistance of our ancestors. These are the crucible of who we are today and signal the crucial date for the study of the evolution of labour relations in Trinidad and Tobago, not 1920.

A description and commentary by Professor Bereton of the situation in relation to Emancipation Act paints the picture graphically:-

> "As we saw, the Act of Emancipation was passed by the British Parliament in 1833 and it became law on August 1, 1834 – Emancipation Day. But while this did technically mark the abolition of slavery, all the formerly enslaved, except children under the age of 6 on August 1, were declared to be 'apprentices' obliged to work for their former owners without wages for three-quarters of the defined working week. This so-called apprenticeship, which the Act said would last for 6 years, really postponed freedom for a few more years. Although the apprentices did have some rights not enjoyed by the enslaved, the system had much more in common with slavery than with freedom.
>
> ...

9 O Wendell Holmes Jr *The Common Law* (1881) p.1.

> So when hundreds of new apprentices gathered in the area of Woodford Square on August 1, they were in an angry mood. 'Point de six ans! (Not six more years!)', they shouted, complaining loudly that they were not given 'full free'. The militia was called out, the soldiers were called from the barracks, over 50 of the 'ringleaders' were sentenced to floggings and in some cases jail. Partly because of the resistance by the people all over the Caribbean to this disastrous apprenticeship scheme, partly through pressure from abolitionists in Britain and in the colonies, it was ended by the government in London two years early, in 1838.
>
> On August 1, 1838 – the real Emancipation Day – apprenticeship ended and the former apprentices gained 'full free' status. In Trinidad, 20,656 apprentices were freed on that day." [10]

But they were freed with nothing.

The authors Deakin and Morris state:-

> "Labour Law stems from the idea of the subordination of the individual worker to the capitalist enterprise; it is above all the law of dependent labour." [11]

In the Caribbean, our history makes this statement even starker than the condition the authors describe from the British perspective. What this means is that the journey for us is more distant and gruelling and the challenges more arduous than that faced by other societies from which we take the cue to our laws. The imperatives upon which our societies were built cannot be forgotten or downplayed. Professor Elsa Goveia makes the point that the slave system, as well as the institution of indentured servitude, had become more than an economic enterprise which could be abandoned when it ceased to be profitable. It had

10 Public Lecture on Emancipation in Trinidad, National Museum, POS, August 2007, p.9.

11 S Deakin & G Morris *Labour Law* 6th edn (Hart Publishing) p.1.

become the very basis of organised society throughout the British West Indies and therefore it was believed to be an indispensible element in maintaining the existing social structure and preserving law and order in the community. [12] This is important to assessing what the Industrial Court of Trinidad and Tobago has achieved in its jurisprudence over the last 50 years and it is therefore important to say a little more. All the contemporary academics of the new University of the West Indies agreed that change had to be radical if it was to be effective and this radical change would neither come from the colonial ruling class nor the local middle class who succeeded them. I like the description given by Professor Goveia of the dilemma which labour faced way into the 20th century up until the time of the introduction of the Industrial Court.

> But, though they were now less physically oppressed, their life chances in the free society, as compared with those of other groups, were not very substantially different from what they had been before. The old community based on slavery had been destroyed. But the emergent free society could only offer them a confused amalgam of opposing social values – on the one hand, practical subordination in a particularistic social structure still based on racial inequality, and on the other, universalist claims to equal status before the law without regard to class or race. As Lord Harris said in 1848, the effect of emancipation was that 'a race has been freed but a society has not been formed.' New guiding principles of order and coherence had still to be decided on. [13]

12 E Goveia *Slave Society in the British Leeward Islands at the End of the Eighteenth Century* (Westport, Connecticut: Greenwood Press, 1980.

13 Id. 331-332.

Times changed but things remained the same – The Industrial Stabilisation Act 1965

In 1965 when the Industrial Stabilisation Act was passed, Trinidad and Tobago as well as the other British West Indies territories had been through several political processes and had to face the challenges of modernisation in a world that had drastically changed from the manner in which the dominant First World states strategised to relate to the other states in the world. We moved through several types of British colonial rule, from party politics, Universal Adult Suffrage, the developing labour movement, political independence to the emergence of executive power in the hands of a coloured, black and Indian middle class. But meaning and self-worth and a sense of ownership did not trickle down to the labouring class. As Professor Rex Nettleford, himself a long time Director of the Trade Union Education Unit of the university at Mona, remarked:-

> "The paradox of Caribbean life is that the more things change the more they remain the same. The vault-like ascent by the society from slavery into freedom and then from colonialism into constitutional independence is yet to be matched within the society by a corresponding progress from cultural inferiority of the vast majority to cultural self-confidence."

The labour unrest and tension by workers, which led to the State of Emergency and the push of the ISA through the legislature was symptomatic not of lawless agitation but a far larger struggle for meaning and self-worth in the matrix of a society that was deemed theirs. Professor M G Smith best sums up the workers' position, writing about that time:-

> "It is evident that despite universal suffrage and party politics in several contemporary Caribbean societies, despite unionization and more liberal industrial laws,

> educational provisions and the like, the majority of the people remain as poorly integrated and as remote and distinct from their superiors as ever, primarily on cultural, linguistic and social grounds, including race and colour, education, wealth and economic activity."[14]

Those at the helm of power misunderstood that this was in truth a campaign for a voice. Dr. Eric Williams recognised this as did the politicians who were contending for power and needed the mass support. Okpaluba tells us that,

> "The unionists were at that stage encouraged by politicians for Dr. Eric Williams has been quoted as having said in 1955 that the employers must "... understand that the day when West Indians were content merely to hew wood and draw water for private investors is gone forever. The worker today requires inducements, incentives and guarantees just as the investor does..." [15]

However, by 1963, when the power base of the new leaders of government was solidified, the Minister of Finance in his budget speech stressed the antithetical position of the country's economy through its industrialisation effort to workers' organisation and workers' say in the matrix of economic power.

> "The trade union movement, quite rightly, today occupies a position of power as never before in our history. It would be a pity if this power were turned into a privilege. For the value of the movement will ultimately depend upon its willingness to resolve the inevitable contradictions between its own group interests and the community interest.

14 M G Smith *Culture, Class and Race in the Commonwealth Caribbean* (Mona, Jamaica: Department of Extra-Mural Studies, UWI 1984).

15 C Okpaluba at 69.

> A ruthless policy of higher wages and salaries and other benefits in a developing country is incompatible with either continuing economic growth or rising levels of employment. It could impair capacity to compete in external markets and weaken the balance of payments." [16]

The individual worker, and more so the collective activities of workers, were now being seen as enemies of the state and the enemy of economic development. It was lost on the politics of the time. But development economics and people-centred polices will only succeed if the citizens of our states **subjectively** experience improvement in their human well-being and are contributors to the effort. Objective economic and social indices, the language of economic and international agencies which has become the linguistic accoutrements of our rulers, may measure change and indicate progress of a kind but will not ensure stability. Only a subjective assessment by the people whose lives are affected will ensure social and political stability and real progress.

Subversive activities and communism scare were rampant before the passing of the Act and was the catalyst for its enactment. It was in this atmosphere that the ISA was tabled for the first time on March 12, 1965, read for the second time on March 18, which not co-incidentally was the same date on which the *Report of the Commission of Enquiry on Subversive Activities* was presented to Parliament. And, by March 20, 1965, the ISA received the Governor-General's assent and was promulgated immediately. The State of Emergency of March 9 was lifted on March 25, 1965.

Thus Okpaluba supports Dr. Zin Henry's conclusion that the ISA "was conceived and introduced not merely as a policy instrument of industrial relations, but also as

16 Quoted by C. Okpuluba, id. 71.

a measure for containing alleged subversive activities and political agitation by trade union leaders through trade union organisations." [17]

In this climate was born the Industrial Court of Trinidad and Tobago – an institution that was given the proverbial basket to carry water to extinguish the flame of dissensus and discontent in the arena of labour relations and leverage objective economic progress through industrial stability. The structure of the Act was the strategy to achieve that end and it was a poor choice. Okpuluba concluded that:-

> "[T]he scheme of the Industrial Stabilisation Act as an instrument of industrial regulation was a total failure. All aspects of industrial relations regulated by the Act proved unworkable as they were completely misconceived. In the final analysis, the ISA could be described as no more than a 'law and order' type of legislation."

Far from being unifying, it was perceived that the objective of the Act was to be "a neutralising force of the powers of a united labour movement." The labour movement was not consulted. It was not to be participatory – the hallmark of good governance and stability. "[Y]our Government have not sought to obtain the views of the Labour Movement on the most far-reaching piece of labour legislation to be brought forward in your time of office", the Trade Union Congress wrote to Prime Minister Dr Eric Williams. This methodology of enactment explains the suspicion with which the ISA was greeted and it was unfortunate that the Prime Minister whose studies presumes and understanding of the angst of the disenfranchised and the long road to achieving a society built on social justice would have countenanced this unfortunate beginnings.

17 Okpaluba 80.

Employment – the Most Critical Component of Democratic Governance

Nonetheless, the establishment of the Industrial Court of Trinidad and Tobago must be considered the most important institutional construct in modern democratic governance in the Commonwealth Caribbean from the point of view of the history of these states which I have recounted. But the most important reason is that employment and labour law stands for a sense of co-ownership of the State which is shared with fellow citizens. While our history is one that recounts a society that was exclusively built for the exploitation of labour and controlled by depriving it of a voice in the institutions of governance, resulting in a lack of correlation between the significance of the contribution that is made by labour to the society and its influence or position in society, yet employment by its very nature is the most important, immediate and unavoidable participation in society. Because when one moves outside of one's immediate family and community through employment, one automatically moves into the sphere of the national society and where you give to get. The fairness of the exchange is a crucial description and measure of how much you are valued in your own society.

Moreover, employment is the major instrument for the creation and distribution of the economic resources of the state. It is perhaps the most significant space where the ordinary citizen finds meaning of citizenship, self-expression, self-worth and dignity – and ultimately self-existence – within the State when the citizen not only participates but is rewarded. ***Employment and labour law stands for a sense of co-ownership of the State shared with fellow citizens.*** When viewed in this manner labour law and industrial relations are pivotal to social change and the Industrial Court as the regulatory institution stands at the apex of transformation and change.

The signal function of the Industrial Court is one of reconstituting relationships in a society where the radical changes which were necessary for the transformation of the society into one in which everyone finds and equal place – to paraphrase the notable words of the national Anthem. After close study and following the work of the Court for many decades, it is no exaggeration that nowhere in the world has the effect of an institution such as the Industrial Court of Trinidad and Tobago been so deeply transformational of the individual sense of civic ownership. But the revolution is unheralded and the feat of the Court in overcoming the seemingly insurmountable obstacles which were laid in the path of the Court by the manner in which it was set up as well as the shortcomings in the first Act, not recognised.

The Industrial Court of Trinidad and Tobago over the last 50 years is a testament to modern democratic governance and orderly change. It has not accomplished this suddenly or in a single action but on a case by case basis, identifying the issues, relating them to real life and \the social values of Trinidad and Tobago and then fashioning remedies to suit. In this manner, the Industrial Court has built an intellectual tradition of protective norms to govern the employment relationship and has created the normative framework for the institutions of the labour market. This is remarkable when one thinks that in most of the Commonwealth Caribbean states and even in the UK, there are predetermined norms found in Labour Codes and such the like, the Industrial Court did not have that kind of pre-packaged assistance.

> "The I.R.A. lays down some, but not all, principles and practice of good industrial relations, e.g. the principle of majority rule of trade unions, good faith bargaining, binding nature of collective agreements, an important

> role of the Court is to lay down and define such principles and practices so that workers, trade unions and employers will be aware of the principles which are applied by the Court." [18]

The Industrial Court is Democracy and Good Governance in its Very Best Expression

The jurisprudence of the Industrial Court has been built with each ordinary citizen having the ability to put forward the contribution of their own circumstances as a consideration in promulgating the rules and conventions which govern this critical aspect of citizenship. Professor Levi explains how this is a high form of democracy, which we must bear in mind as we construct new institutions to carry forward our social, political and economic development:-

> "What does the law forum require? It requires the presentation of competing examples. [19] The forum protects the parties and the community by making sure that the competing analogies are before the court. The rule which will be created arises out of a process in which if different things are to be treated as similar, at least the differences have been urged. In this sense the parties as well as the court participate in the law-making. In this sense, also, lawyers represent more than the litigants.
>
> Reasoning by example in the law is a key to many things. It indicates in part the hold which the law process has over the litigants. ***They have participated in the law-making. They are bound by something they helped to make. Moreover, the examples or***

18 TD No. 72 of 2000 Union of Commercial and Industrial Workers v. El Dorado Consumers Co-operative Society Limited.

19 By 'competing examples' one means merely the particular situation in which the litigants before the Industrial Court have found themselves and on which they are urging the Court to rule, thereby creating a rule for the particular circumstance.

> ***analogies urged by the parties bring into the law the common ideas of the society.*** The ideas have their day in court, and they will have their day again. This is what makes the hearing fair, rather than any idea that the judge is completely impartial, for of course he cannot completely be. Moreover, the hearing in a sense compels at least vicarious participation by all the citizens, for the rule which is made, even though ambiguous, will be law as to them." [20]

The rule-making in industrial relations by the Industrial Court is therefore even more democratic and participatory than enactments made in Parliament which are usually the function of a decision of Cabinet carried out by the legislative drafting department of the Parliamentary Counsel. The Industrial Court, by having to bring to bear its broad standard of adjudication in accordance with "equity, good conscience and the substantial merits of the case before it, having regard to the principles and practices of good industrial relations" necessarily reasons inductively. The inductive process of reasoning rather than the deductive has the great potential of looking at specific instances and drawing from them logical inferences and lessons that is based on the unique and shared experiences of the Republic of Trinidad and Tobago.

In this task the Industrial Court has neither been shy or modest and quite rightly so. Because if it does not do it, experience has shown that it will be done for us based on the shared experience of other foreign peoples. Sound logical inferences are fully accepted as the basis for judicial activism. Because it is reasoned – unlike parliamentary legislation, which requires no compelling reason or any at all, gives legitimacy and a justification for the rules and principles that the Industrial Court has laid down over the past 50 years, sometimes controversially. But

20 Edward Levi *An Introduction to Legal Reasoning* (University of Chicago Press 1949) p. 5.

the point that the rule making is participated in by the ordinary citizen, both employee and employer, and their advocates who skillfully advance the respective interests, accords with the most critical feature of good governance in the creation of institutions – participation. The Industrial Court has been the epitome of transparency and accountability the other two ingredients of good governance.

The Framework of Industrial Relations Act

But much credit must also be reserved for the ideological framework of the Industrial Relations Act which replaced the ISA. The IRA has been a work in progress and there has been great sensitivity to legislative reform and amendment to improve the legislation. Again, in no other legislative area in Trinidad and Tobago has there been such monitoring and re-evaluation to ensure that the legislation is producing the required effect. While the monitoring is informal, this is typical of democracies and in this case it is effective. Professors Seidman states:-

> "In the largest sense, democracy itself constitutes a gigantic, if somewhat unsystematic, monitoring and evaluation system. Constituents whose toes a law's implementation pinches can and frequently do complain to their legislative representatives." [21]

This has been the experience of the IRA and it is a model of democracy in this regard.

The pivotal core of the jurisprudence of the IRA is described by s 10 (3) of the Act:-

> "Notwithstanding anything in this Act or in any rule of law to the contrary, the Court in the exercise of its powers shall –

21 A Seidman, R Seidman & N Abeysekere *Legislative Drafting for Democratic Social Change* (2001) p 114.

(a) Make such order or award in relation to a dispute before it as it considers fair and just, having regard to the interests of the persons immediately concerned and the community as a whole;

(b) Act in accordance with equity, good conscience and the substantial merits of the case before it, having regard to the principles and practices of good industrial relations."

In addition, the jurisdiction to give relief to an employee who has been dismissed adds significantly to the ability to weave a jurisprudence that fits within the unique moral values and legitimate expectations of citizenry which employment represents as discussed above in constructing a just society. Section 10(5) in giving the Court the power to exercise a wide discretion to make an award provides the platform for filling in the grid of moral values that must underlie any national law:-

> "An order under subsection (4) may be made where, in the opinion of the Court, a worker has been dismissed in circumstances that are harsh and oppressive or not in accordance with the principles of good industrial relations practice."

In our ex-colonial states based on the English common law, the doctrine of precedent and the slavish adherence by our judges and attorneys to the value of case law precedents from elsewhere continues to be the route whereby the values of societies that are not our own creep in to undermine the sovereignty of our self-definition of our society.

Additionally, and this is key, the way is paved for cognitive accessibility to the court by the ordinary citizen which the eccentric complexity of the rules and procedure of the regular courts to which they have unyieldingly clung, which elevates form over substance does not provide. Therefore it is critical to the success of the Act that sections 9(1) and 10(6) of the Act restrict the intrusion of the methodology and ideas of the regular courts into the jurisprudence being forged by the Industrial Court. Section 9(1) provides:-

> "In the hearing and determination of any matter before it, the Court may act without regard to technicalities and legal form an shall not be bound to follow the rules of evidence stipulated in the Evidence Act, but the Court may inform itself on any matter in such manner as it thinks just and may take into account opinion evidence and such facts as it considers relevant and material, but in any such case the parties to the proceedings shall be given the opportunity, if they so desire, of adducing evidence in regard thereto."

Section 10(6) ousts the jurisdiction of the regular courts to question the judgment of the Industrial Court in language that is pellucid and strong.

> "The opinion of the Court as to whether a worker has been dismissed in circumstances that are harsh and oppressive or not in accordance with the principles of good industrial relations practice and any order for compensation or damages including the assessment thereof made pursuant to subsection (5) shall not be challenged, appealed against, reviewed, quashed or called into question in any Court on any account whatsoever."

This interdiction is repeated with respect to any proceedings before the Court, except in limited circumstances. Section 18(1) provides:-

> "Subject to subsection (2), the hearing and determination of any proceedings before the Court, and an order or award or any finding or decision of the Court in any matter (including an order or award) -
>
> 1. shall not be challenged, appealed against, reviewed, quashed or called in question in any Court on any account whatsoever; and

2. shall not be subject to prohibition, mandamus or injunction in ay Court on any account whatever."

The dispensation of justice in the Industrial Court without the plank of older tradition on which to rely becomes a pragmatic exercise. The task is rendered even more complex by its super-wide jurisdiction and broad objectives stated in the IRA. The doctrinal structure of industrial relations jurisprudence embraces a close consideration of many disparate issues, considerations and sectorial concerns. Ideas must be drawn from many areas. Indeed in a phrase the ultimate function of the Industrial Court is in fact a reconstitution of relationships in the society, not only the relationship between persons in diverse roles but also the relationship between organisations, government and governmental institutions, within the context of economic efficiency and fundamental social and economic rights, voluntary sources and particular institutions as well as the overarching concern with meeting international standards which our country has committed itself to as a matter of international law.

The Industrial Court stands at the apex of many strands that must be fused into, and become, to use Professor Goveia's words, "new guiding principles of order and coherence" and yet do so without disruption. The background is the complex economic, political and social environment and constructs in Trinidad and Tobago. Within this is the divide between individual labour law and collective labour law. Then the various strands which affect their regulation:-

1. Law of contract
2. Common law
3. Regulatory legislation
4. Collective bargaining
5. The business enterprise
6. Workplace custom and practice

Charting the Jurisprudence

The road to charting the jurisprudence depends a great deal on the leadership of the Court. Despite the imperfections of the ISA, the appointment of Sir Isaac Hyatali as the first President of the Industrial Court was a master stroke of genius of the jurisprudence of the Court. The initial business was to disabuse everyone that the Court lacked independence from the Executive and to establish that it is committed to justice to all citizens. In his first Annual Report he repeated that ***"publicly and emphatically that this Court is an independent Court – free from the control, directions or influences of the Executive, members of Parliament, political parties and personalities and all pressure groups and combines, guided or misguided that may appear on the scene now or hereafter"***. He continued:-

> "Let all citizens of our country be assured of this and let them also be assured that those who seek justice at our hands will not do so in vain."

Even where there was no provision for reinstatement of workers in the ISA, as President of the Court, Sir Isaac boldly led the Court to exercise that jurisdiction and was unrestrained in his criticism of the judgment of the Court of Appeal which ruled this ultra vires. Sir Isaac tirelessly campaigned to have amendments made to the Act and, to a large degree, much of the improvements to the legislation leading ultimately to its repeal and replacement by the IRA was foundationally laid by Sir Isaac Hyatali. He was clear on the role of the Court to promote 'social justice' from the first years of its existence.

> "The large number of trade disputes that have been and are continuing to be referred to the Court reflect either confidence in ***its dedication to the cause of dispensing social justice*** without fear, or favour, affection or ill will...." [22]

22 *Annual Report 1966-1967* p. 16 para 19.

The current President, H H Mrs. Deborah Thomas-Felix, has continued to lead the Court in the path of this noble tradition of creating jurisprudence for the Industrial Court which is tailored to meet the values of every citizen of the Republic and safeguarding the economic viability of the country. In her first Annual Report as President she summed up the role of the Industrial Court.

> "The Industrial Court, as the final arbiter of employment issues in this country continues to serve as an invaluable instrument for social justice. This Court, from my perspective, continues to be the glue of human dignity, equity and fairness which permeates into this mosaic of employment relationships in Trinidad and Tobago and holds it together. It is therefore important for us to always remember the history of the Court and the importance of its role in this society." [23]

Like her first predecessor, she takes the platform of President of the Industrial Court to be a voice in relation to issues and trends which affect the employment of citizens of Trinidad and Tobago. For example, in 2013, she expressed "deep concern regarding the widespread use of short-term and fixed-term contracts of employment in the public sector." The President clearly appreciated that principles that may pass as fair and just in some other and larger jurisdiction, is not necessarily so in Trinidad and Tobago. In this small state the Government is a major employer upon whom the citizen depends and it is critical to social inclusion. Justice therefore is crucial in this area of employment relations.

> "Given the importance of the Government as employer and the role of the public sector in national development, we should strive for employment and human resources policies and practices that would

23 The Industrial Court of Trinidad and Tobago *Annual Report October 2011- September 2013* at p.6.

> foster an efficient and productive public sector that delivers high-quality services and supports good stewardship."

In this regard, we are kindred spirits. I observed some time ago:-

> "The public service occupies a distinct, obvious and critical role in Caribbean life: political, social, cultural and economic. It is well known that in all these societies, a government job is perhaps the most important channel of participation in the democratic governance of the state by ordinary people who would typically be without status, power or influence. Government is by far the largest and most reliable employer. A government job is a source of status at every economic level and also a source of economic stability to an impoverished family or community. The district constable or police officer, the teacher or nurse, the postmistress or clerk, even the labourer or domestic servant employed to government is the link to participation in the official society both from a democratic and a cultural perspective." [24]

The Rights-Based Approach

The question becomes the precise manner in which the Industrial Court has exercised this generous jurisdiction to give credence to the claim that it has forged a jurisprudence of social justice which has impacted society. The President of the Court has recently stated:-

> "I believe that social inclusion, equity and fairness are necessary precursors for building a stable industrial relations environment and by extension a vibrant and prosperous economy. The challenge I daresay for this country and many countries is how to achieve

24 L. Jackson *The Fourth Estate: Towards a Caribbean Constitutional Ideology of the Independent Public Service* (unpublished).

> sustainable inclusive growth and development for all citizens. It is my respectful view that, economic growth will be irrelevant if it does not take into account the betterment of each and every section of the society. Sustainable inclusive growth can only be achieved when we combine policies for economic development with those of social justice and inclusive growth for all groups particularly those which are most vulnerable."

In reviewing the jurisprudence of the Industrial Court, this objective has been advanced by taking the modern rights-based approach to the resolution of conflicts and the dispensation of justice. This is in keeping with the modern movement of international society. The strong provisions of the Industrial Relations Act of Trinidad and Tobago, the history of agitation and the personnel of the Court has led to the development of a jurisprudence of rights-based approach to the adjudication of employment relationship disputes.

In *Caroni (1975) Limited v Association of Technical Administrative Supervisory Staff*, [25] de la Bastide CJ made clear the breadth of the jurisdiction of the court:-

> "The wording of S 10(6) is very explicit. However reluctant this court may be to accept that its jurisdiction has been ousted by an Act of Parliament and that it is thereby denied the opportunity of investigating an alleged injustice and correcting it, if found to exist, the intention of Parliament is too clear in this instance to be deflected by any presumption of law or canon of construction. It is clearly the duty of this court to give effect to it. We must not be tempted to do otherwise by pictures painted of the gross injustices which may be perpetrated if we recognise and accept the restriction which Parliament has imposed on our right to interfere. In any case, s 10(6) does not oust any

25 (2002) 67 WIR 223, 225-226.

pre-existing jurisdiction of the Court of Appeal. The Industrial Court is a comparatively recent creation of statute, and so is the right given to appeal from it to the Court of Appeal. The intention of Parliament, clearly expressed in s 10(6), is that the question whether the dismissal of a worker is in any case harsh and oppressive and contrary to the principles of good industrial relations practice, should be reserved to the Industrial Court. What distinguishes a dismissal that is harsh and oppressive from one that is not, is a matter which the Act clearly regards as grounded not in law, but in industrial relations practice. The practice, which is not codified in our jurisdiction, is to be determined and applied to the facts of each case by the Industrial Court. The policy of the statute is obviously to entrust that function only to judges of the Industrial Court who come equipped with experience of, and familiarity with, industrial relations practice. This is a qualification which judges of the Supreme Court do not necessarily or even ordinarily have. It is considerations like these which presumably underlie the prohibition in s 10(6) against the Court of Appeal reviewing the decision of the Industrial Court that the dismissal of a particular worker does, or does not, have the quality which triggers the grant of the remedies of compensation and reinstatement.

A harsh and oppressive dismissal is something which, according to the Act, may be identified only by the Industrial Court.

It does not matter whether the party challenging the decision of the Industrial Court on this issue claims, not merely that the decision was against the weight of the evidence, but goes further and claims that no reasonable judge properly directed could have come to the same conclusion, having regard to the evidence. In the latter case, the ground of appeal has graduated from a question of fact to a question of law; but it is nonetheless barred by the prohibition contained in s

> 10(6). This is not to say that a decision of the Industrial Court as to whether a dismissal is harsh and oppressive is so sacrosanct that it can never be challenged on any ground whatever. If, for instance, there has been some procedural irregularity which involves a breach of the rules of natural justice, then clearly an appeal would lie to the Court of Appeal, notwithstanding s 10(6). In such a case it would be the process by which the Industrial Court reached its opinion and not the opinion itself that was challenged."

But the proof of the pudding is in the actual adjudication by the Industrial Court itself – the use of an understanding of the rights-based approach as the interpretative lens through which disputes are resolved. Workers do not merely have a claim or remedy as Fernandes seem to say they have a right to property in their job. In *Union of Commercial and Industrial Workers v El Dorado Consumers Co-operative Society Ltd,*[26] H H Ramsubeik summed up the approach and commitment of the Court.

> "The idea still persists in some quarters that it is possible to terminate a worker's employment by merely giving him the required notice under the contract of employment. This was true under the common law but termination of workers by notice alone is insufficient under the Act. This whole question was discussed as long as 1965 in Trade Dispute No. 2 of 1965 between the Civil Service Association and the Marketing Board but such submissions continue to be made.
>
> In addition, an employer must have an acceptable reason for terminating the worker's employment. Under the common law, the employer had the right to terminate without assigning a reason for the termination. This is not acceptable under the Act.

26 TD No. 72 of 2000 Union of Commercial and Industrial Workers v El Dorado Consumers Co-operative Society Limited. p. 15.

> An employer must have a valid reason for dismissal which must be connected with the worker's conduct or capacity to perform the work.
>
> Additionally, an employer must inform a worker of the true reasons for his dismissal. There was no requirement under the common law for an employer to give a reason for a worker's termination. He just had to inform him of the termination. By the principles of good industrial relations practice, however, an employer must give a worker the true reason for his dismissal.
>
> An employer must also give a worker an opportunity to be heard before a dismissal becomes effective. In Trade Dispute No. 68 of 1980 between Trinidad and Tobago Television Co and Communication, Transport and General Workers' Trade Union, H H Braithwaite said: "It is an understatement to say the common law rights of an employer have been circumscribed. For all practical purposes they have almost been completely eroded out of existence"."

In *Fernandes (Distillers) Ltd v Transport and Industrial Workers' Union* Wooding CJ emphasised the historical common law prerogative of the employer as owner of the worker singularly as a factor of production without any recognition of a right of the worker to his work. In forceful language Wooding CJ said:-

> "And I cannot too strongly stress that the issue was not whether the company could justify the legality or propriety of the dismissal."

This is in stark contrast to the recent decision of the Industrial Court in *Trinidad and Tobago National Petroleum Marketing Co Ltd and Oilfields Workers' Trade Union.*[27]

27 TD No. 717 of 2013 and IRO No. 23 of 2013 (Consolidated) between Trinidad and Tobago National Petroleum Marketing Company Limited and Oilfields Workers' Trade Union.

> "It is noteworthy that this country does not have a labour code to give detailed guidance to employers, workers and trade unions regarding the day to day conduct of their relationships. Instead the legislature has provided overarching principles and has emphatically positioned the Industrial Court as guardian of the national standards of what constitutes good industrial relations principles and practice. Thus, the importance of the role of the Industrial Court in issuing guidance to shape the industrial relations jurisprudence in the country cannot be over emphasised."

In that case 68 workers were dismissed – equivalent to the discharge weapon of mass destruction in such a small society. In rejecting the dismissal of the workers as a product of arrogance and intransigence and a violation of natural justice, the court insisted that "industrial common sense causes us to examine the extent to which Management's own action or omission call into question the reasonableness of the decision to suspend the workers and then to dismiss them." The Court ordered the reinstatement of all the workers without loss of pay, benefits or seniority and also an award of damages. While the matter is the subject of an appeal before the Court of Appeal, in reliance on what we have said above, whatever conclusion the Court of Appeal come to would be irrelevant to the vindication of the rights of the workers in the Industrial Court and the role and function of the Industrial Court. The perception of the workers was that they matter and have a voice to assert their position in the institutional arrangements of the state. [28]

The overall conclusion is that the Court has adopted a rights-based approach to the rights of employees to a proprietary interest in their employment.

28 The Court of Appeal upheld the decision in this matter.

Sharma CJ has said of the role of the Industrial Court:-

> "[25] What is of critical importance is the fact that in addition to conferring this jurisdiction on the Industrial Court. The legislature expressly ousted the Court of Appeal's jurisdiction in certain matters considered essential to determining good industrial relations practice. These matters are ones considered to be questions of fact and determinations based on the evidence which the members of the Industrial Court are best qualified to answer. This is consistent with the fact that the legislature vested the Industrial Court with the responsibility of ensuring that good industrial relations practices are maintained in employment relationships." [29]

This is important because as Michael Freeman notes about rights in another context:-

> "Rights are important because they recognize the respect the bearers are owed. To accord rights is to respect dignity: to deny rights is to cast doubt on humanity and integrity. Rights affirm the Kantian principle that we are ends in ourselves and not means to others' ends. It is, therefore, important that, as Ronald Dworkin so eloquently reminded us, we see rights as 'trumps'. They cannot be knocked off their pedestal because it would be better for others, or even society as a whole, were these rights not to exist." [30]

The property interest of the worker in his job has been enhanced by the Industrial Court acting under the IRA while taking care of the multiplicity of other motivations for the Act. All rights, including property rights are a balance between the public interest and the individual and the question is always the margin of appreciation or proportionality with regard to the burden on the

29 *Caribbean Development Company Limited v National Union of Government and Federated Workers*, Carilaw TT 2003 CA 61, per Sharma CJ [24]-[25].

30 M. Freeman *What's Right with Rights* Int. J.L.C. 2006, 2(1), 89-98, 89.

individual employee. In this regard the cases have shown that the Industrial Court has not hesitated to act where the burden on the worker was excessive in relation to the options available to the employer and the manner in which it has been exercised in the process.

Indeed, one can be bold enough to say that without the provision of social rights in the Constitution, a credible argument can be put forward that the work of the Industrial Court under the IRA has resulted in an effective constitutionalisation of employment law. This conclusion is more tempting when it is coupled with the panoply of legislative regulatory norms of the employment relationship which is backed up by a strong remedial regime, protected from the common law interference of the courts. The provision of the substantive rights and the provision of broad discretionary remedies to vindicate these rights have effectively created property rights in employment and the requirement of good governance – participation, transparency, accountability, fairness, reasonableness and proportionality.

Conclusion

The Industrial Court over the last 50 years has been from beginning to end the stalwart of good governance and social justice in the Republic of Trinidad and Tobago. As a home grown institution and not the replica of a precedent to be found elsewhere it is a model for democracies not only in this region but throughout the world. One can easily measure the quantitative effect of the Court by looking at the state of industrial relations today compared with the turbulent times of 1965. On the other side, it is difficult to measure the mostly qualitative impact as regards the feelings of the citizen in terms of participation and as this current President of the Court consistently reminds us "social inclusion". It is fitting to close with the words of the first President Sir Isaac Hyatali who so well established the firm foundations for the achievements of the Court, quantitative and qualitative. This shows that the achievements are not new but occurred from the very start of the Court's existence.

But let Sir Isaac Hyatali tell us himself:-

> "Having regard to the results achieved since then [the period preceding the Act], there is justification for observing that true economic and other cherished foundations of the Country have been preserved and fortified by the establishment of an impartial judicial system to settle in a peaceful and civilised manner trade disputes which it was the fashion to resolve theretofore by costly and ruinous industrial warfare. Indeed the industrial peace which has reigned in the society even since the enactment of the Act eloquently bespeaks the extent to which its objects have been achieved and needs no further elaboration from me."

Final words indeed! The Industrial Court eloquently speaks for itself with regard to its achievements and needs no further elaboration from me." [31]

31 Dr. Leighton M. Jackson has over 31 years of experience lecturing law in the Caribbean region and is the former Dean of the Faculty of Law, University of the West Indies (UWI), Mona Campus. His broad area of expertise includes Employment and Industrial Relations Law, Family Law, Constitutional Law, Human Rights Law, Real Property Law and Legal Methods, Research and Writing.

Dr. Jackson attained his doctorate at the Osgoode Hall Law School, Canada, Masters of Law degree (LLM) at the University of Sydney, Australia and his undergraduate law degree at UWI. He also spent a brief time at Boston University School of Law in the legislative drafting programme.

Having been admitted to the Bar in Jamaica and the United States, Dr. Jackson has practiced extensively in several jurisdictions. He was admitted to the United States District Court, Eastern and Southern Districts of New York in 1990, the United States Court of Appeal (2nd circuit) in 1991 and the Supreme Court of the United States in 1993. Dr. Jackson was the Principal Law Clerk to the Deputy Chief Administrative Judge in New York Office of Court Administration and served as Senior Appellate Court Attorney in the Appellate Division of the Supreme Court of New York.

Chapter II

Management Prerogative

The issue of management prerogative is an ongoing debate in the workplace as business owners seek to assert power and control and workers seek to assert their rights to equity and fairness.

"Oxford Reference" defines management prerogative as, "the concept of the right of managers to control and direct the work process, unhindered by interference from employees, trade unions, or the law."

The following is a speech which I delivered in 2013 which contains my personal perspective on the topic and what I consider to be the fundamental principles of management prerogative.

> **"Management Prerogative: Concept or Reality?**
>
> The management of a business is principally a property right of its owner/s. Hence, enterprises possess inherent autonomy to direct their business operations efficiently and without unnecessary interference from either the government or workers, except as may be provided by law. This essentially is the rationale for the exercise of management prerogatives. Management prerogative is

the right and unqualified authority which reside with employers and management to exercise their discretion in certain areas of decision-making in the business without discussions with or the agreement of a third party. Business owners have the right to receive reasonable returns on investment and an inherent right to expand and grow their business as they wish.

Management prerogatives include the right to hire, promote, suspend, or dismiss employees, the right to direct the work of employees; and the right to establish policy. Management has the right to increase or reduce the workforce in support of the particular business and based on the availability of financial resources and to determine and decide on issues such as products availability, price and business methods. Management prerogatives are not subject to negotiations with any Union and are usually expressly stated in collective agreements. The employer's right to conduct the affairs of the business, according to his or her own discretion and judgment, is well-recognised and accepted as an inherent part of any employment relationship. Employers therefore enjoy a great deal of latitude to regulate all aspects of employment.

Historically, the relationship between employer and worker was one of power and control on the one hand and subordination and discipline on the other. The period of the Industrial Revolution in the 18th century which impacted on the lives of citizens in many countries and on social systems worldwide: was characterised by power, control, subordination and discipline in the place of work. These were the essential and managerial functions in employment relationships and management prerogatives were quite extensive in the days of old.

Today the management structure in most organizations remains hierarchical and the elements of control, subordination and discipline from centuries ago continue to exist. Workers to a large measure resist the control of management and the relationship between managerial control and this resistance cannot be understood without considering the nature and distribution of power between the parties. Managerial prerogatives have been one of the most divisive factors between labour and management, due to workers making an effort to challenge the authority of the manager, and the manager's attempts to maintain power and control.

Workers and Trade Unions generally acknowledge the role of management to manage, however, they do not usually consider the managerial functions as a "right' but as part of the job managers are paid to do. Management uses the term management prerogative to defend its role in the workplace, while trade unions use this term to place an element of responsibility upon management.

The evolution of industrial relations and globalisation are reshaping the world of work in profound ways and altered the approach to management prerogatives in businesses. Globalisation has brought with it the diffusion of innovations and novel technologies, the rapid flow of ideas and the internationalization of business and business processes; there is also the increased emphasis on skills, quality and productivity.

Globalisation also has an impact on Human Resource Management policies and practices in the workplace. Contemporary Human Resource Management is moving towards:-

> "A change in power relations and highlights the supremacy of management. The management prerogative is rediscovered but in place of command and control the emphasis is on commitment and control as quality, flexibility and competence replace quantity, task and dumb obedience. To put it another

> way: the managerial agenda is increasingly focused on innovation, quality and cost reduction."[32]

Today management prerogatives have been circumscribed by modern industrial relations principles and practices that speak to fairness, equity and the protection of fundamental human rights. Management is charged with the corporate responsibility to respect human rights, that is, to act with due diligence to avoid infringing the rights of others. It is therefore the duty and responsibility of employers to find a proper balance between the exercise of management prerogatives and respecting and upholding the rights of workers and the law.

In Trinidad and Tobago employment relationships are governed to a large measure by a robust legal framework and by international standards that help to promote a strong social dimension to industrial relations and places labour relations in an economic context. This country has been adhering to global standards in the promotion and fostering of international best practices; and the Industrial Court plays the role as an impartial arbiter.

Let us briefly examine the legal framework of Industrial Relations in this country and the role which the Industrial Court continues to play. You may agree that much of what governs conduct and the core rules at the workplace in Trinidad and Tobago, and I daresay in many jurisdictions, is the content of individual collective agreements, informal understandings, the employee handbook and other formal instructions that originate within the workplace. It is safe to say that the day-to-day rules of the workplace are largely generated from within the individual organisations.

32 John Purcell "Human Resources Management – Implications for Teaching, Theory, Research and Practice in Industrial Relations" (Paper presented at the Ninth World Congress of the International Industrial Relations Association, August-September, 1992, Sydney, Australia).

Legislation such as the Industrial Relations Act, the Maternity Protection Act and the Retrenchment and Severance Benefits Act define the legal parameters within which parties must operate. Their relevance assumes significance when there is a need to ensure that legal and equitable standards are maintained at the place of work. The legal framework consists not only of *"labour laws"* that govern the workplace. One must also look to constitutional law, civil law, the *"common law"*, company law and even the criminal law. In addition, International Conventions, many of which this country has ratified, help to determine the international best practices and acceptable standards to be adopted by both parties at the workplace.

From the perspective of the Industrial Court, the legal framework from which we operate is a fundamental guarantee for the protection and for upholding the rights of employers and workers in order to have fair and equitable resolutions to disagreements. It is our view that it is in the enlightened self-interest of both the employer and the worker to adopt and adhere to industrial relations practices which are in accordance with the laws of this country and international labour standards.

One of the roles of the Industrial Court is to guide parties, through its judgments, on how to find and achieve a balance in the exercise of management prerogatives. The Court has pronounced in several of its judgments that the exercise of management prerogatives must be in accordance with the legal procedural requirements intended as safeguards against their abuse.

Let us quickly examine two scenarios: assume that for financial reasons a Company decides to retrench its workers, a decision which is entirely within its prerogative to make. However, the exercise of that prerogative must be conducted within the limits and confines of the law. The second scenario is as follows: employers inherently have the right to discipline workers, which I imagine is a routine and sometimes daily exercise of management prerogative. However, the law provides that disciplinary action can only be for just cause, simply put, the law does not condone the whimsical and arbitrary use of management prerogative. Unlike some jurisdictions where there is no written legislation, this country provides statutory safeguards to prevent employers from treating workers unfairly and without just cause.

The legal framework does provide for and preserves the processes for the exercise of management prerogatives by employers. However, these prerogatives cannot and ought not to be exercised without due consideration of the rights and obligations of both parties. The exercise of management prerogatives requires due regard to the principles of good industrial relations and international best practices. Employers should therefore be guided in their deliberations and in the exercise of management prerogatives by principles of equity, fairness and good industrial relations.

In the local context, the unfettered prerogatives which management once enjoyed historically have been circumscribed over time by the laws of this country and by international best practices and standards. Trinidad and Tobago has repealed the Masters and Servants Ordinance and is part of the international community which subscribes to a body of national laws and international standards which speak to justice and equity at the workplace. These are standards that have been adopted by employers and workers worldwide. In my respectful view, it is in a company's interest to adopt and embrace the principles of corporate responsibility that encourage compliance with the spirit of the law, ethical standards, and adherence to international norms. Those principles will ultimately redound to the efficient use of the company's human resource and to the overall success of the business.

To answer the question is "management prerogative" a concept or reality; if the question has not already been answered; I will say that management prerogative is not a mere concept but a reality which is necessary in the operation of any business. Management needs to be allowed to make decisions about the day-to-day operations of the business and its future without the interference of workers or their representatives.

The Industrial Court of Trinidad and Tobago in I.C.A. 8 of 1995 stated that:-

> "management prerogatives are inherent in the very fabric of employer/employee relationships. They are the unwritten and unspoken part of every contract of employment, and indeed they came into being on the very first day that one human being engaged another in a contract of service."

However, these prerogatives are circumscribed by the laws and legal framework of this country. As a consequence, there is a need for employers to appreciate the difference between management prerogatives and the rights of employees to participate and assist in achieving and preserving industrial peace for their mutual benefit.

Employers' organisations such as the ECA play a very important role in influencing employment relationships. These employer's organisations examine the internal workings of the businesses of their members and advise and guide their membership on best practices and standards in the workplace. In so doing they assist in raising awareness about changes in the law and in enhancing the capacity of their members to deal with developments in their operating environment.

I am sure that the ECA's message is similar to mine, which is, that management prerogative is a reality in the global economy and in this country, but it must be balanced with fairness, good industrial relations principles and practices and corporate responsibility based on international labour standards and the laws of this country. Employers must be ever mindful of the duties, obligations and rights of workers and the duties, obligations and rights which they possess as employers when asserting management prerogatives.

Earlier this year, the international business community submitted a report to the UN on 'Corporate Sustainability and the United Nations Post-2015 Development Agenda'. In that Report business representatives acknowledged that:-

> "Companies ... are increasingly aware that they need to earn and maintain a social license to operate, as well as a legal one. Corporations face increasing expectations from stakeholders to manage their societal impacts, including on human rights [and] labour ..."

I have no doubt that considerations of this kind would be uppermost in the minds of management worldwide, including in this country, as they exercise their prerogative. As you traverse the employment relationship, always bear in mind that duty and obligations cannot be separated from respect of rights at work as human rights." [33]

Jurisprudence on Management Prerogative

As I mentioned before, it is my view, that management prerogatives are circumscribed by the laws and legal framework of a country. There are many instances where the issue of management prerogative has been addressed by the Industrial Court of Trinidad and Tobago

33 "Local Judicial Perspective: Management Prerogative: Concept or Reality?" delivered by Her Honour Mrs. Deborah Thomas-Felix, President of the Industrial Court of Trinidad and Tobago at the ECA/ESC Conference on 16th October, 2013.

through its judgments, a few of which are mentioned hereunder in this Chapter.

In 1971, some 40 years ago, H H Braithwaite Vice President (as he then was) stated the following on the issue of management prerogatives in **Halliburton Tucker Limited and Oilfields Workers' Trade Union:-**

> "We find it rather startling and disappointing that this proposition could be advanced to us that an employer's prerogative entitles him to alter unilaterally at his whim and fancy the methods under which work is carried out in his establishment. It seems to us to take no account whatsoever of the course and practice of industrial relations or the elementary principles of industrial psychology, social psychology or individual psychology for that matter. We reject this and support the contention of the Union that when an industrial agreement governing the terms and conditions of employees is entered into, an employer is certainly not acting properly if he proceeded to unilaterally make material changes in the methods used in the performance of work covered by such an agreement... We are satisfied from the evidence that the introduction of a sandblasting machine into the work of spray painting was a major and drastic change in the circumstances under which Lynch had been working for ten years. We consider that since the question whether it was right that he should be called upon to do sandblasting was under discussion between the Union and the Company, it was improper of the Bulk Plant Superintendent, while that state of affairs was admittedly within his knowledge, to order Lynch to use the sandblasting machine. We consider that the Company was wrong in any event to issue such an order and in the event unilaterally make such a drastic and material change in the content of his work."[34]

34 TD No. 105A of 1969 Halliburton Tucker Limited and Oilfields Workers' Trade Union.

H H Braithwaite, President also stated in **Trinidad and Tobago Television Company Limited and Communication, Transport and General Workers' Trade Union** that:-

> "It is an understatement to say the common law rights of an employer have been circumscribed. For all practical purposes they have almost been completely eroded out of existence."[35]

In **Bank Employees Union and Republic Bank Limited,** H H Elcock in his dicta stated that management prerogatives are inherent in the very fabric of employer/employee relationships:-

> "This is an appropriate juncture for us to put the matter in proper perspective with a few general remarks about the matter of management rights and prerogatives (hereinafter referred to simply as "management rights"). These rights are invariably mentioned in collective agreements between employers and unions, but they could just as easily be omitted, for they are not derived from or conferred by such agreements. Rather they are inherent in the very fabric of employer-employee relationships. They are the unwritten and unspoken part of every contract of employment, and indeed they came into being on the very first day that one human being engaged another in a contract of service. [36]

In the dicta of **Oilfields Workers' Trade Union and Trinidad Cement Limited,** I addressed the issue in the following way:-

> "We do not question the managerial prerogative which a Company has to organize and reorganize its business but this must be balanced with the right of the worker to job security, equity and fairness, and above all, to the processes that are laid down by the various legal principles, especially the provisions of the IRA which

35 TD No. 68 of 1980 Trinidad and Tobago Television Company Limited and Communication, Transport and General Workers' Trade Union.

36 ICA No. 8 of 1995 Bank Employees Union and Republic Bank Limited.

> mandate adherence to the principles and practices of good industrial relations, as that term has come to be understood, so as to ensure industrial peace...When faced with harsh economic circumstances, as it is alleged in this case before us, there are several strategic options which are available to the parties. Some are in the exclusive remit of the managerial prerogative, while others require the consent and cooperation of the workers both in their individual capacity as well as in their collective capacity where the workers are part of a bargaining unit subject to a collective agreement."[37]

In **Transport and Industrial Workers' Union and Trinidad Distributors Limited**, H H Elcock examined the principle of restructuring and retrenchment as a management prerogative, and he held inter alia:-

> "We hasten to add that we are fully cognisant of the fact that employers are free and entitled to organize and/or reorganize and/or restructure their business operations as they see fit, this being one of the rights and prerogative of management that are expressly recognised by law. We would also say that where an employer chooses to reorganize or restructure his business to any appreciable degree it is usually extremely difficult for an outsider, be it a Union or a Court, to successfully challenge the genuineness of the resultant reorganization. However, where the reorganization or restructuring appears to be quite superficial, in choosing as it does the mere reallocation of storage space for goods and the redeployment of managers it is in our opinion, incumbent upon an employer to furnish an aggrieved worker (and consequently to this Court) a much more convincing and satisfactory explanation."[38]

37 GSD IRO No. 36 of 2018 Oilfields Workers' Trade Union and Trinidad Cement Limited.

38 TD No. 4 of 1991 Transport and Industrial Workers' Union and Trinidad Distributors Limited.

In **Oilfields Workers' Trade Union and Trinidad and Tobago National Petroleum Company Limited,** H H Mahabir also considered the principle and stated:-

> "It is not disputed that retrenchment is a valid management prerogative. It is however, subject to faithful compliance with the substantive and procedural requirements laid down by the RSBA, jurisprudence and the principles of good industrial relations practices. The right of an employer to dismiss an employee differs from and should not be confused with the manner in which such a right is exercised. It is incumbent that an employer exercises its prerogative to retrench employees in good faith for the advancement of its interest (for instance to restructure for efficiency) and not to defeat or circumvent the employees right to work and thereby earn a livelihood."[39]

39 TD No. 3 of 2001 Oilfields Workers' Trade Union and Trinidad and Tobago National Petroleum Company Limited.

Chapter III

Fixed-Term Contracts

Generally speaking, when we speak about employment contracts of an indefinite duration, we refer to the general (standard) form of employment contracts.

Fixed-term contracts, by their very nature, constitute the exception to the general form of employment contracts. The legal implications of fixed-term contracts have been examined by Courts globally; here in our twin island Republic, the Industrial Court adjudicates upon many of these contracts.

THE EMPLOYMENT RELATIONSHIP

Contract *of* Service vs Contract *for* Service

In the world of work, employment is characterised either by a contract **of** service or a contract **for** service. On the one hand, persons who are employed under a contract **of** service are considered to be employed for an indeterminable or indefinite period and they are regarded as permanent workers. Contracts of service can be expressed or implied and (if they are expressed) they can be oral or in writing. A main feature of a contract of service is that the workers are "controlled" by their employers in the sense that they must perform the tasks they are instructed to do, they are expected to report to work at a specific place, during specific hours and on specific days. Moreover, they have the right to certain leave (vacation, sick, injury, maternity and paternity) and they can enjoy additional benefits such as travelling, study leave, health insurance and pension benefits. Many of these workers maintain an employment relationship with their employers for a number of years, some until retirement. This is so, particularly, for those workers who are employed in the public sector and with the protective services.

On the other hand, persons who are engaged under contracts **for** service are independent contractors (self-employed), they are engaged for a fee to carry out an assignment or a project, usually by a specified date. The relationship between the parties in this type of contract ends when the project, or assignment is completed or at a specified date stipulated in the contract. Persons who are engaged in this manner are engaged under fixed-term contracts and work under contracts for service.

It is useful to note, that while parties in both types of contractual relationships have rights and responsibilities, persons who are engaged under contracts for service are not regarded as employees but as independent contractors or self-employed. Moreover, whereas permanent employment contracts can only be terminated in specific grounds, fixed-term contracts are temporary in nature and are regarded as short term employment which automatically expire at a predetermined point in time, this is referred to in law as the effluxion of time.

The authors of *"Commonwealth Caribbean Employment and Labour Law"* state:-

> "Today, a determination as to whether or not an employment contract/contract of service exists will be made by the courts having regard to the express and implied terms of the contract. Reliance may also be had on statutory provisions, collective agreements, and rules of the organisation, disciplinary codes and

> the job description of the individual....On 15th June 2006, the ILO adopted the Employment Relationship Recommendation with a view to urging member States to adopt national policies for the protection of workers in an employment relationship. It was recognised that for this national policy to promote economic growth, job creation and decent work, it was important to consider the definitions of employer, employee and their inter-correlation in the employment relationship." [40]

Let us examine some of the cases to see how the Courts interpret *contracts of service* and *contracts for service.*

In the English case of **WHPT Housing Association Ltd. v Secretary of State for Social Services**, Webster J. held that:-

> "The difference between a contract of service and one for services must reside, essentially, in the terms of the principal obligation agreed to be undertaken by the employee .....In the contract of service, it seems to me, the principal obligation undertaken by the employee is to provide himself to serve; whereas in a contract for services, the principal obligation is not to provide himself to serve but his services for the use of the employer." [41]

As Hariprashad-Charles J stated in **Ian Charles and The Board of Governors of the H. Lavity Stoutt Community College**:-

> "In order to qualify as a fixed-term contract, the date of termination must either be stated or must be ascertainable from the context or the other terms of the contract." [42]

---

40 Natalie Corthesy and Carla- Anne Harris-Roper, Commonwealth Caribbean Employment and Labour Law (Routledge 2014) 93.

41 (1981) ICR 737.

42 Claim No. BVIHCV2010/0049 Ian Charles and The Board of Governors of the H. Lavity Stoutt Community College.

In **Banking, Insurance and General Workers Union and Air Canada**, H H Aberdeen posits on page 14 of the judgment:-

> "Over the years, both common law and Labour courts have attempted to grapple with this difficult question of deciding whether a person was an employee and therefore working under a contract of service, or whether he/she was self-employed or an independent contractor and therefore working under a contract for services. In the course of these attempts, a number of principles and tests have been developed as useful tools in the determination of this issue. The Court has, in the past, relied on and employed some of these principles and tests...
>
> The Court identified various criteria which have been applied in order to distinguish a contract of service from a contract for service (i.e. an employee from and independent contractor) and concluded that in deciding whether a contract of service exists it must look at the reality of the relationship; that it is not necessarily bound by the label or description which the parties themselves give to the relationship and that it is entitled to look at the surrounding facts and come to its own conclusions on the facts. The Court went on to posit the view, that no one test is conclusive and that one will have to look at all the elements of the relationship in determining the issue. The Court then set out some of the more important elements that should be considered as follows:-
>
> (i) The employer's right of control;
>
> (ii) The employee as an integral part of the business;
>
> (iii) The chance of profit and the risk of loss by the person who undertakes the work;
>
> (iv) Ownership of the instruments;
>
> (v) The entitlement to exclusive service;
>
> (vi) The payment of wages, sickness pay, and holiday pay and by whom payment is made;

(vii) The power of selection and appointment;

(viii) The power to suspend and dismiss;

(ix) The power to fix the place, time of work and the times at which holidays are taken;

(x) The deduction of PAYE etc;

(xi) The intention of the parties;

(xii) The view of the ordinary person." [43]

In **Banking, Insurance and General Workers Union and Tobago House of Assembly** upon which I presided together with H H Achong and H H Aberdeen, I explained the following:-

> "The vast majority of employment contracts are of a permanent nature, meaning that they are of indefinite duration in relation to the date of their termination. At common law, however, any employment contract may be terminated by either party giving notice. In relation to the use of fixed-term contracts genuine motives exist for using it instead of the indefinite contract.
>
> As Gwyneth Pitt in her book 'Employment Law' explains in relation to the UK:-
>
> > "Sometimes an employer may have a genuinely short-term need for workers and in these circumstances, will wish to employ the worker for that specific period only. Examples might be catering staff to work during Wimbledon fortnight, fruit pickers to bring in the harvest, someone to cover another employee's maternity leave or a builder to work on a construction project." [44]
>
> As the learned author continues, it does make sense for employers to be able to make use of fixed-term contracts when there is a genuine short-term need. However, it is capable of abuse by using a succession of short fixed-term

43 TD No. 90 of 2001 Banking, Insurance and General Workers Union and Air Canada.

44 Gwyneth Pitt, *Employment Law* (6th Edition Thompson/Sweet & Maxwell) 3-020.

contracts, because at common law at the end of the defined term the contract would terminate automatically and the protection of the employee in terms of, for example, redundancy and unfair dismissal would be negated and the employers avoid incurring the responsibilities which they would have to a permanent employee." [45]

It is always important to note that fixed-term contracts end, not by what is considered to be a termination or a dismissal, by either of the parties, but they end automatically with the effluxion of time. Therefore, technically, there is no dismissal of the person who is engaged under such a contract.

Who is a Worker?

Before I continue to examine fixed-term contracts and the jurisprudence which has developed on the topic, we must give due consideration to the meaning of "*worker*" in the industrial relations context in Trinidad and Tobago.

The IRA provides that subject to subsection (3), a worker means:-

"*a. any person who has entered into or works under a contract with an employer to do any skilled, unskilled, manual, technical, clerical or other work for hire or reward, whether the contract is expressed or implied, oral or in writing, or partly oral and partly in writing, and whether it is a contract of service or apprenticeship or a contract personally to execute any work or labour;*

b. any person who by any trade usage or custom or as a result of any established pattern of employment or recruitment of labour in any business or industry is usually employed or usually offers himself for and accepts employment accordingly; or

45 TD No. 21 of 2015 Banking, Insurance and General Workers Union and Tobago House of Assembly. This decision was appealed and upheld by the Court of Appeal.

c. *any person who provides services or performs duties for an employer under a labour only contract, within the meaning of subsection (4)(b); and includes*

d. *any such person who -*

   i. *has been dismissed, discharged, retrenched, refused employment, or not employed, whether or not in connection with, or in consequence of, a dispute; or*

   ii. *whose dismissal, discharge, retrenchment or refusal of employment has led to a dispute; or*

e. *any such person who has ceased to work as a result of a lockout or of a strike, whether or not in contravention of Part V, as the case may be."* [46]

Simply put, the main feature of a worker within the meaning of the IRA is that he/she is under a contract with an employer, whether the contract is expressed or implied, oral or in writing, whether it is a contract of service or apprenticeship or a contract personally to execute any work or labour. Under the statutory definition, a worker is therefore an individual who has entered into or works under a contract of service with an employer. By implication, the statutory definition does not extend to self-employed persons and independent contractors; these are individuals who are generally contracted to work on the basis of a contract for service.

Additionally, the Industrial Court of Trinidad and Tobago has the jurisdiction to adjudicate upon cases involving fixed-term contracts. In so doing, the Court is guided by the principles and practice of good industrial relations in its determination of whether or not the expression "fixed-term" is a label or a disguise, or whether it is a genuine fixed-term arrangement between the parties.

46 Industrial Relations Act Chapter 88:01 of the Laws of Trinidad and Tobago.

As I stated in **Banking, Insurance and General Workers Union and Tobago House of Assembly**:-

> "Read together, the failure to renew a contract falls squarely within the Court's jurisdiction. This case is a dispute concerning the re-employment of a worker within the meaning of the Act and is properly referred to this Court for determination. As such, this Court is mandated, "notwithstanding any other rule of law to the contrary", including the common law in relation to fixed-term contracts, to determine the matter based on the principles stated in the Act.
>
> It means therefore that the attempt by the Assembly to use the concept of fixed-term contract to oust the jurisdiction of this Court, which in its legislative judgment Parliament has so broadly stated and strongly insulated, fails from the outset.
>
> This is not to say that a fixed-term contract is not recognized in our law or by this Court or that in every case of the automatic termination of a fixed-term contract there arises a successful claim of unfairness, if it is not renewed. The precedents of this Court demonstrate that, like all other disputes coming before this Court, the resolution will depend on the facts and circumstances of each individual case and an assessment made on the whole of the evidence regarding whether the treatment of the worker by the employer is harsh and oppressive or not in accordance with the principles and practices of good industrial relations.
>
> Put another way, even if a contract is upheld as one for a fixed-term, where there is a dispute in relation to that contract that this Court is called upon to resolve, the conduct of the parties under that contract will be assessed by the criteria laid down in the IRA by which this Court must determine all disputes and the Court will make its awards or orders according to its factual findings and its application of those principles.

In the exercise of our jurisdiction under the IRA, specifically in relation to resolving disputes in relation to fixed-term contracts measured by the guiding principles enumerated in section 10 which we are compelled to follow, we adopt the oft-repeated words of Phillips, J in Terry v East Sussex County Council [47], said in relation to their own statutory provisions but just as apt to what this Court is empowered to do in resolving these disputes:-

> "What an industrial tribunal must do is to ensure that the case is a genuine one where an employee has to his own knowledge been employed for a particular period, or a particular job, on a temporary basis....At one end is the plain case where a person, for example, a school teacher, is employed to fill a gap where somebody is absent, and it is made plain at the moment of engagement that he is only being employed during the period of the absence of the person he is temporarily replacing. At the other end is the case of the employee who is engaged on a short fixed-term contract, perhaps described as 'temporary,' in an employment where as a general rule the employees are engaged on a weekly basis and where there is no particular end served by the employment being arranged in the manner in which it has been. In between, there will be every possible variety of case...The great thing is to make sure that the case is a genuine one, and for industrial tribunals to hold a balance. On the one hand, employers who have a genuine need for a fixed-term employment, which can be seen from the outset not to be ongoing, need to be protected. On the other hand, employees have to be protected against being deprived of their rights through ordinary employments being dressed up in the form of temporary fixed-term contracts." [48]

47 [1976] ICR 536, 541-542.

48 TD No. 21 of 2015 Banking, Insurance and General Workers Union and Tobago House of Assembly. This decision was appealed and upheld by the Court of Appeal.

In **Banking, Insurance and General Workers Union and Royal Bank of Trinidad and Tobago Limited**, H H Khan, President, held that:-

> "A worker who serves an employer pursuant to a fixed-term contract is a worker within the meaning of the Industrial Relations Act ("the Act") unless specifically excluded by law. Further, it is well settled that a failure to renew a fixed-term contract upon its expiry can be a dismissal which is harsh and oppressive or not in accordance with the principles of good industrial relations practice."[49]

In **Banking, Insurance and General Workers Union and Maraj and Sons Limited**, I examined the dicta of several judgments to determine the nature of the contract and whether the label ascribed to the employment contract of Ms. Ramroop was a reflection of the true relationship, I stated as follows:-

> "In the case of Ready Mixed Concrete (South East) Limited v Minister of Pensions and National Insurance (1968) 1 All ER, Mac Kenna J. suggested the following as an appropriate test to determine whether a contract of service exists:-
>
> > "A contract of service exists if these three conditions are fulfilled
> >
> > i. The servant agrees that, in consideration of a wage or other remuneration, he will provide his own work and skill in the performance of some service for his master;
> >
> > ii. He agrees, expressly or implied that in the performance of that service he will be subject to the other's control in a sufficient degree to make that other master;
> >
> > iii. The other provisions of the contract are consistent with its being a contract of service."

49 TD No. 216 of 2001 Banking, Insurance and General Workers Union and Royal Bank of Trinidad and Tobago.

It is clear that condition (i) aforesaid embodies a test of mutuality of obligation which have been accepted by the courts as one of the most important tests of the nature of the employment. As Mac Kenna J. stated later in the said Ready Mix case (supra)

> "there must be a wage or other remuneration. Otherwise there will be no consideration, and without consideration no contract of any kind. The servant must be obliged to provide his own work and skill."

In Market Investigation Limited v Minister of Social Security (1969) 3 All ER 732 Cooke J summarised this test in the following terms:-

> "Is the person who has engaged himself to perform these services performing them as a person in business on his own account? If the answer to that question is "yes", then the contract is a contract for services. If the answer is "no", then the contract is a contract of service. No exhaustive list has been compiled and perhaps no exhaustive list can be compiled of the considerations which are relevant in determining that question nor can strict rules be laid down as to the relative weight which the various considerations should carry in particular cases. The most that can be said is that control will no doubt always have to be considered, although it can no longer be regarded as the sole determining factor; and that factors which may be of importance are such matters as whether the man performing the services provides his own equipment, whether he hires his own helpers, what degree of financial risk he takes, what degree of responsibility for investment and what management he has, and whether and how far he has an opportunity of profiting from sound management in the performance of his task. The application of the general test may be easier in a case where the person who engages himself to perform the services does so

> in the course of an already established business of his own; but this factor is not decisive..."

Miss Ramroop was asked by Counsel for the Company whether she was employed as an independent contractor and she responded in the affirmative. It is clear that the way the parties choose to label their relationship is not conclusive evidence of the type of relationship which existed especially when the evidence suggests that the legal nature of their relationship differs from the labels the parties have attached to it.

In Young and Woods Limited v West [1980] IRLR 201 CA an employee chose to be paid as a self-employed person as opposed to different methods of payment when he was "hired." No deductions were made from his pay for tax, he was responsible for his own National Insurance contributions and he did not receive any holiday pay or sickness benefit from the Company. Moreover, the agreement was made with the knowledge of the Inland Revenue who treated him for tax purposes as self-employed. However when the employee's services were terminated by the company and he complained of unfair dismissal, a tribunal held that he was an employee as defined by the statute and entitled to bring a claim for unfair dismissal. The Court of Appeal upheld the industrial tribunal's decision stating per Lord Justice Ackner;

> 'It is by now well settled law that the label which the parties chose to use to describe their relationship cannot alter or decide their true relationship, but in deciding what the relationship is, the expression by term by them of their intention is relevant but not conclusive.'
>
> When we examine all of the evidence which is before the Court, both the Company and the Union agree that Miss Ramroop was employed to be a supervisor of the store at Broadway, they also agree that she

> had to undergo a period of training at the Frederick Street Head Office prior to her assuming duties at the Broadway Store. She was required to sign a daily register at work and she worked from 8:00 am to 5:00 pm like all of the other employees. She was paid the sum of five thousand dollars ($5,000) monthly and when she did not report to work for a day there was no deduction of a day's pay from the said sum which the Company paid to her. There was no written contract between the parties and apart from the method of payment there is no evidence before the Court to suggest that there was a difference between her and any other supervisor or worker in the Company and there is certainly no evidence to suggest that she was an independent contractor. It appears from the evidence that Miss Ramroop provided herself to serve the Company. We, find therefore on the totality of the evidence that the relationship of employer/employee existed between the parties.
>
> We find that Miss Ramroop is a worker within the meaning of the Industrial Relations Act Chapter 88:01 and that a contract of service existed between the parties. The label "independent of contractor" which has been used to describe her does not in any way reflect the true nature of the relationship which existed between her and the Company."[50]

Some other Features of Fixed-Term Contracts

As stated before, fixed-term contracts, by their very nature, are not intended to be permanent but rather temporary and short term arrangements. The main features of these types of contracts are that they contain a commencement date, and usually a specified date of expiration. Many fixed-term contracts, particularly those from the private sector, contain commencement dates, expiration dates and

50 TD No. 181 of 2004 Banking, Insurance and General Workers Union and Maraj and Sons Limited.

a clause which provides that each party has the right to terminate the contract before its expiration by providing a notice. Should such a clause form part of a fixed-term contract of which parties to the contract agreed will come to an end at a specified date with the effluxion of time?

The dicta of Lord Denning MR in the House of Lords case of **BBC v Ioannou** are instructive and thought provoking on this issue:-

> "In my opinion a 'fixed-term' is one which cannot be unfixed by notice. To be a fixed-term the parties must be bound for the fixed-term stated in the agreement: and unable to determine it by notice on either side. If it were only determinable for misconduct, it would, I think, be a fixed-term – because that is imported by the common law anyway. But determination by notice is destructive of any 'fixed-term'." [51]

In **Dixon v BBC** the English Court of Appeal held that a contract is for a "fixed-term" even though the contract contains a provision which states that it may be terminated by notice on either side before the expiration of the term of the contract. [52]

In contrast, while the dicta on **Bank and General Workers' Union v. Home Mortgage Bank** explain in part the practice of good industrial relations which relate to short-term contracts, HH Khan asserted that every contract of employment, whether short-term or of indefinite duration, may be terminated by notice. He did not address, however, the issue of a clause within a "fixed-term" contract which provides for termination by notice on either side:-

> "We find that the Employer's failure to give such reason or reasons was in breach of the principles of good industrial relations practice. It does not matter that the contract was a short-term contract. The Act's protection applies to all persons who work under contracts of employment, regardless of the duration of the contract. In our opinion,

51 [1975] 2 All ER 999.

52 [1979] QB 546, [1979] ICR 281, [1979] IRLR 114, CA.

> it is just as possible for an employer to dismiss a worker under a short term contract of employment harshly and oppressively or contrary to the principles of good industrial relations practice as he can in the case of a worker under an indefinite contract of employment. The length of the employment under the contract is of no significance. Every contract of employment, whether short-term or of indefinite duration, may be terminated by notice. If an employer dismisses a worker under a short-term contract of employment harshly or oppressively or contrary to the principles of good industrial relations practice, the Court will take the duration of the contract into account for the purpose of assessing the quantum of damages to be paid by the employer but its short-term character is no defence in such a situation." [53]

Denning L.J. (as he then was) in **Stevenson Jordan and Harrison Ltd v Macdonald and Evans,** gave examples of the integration test which is also used to determine the type of contract of employment and reasoned:-

> "But in Cassidy v Ministry of Health, Lord Justice Somervell pointed out that that test is not universally correct. There are many contracts of service where the master cannot control the manner in which the work is to be done, as in the case of a captain of a ship. Lord Justice Somervell went on to say. "One perhaps cannot get much beyond this 'Was the contract a contract of service within the meaning which an ordinary person would give under the words" I respectfully agree. As my Lord has said, it is almost impossible to give a precise definition of the distinction. It is often easy to recognize a contract of service when you see it, but difficult to say wherein the difference lies. A ship's master, a chauffeur, and a reporter on the staff of a newspaper are all employed under a contract of service; but a ship's pilot, a taxi-man and a

53 TD No. 140 of 1997 Bank and General Workers' Union v Home Mortgage Bank.

> newspaper contributor are employed under a contract for services. One feature which seems to run through the instances is that, under a contract of service, a man is employed as part of the business, and his work is done as an integral part of the business; whereas, under a contract for services, his work, although done for the business, is not integrated into it but is only accessory to it." [54]

Strictly speaking, when a fixed-term contract ends, the contract of employment and the employment relationship end; the parties go their separate ways and there is no legal duty or obligation for re-engagement on the part of anyone. Indeed, only when there is a contention by the parties on whether or not the employment is a genuine fixed-term contract or permanent employment, that the issue is brought to the Courts for resolution. The Courts examine the employment relationship between the parties to determine its true nature, and then ascertain, whether the employer had a duty or obligation to the person employed. In other words, the Courts determine whether or not there exists a fixed-term contract (and therefore temporary employment) or permanent employment for an indeterminate period.

As I stated in **Oilfields Workers' Trade Union and University of Trinidad and Tobago Limited:-**

> "While normally and without more, there is no legitimate expectation in law for the renewal of a fixed-term contract and therefore an employer has no duty or obligation to a worker at the end of the term of such a contract, which expires with the effluxion of time in accordance with the principles of good industrial relations practice, the Court must examine the facts of each trade dispute to ascertain the true nature of the contract of employment which exists between the parties to determine whether the contract of employment is fixed-term in nature or of an indefinite duration." [55]

54 [1952] 1 T.L.R. 101.

55 TD Nos. 48 and 188 of 2015 Oilfields Workers' Trade Union and University of Trinidad and Tobago Limited.

In **Transport and Industrial Workers' Union and National Maintenance Training and Security Company Limited**, I upheld the Company's submission that the contract was for a fixed-term and I ruled that the person was employed on a short term contract and she therefore was not a permanent employee:-

> "The Union asserted that the worker was interviewed for the position of Clerk which is a permanent position and she was appointed to work as a Clerk. The Company argued that the worker was employed on a temporary basis (on 3 months contracts) as a Clerical Assistant to assist in clearing a backlog which existed at the time. The Company stated that there exists a policy within the Company of employing extra workers to perform specific tasks for specific period from time to time. These workers are temporary workers and their jobs are not among the jobs listed in the Collective Agreement...the worker was employed as a temporary worker by the Company and she knew or ought to have known this. Further, that there is no duty on the part of the company to confirm the worker to a permanent status after three (3) months since she cannot be regarded as a worker on probation for the purposes of the provisions of the Collective Agreement. The Court held that in all of the given circumstances when the worker's term of employment expired in March 2002 there was no duty on the Company to extend her employment for a further period. We held that "the decision for the Company not to rehire her and/or extend her term for a further three months cannot be considered unreasonable, harsh or oppressive and it is not contrary to good industrial relations practices." [56]

56 TD No. 97 of 2003 Transport and Industrial Workers' Union and National Maintenance Training and Security Company Limited.

H H Ashby in his dicta in **Communication Workers' Union and Telecommunications Services of Trinidad and Tobago** acknowledged that fixed-term contracts end with the effluxion of time:-

> "The letters from TSTT to the worker are fixed-term contracts which terminate by the effluxion of time. While the evidence of the worker's shortcomings explains why TSTT did not give further extensions, there was no reason for TSTT to treat the end of his employment as a dismissal for cause. The decision by TSTT not to extend further the worker's term contract when it expired on March 31, 2004 was neither wrong in law nor an act that is not in accordance with good industrial relations practice." [57]

It is noteworthy that the exercise which a Court undertakes to ascertain whether a contract is fixed-term or not, is a fact finding exercise. The Court scrutinises the evidence about the nature of the employment contract in order to ascertain the true relationship which the parties to the contract shared over time.

Permanent Employment or Fixed-Term?

However, there are employment relationships which may appear to the simple observer to be normal permanent employment, until the employer declares the relationship to be a series of "temporary" engagements by the use of fixed-term contracts, and brings an end to the relationship. The Court will not only examine the "temporary" contracts to understand their true legal meaning, but will also ascertain the terms and nature of the employment relationship to see if they are in conformity with the principles and practice of good industrial relations.

The dicta in **Bank and General Workers' Union v. Home Mortgage Bank** speak to the practice of good industrial relations as it relates to short term contracts:-

57 ESD TD No. 55 of 2006 Communication Workers' Union and Telecommunications Services of Trinidad and Tobago.

> "The principles of good industrial relations practice dictate that no worker's employment may be terminated except for a valid reason connected with his capacity to perform the work which he was employed or which is founded on the operational requirements of an employer's business. These principles are enshrined in writing in Convention No.158 of the International Labour Organisation ("I.L.O. Convention No.158"). I.L.O. Convention No.158 has put in written form long standing principles of good industrial relations practice and it is of no consequence that the Convention has not been ratified by Trinidad and Tobago. It is not applicable as part of the domestic law of Trinidad and Tobago but as evidence of principles of good industrial relations practice which have been accepted at an international level."[58]

The following are considerations and guidelines which were stated in **Banking, Insurance and General Workers Union and Tobago House of Assembly** mentioned before which can be useful:-

> "We begin with the statement of McPherson JA in Ceccol v Ontario Gymnastic Federation as a guide.
>
>> "A court should be particularly vigilant when an employee works for several years under a series of allegedly fixed-term contracts. Employers should not be able to evade the traditional protections of the ESA and the common law by resorting to the label of 'fixed-term contract' when the underlying reality of the employment relationship is something quite different, namely continuous service by the employee for many years coupled with verbal representations and conduct on the part of the employer that clearly signal an indefinite-term relationship." [59]

58 TD No. 140 of 1997 Bank and General Workers' Union v Home Mortgage Bank.

59 2001 CANLII 8589 (ON, CA).

The principle emanating from this case is that describing the job as temporary or a 'fixed-term' contract is just one factor to be considered. The reasonable expectation of the employee as to the likelihood of renewal is another factor that has to be considered. The considerations to be weighed in finding if such a reasonable expectation exists are:-

(1) Whether it was the ordinary kind of short-term fixed contract, based on the kind of work the employee is employed to do and where he is employed to do it as well as the manner in which workers similarly situated are treated;

(2) Whether there was a genuine purpose for organising the employment relationship on a temporary fixed-term basis;

(3) Whether the purpose for organising the employment relationship on a fixed-term basis is either obvious or clearly brought to the attention of the employee at the time the relationship commenced and there is no subsequent contrary course of conduct that would undermine this understanding;

(4) Whether that purpose in fact came to an end, because the task he was employed to do was completed or the post was abolished or funding expired or the kind of work that the worker was engaged to do is no longer available.

Three additional points may be made pertaining to fixed-term contracts.

The first is that it is not sufficient for the employer merely to show that the employee had signed what may be a regular relationship 'dressed up' as a fixed-term contract. This must be supported by the other consistent circumstances of the case so that there can be no basis upon which the employee could contend that he had a reasonable expectation of renewal.

Secondly, since this is a situation where the reasons for creating the situation or for not renewing lie in the possession of the employer, the burden of proof will initially have to be discharged by the employer by presenting evidence of the details of the situation. The reason for the decision not to renew like a dismissal "*is a set of facts known to the employer, or it may be of beliefs held by him, which cause him to dismiss the employee and that, accordingly, when determining a reason for dismissal, one must go to the thought processes of the employer.*" Therefore the evidence regarding the circumstances and reasons for non- renewal as well as the practices of the organisation must be led by the employer.

Thirdly, the manner in which the decision regarding non-renewal must also comport with good industrial relations practice. The implied duty of respect, trust and confidence imposes on the employer the need to ensure that there is a peaceful environment which is obtained through consultation and communication, the bedrock upon which our industrial relations practice is built. This also lends to the orderly management of a business. Thus the right to consultation in terms of good industrial relations practice is dependent not so much on an implied or express term in the employment contract but is an obligation with a corresponding right imposed on both parties to an employment relationship to meet the standard of good industrial relations practice dictated by the statutory scheme." [60]

60 T.D. No. 21 of 2015 Banking, Insurance and General Workers Union and Tobago House of Assembly. This decision was appealed and upheld by the Court of Appeal.

Month to Month Contracts and Legitimate Expectations

An interesting feature has emerged in organisations whereby some employers, at the expiration of what has been labeled as a fixed-term contract, retain the services of the person on a "month to month" basis without the formality of a written contract. In addition, that person continues to perform the same duties and functions for the same wage as he/she did under the expired contract.

What is the legal effect when a fixed-term contract expires and the person continues to work for the employer on a "month to month basis" under the same terms of employment? In my view, this new arrangement/relationship can be deemed, based on the particular facts, to be employment for an indeterminable period, namely permanent employment.

In **Public Services Association of Trinidad and Tobago and Housing Development Corporation**, H H George-Marcelle examined what were referred to as "month to month contracts" and noted:-

> "Three workers in this case were terminated however; special importance is paid to a worker, who was first employed with the National Housing Association (NHA) as a Customer Service Representative in around the year 2002. She worked continuously on a series of fixed-term contracts of employment and subsequently for the Housing Development Corporation. Three months prior to the end of her contract, the worker gave notice in writing of her desire to have her contract renewed, pursuant to Clause 15 of the contract. At the end of the contract the worker proceeded on vacation leave and upon her resumption of duty by letter dated 8th October 2010 she was advised that her services would be retained on a month to month basis from October 1st 2010 until advised in writing. The worker was dismissed on October 14th 2011."

H H George-Marcelle said the following about the "month to month" arrangements:-

> "The month to month contract created in the minds of the workers a legitimate expectation that their original contracts of employment would have been renewed. Under the circumstances, the Court had no other choice but to determine that a new contract of employment had begun and the services of the workers were subsequently terminated in a harsh and oppressive manner not in keeping with good industrial relations practice." [61]

Another example of an employment relationship which is labelled as fixed-term, and at the end of the contract the person continued to be employed on a "month to month" basis for a year, is the case of **Oilfields Workers' Trade Union and University of Trinidad and Tobago** where, after two consecutive three year contracts ended, the person continued to be employed by the University on a month to month basis, performing the same functions as he did under the previous contracts.

The following is part of my ruling:-

> "An examination of the facts in this Trade Dispute reveals that the worker was employed on two consecutive three year contracts during the period of 2007 to 2013 with no break in service at the end of the initial contract. The first contract ended on 13th May, 2010 and during the period when there was no contract in place, the worker continued to be employed without any interruption or break in service until 23rd August, 2010, the commencement date of the second written contract. The full effect of this arrangement is that he worked uninterrupted for more than six years and at variance to the terms of his written contracts. The University has not properly explained to the Court why the worker continued to be employed

61 TD No. 250 of 2012 Public Services Association of Trinidad and Tobago and Housing Development Corporation.

> uninterrupted at the end of one contract for some three months before a new contract was in force and further, why when the second contract ended in August, 2013, did he continue to work on what has been described as a "month to month contract" with the same terms and conditions as in the contract.
>
> The Attorney at Law for the University argued that the worker was on fixed-term employment which expired and he then continued to be employed on a "month to month" contract until August, 2014; this month to month contract was not in writing. We are at pains to ascertain what is meant by a "month to month" contract in this context, when the reality of the employment relationship between the parties for more than 7 years is that there was continuous service by the worker and the verbal representations from the management of a further renewal with a salary increase. This in our view can only be defined as an indefinite term arrangement dressed up as fixed-term employment." [62]

In **Communication Workers' Union and Mr. Cooper, Permanent Secretary to the Prime Minister, Office of the Prime Minister,** H H Jack considered the nature of the employment relationship and reasoned:-

> "The contract ended with the effluxion of time and the terms of a gratuity payment upon its expiration was satisfied. The Worker fulfilled a fixed-term contract which ended following which he was employed on a month to month basis. There is no evidence provided that he complained of this arrangement until it ended and he failed to secure another fixed-term contract.
>
> The Court is unable to disregard the evidence before it that forms the basis for the Worker's failure of the security

62 TD Nos. 48 and 188 of 2015 Oilfields Workers' Trade Union and University of Trinidad and Tobago Limited.

> vetting. In fact, it is this information that is the premise of the Employer's decision not to offer the Worker a new contract and not his performance...We are therefore of the view that the Worker's termination was neither harsh nor oppressive or contrary to good industrial relations practice. His termination occurred with the expiration of his contract and was not based on his performance as intimated by the Union. His failure to secure a new contract had everything to do with the results of a new security vetting system that was introduced by the Employer." [63]

Retirement Policy and Performance Appraisals vs Fixed-Term Contracts

Can a Retirement Policy be introduced in a fixed-term contract after the commencement of that contract, and more importantly, can retirement be a term of fixed-term employment? I examined this issue in the judgment of **Oilfields Workers' Trade Union and University of Trinidad and Tobago Limited**:-

> "The University stated, inter alia, that: The Board of Governors approved and the University implemented Policy Ref. No HR 22 Retirement on October 18, 2012. According to this new policy, the age of retirement for non-academic staff is sixty-five (65) years. The University explained that retirement takes effect at the end of the employment contract or at the end of the academic year, whichever is more convenient to the operations of the University. The Retirement policy makes provision for the University to offer at its sole discretion Post-Retirement contracts of employment to employees who have exceeded the normal retirement age, in order to facilitate succession planning or to retain specialised skills that are

63 TD No. 227 of 2012 Communication Workers' Union and Mr. Cooper, Permanent Secretary to the Prime Minister, Office of the Prime Minister.

> not available among the University's existing resources. The worker reached the age of 65 years and therefore he was subject to the terms of the retirement policy. The University also maintained that the worker was on fixed-term employment and noted that after the expiration of the second fixed-term contract of employment on August 22, 2013, he continued to be engaged by the University on a month-to-month basis without a contract".

The Court reasoned that:-

> "The question arises whether a retirement policy which does not exist as a term in a fixed-term contract can be included during the life of the contract without prior agreement or consultation. The University cannot have it both ways. The University cannot on the one hand say that there exist a fixed-term contract, the terms of which are binding on parties and which comes to an end with the effluxion of time and that the parties are confined to operate within the terms of that contract, then on the other hand, say that there is a retirement policy which though is not a term of the contract and which was introduced without proper consultation, must be adopted and applied to the worker's employment contract in a similar manner as is done with a person on an indefinite term contract.
>
> A retirement policy which does not form part of a fixed-term contract cannot be included in a unilateral manner by the University. Further, as with all fixed-term employment, retirement is not an issue; the contract ends with the effluxion of time and therefore the employer has no duty or obligation to provide retirement benefit and other benefits which may arise in cases of retirement.
>
> Retirement in the industrial relations context contemplates that there exist a contract of service which is indefinite in nature between parties and which has ended after a period of service. Further, Article 5 of the

> ILO Termination of Employment Convention, 1982, states that age, subject to national law and practice regarding retirement, should not constitute valid reasons for termination."

Another issue which arose in this case was the importance of a performance appraisal in a fixed-term contract.

> "The evidence is that on the 5th July, 2013, a performance appraisal was prepared by the worker's supervisor and a recommendation was made that he be given a new three-year contract with an increase in salary. The Performance Appraisal gave the worker a Grade 5 out of a total of 6 grades in leadership. There is no written provision in the two employment contracts between the parties for a performance appraisal to be done before the expiration of a contract and there is also no evidence to suggest that such an arrangement had been agreed upon beforehand by parties when they entered into any of the contracts. A performance appraisal is usually done if there exists a contract of service between the parties and it is used as a tool to assist the employer in the evaluation of a worker's performance. It is curious that in this case, a performance appraisal was done under what the University considers to be a contract for services, namely as part of fixed-term employment. This performance appraisal with the recommendations was also done when the worker was about to attain age 65." [64]

In **Oilfields Workers' Trade Union and Chief Personnel Officer, Ministry of Education**, H H Soverall stated:-

> "The Employer referred to a number of judgments both local and foreign and also Halsbury readings in its Closing Submission in support of its case that the workers were on fixed-term contracts which naturally came to an end

64 TD Nos. 48 and 188 of 2015 Oilfields Workers' Trade Union and University of Trinidad and Tobago Limited.

with the effluxion of time and contained no claims for automatic reemployment or for automatic renewal. Those references were read subject to the similarity in the inherent facts and evidence. However, in this instance, there were distinguishing facts between the instant matter and the authorities under reference.

The distinguishing factors are:-

i. the number of contracts,

ii. the completed performance appraisal of the workers with the Principal, recommendation to renew the contracts, and

iii. the precedent established in the past to renew the contracts on the basis of the performance appraisal.

Starting with the last factor, on the renewal on the basis of performance appraisal, Ms. Kangoo, the Union's witness, testified that the Principal would have told her in 2007, the beginning of the last contract, that the appraisals were being done in order to renew her contract and her contract was eventually renewed on that basis and she continued to work. This was not challenged by the Employer... This testimony was corroborated by Ms. D. Bourne, the Employer's witness and their Senior Human Resource Officer when she admitted in response to the Court that the contracts were renewed in 2007 on the basis of the performance appraisal...Indeed, without more, the precedent has been established and is applicable for all such future instances relative to the renewal of contract... Moreover, the question arises as to the reason for requiring performance appraisals of purportedly contract workers. The answers are two-fold namely:-

i. for an increase in salary, an event which rarely takes place and/or

ii. for continued employment.

We know for a fact that there was no increase in salary, for whatever reason. By a process of elimination, it is therefore for the purpose of continued employment."[65]

Fixed-Term Contracts vs Maternity Protection

In **Oilfields Workers' Trade Union and Ministry of Education and the Chief Personnel Officer**, I considered the rights of a worker to maternity benefits and the labelling of a contract as fixed-term to deprive the worker of those benefits. The facts and dicta have been abridged and they are as follows:-

> "On 14th September, 2004 the Worker was employed on a three year contract with the Ministry as a School Clerical Officer. At the end of that first contract in 2007, the parties continued their employment relationship when the Worker entered into a second contract for a further term of three years. In December 2009, during the period of her second three year contract, the Worker became pregnant and her expected date of delivery was August 2010. It is the Union's evidence that the Worker submitted a Leave Application Form to the Ministry dated 15th July, 2010 wherein she sought to obtain ninety-three days leave (vacation and maternity leave). According to the Union, the Worker was advised by the Ministry's personnel that her contract was ending on 16th September, 2010 and she should therefore re-submit her leave application. She was further advised that instead of applying for ninety-three (93) days leave she should apply for thirty-five (35) days leave which will take her to the end of the contract.
>
> The Worker testified that she was also advised by the Ministry's personnel that the changes to the number of days on the Leave Application Form (from 93 to 35) will not affect her maternity leave entitlement. She testified

65 TD No. 384 of 2010 Oilfields Workers' Trade Union and Chief Personnel Officer, Ministry of Education.

that she was further advised that vacation leave must be taken within the period of the timeframe of the contract. However, with respect to an application for maternity leave she was told "maternity leave was maternity; I would still be entitled to the maternity leave". The Worker re-submitted her Leave Application Form as directed by the Ministry's personnel for thirty five (35) days leave. However, when she proceeded on leave on 13th August, she did not receive the full maternity leave benefits of 13 weeks; instead she received maternity leave benefits for the period 13th August to the 16th September 2010. The Union's case is that the remainder of the Worker's maternity leave entitlement is due and owing.

The CPO argued that the Worker's contract was for a fixed term which ended with the effluxion of time, additionally:-

> "In the instant matter, **the Worker's contract of employment was a fixed-term contract with a start date of September 17, 2007 and an end date of September 16, 2010**. (emphasis ours). To this end, it is submitted that all entitlements and benefits, including the Maternity benefits that the Worker would have been entitled to while the contract subsisted, came to an end as soon as the contract determined by effluxion of time on September 16, 2010."

In order for the Court to determine the true legal nature of the employment relationship which existed between the parties, we need to examine the legal framework and the protection which the law provides for pregnant women. The Court also needs to ascertain what is the true legal import of the "fixed-term" contract which has been cited by the CPO.

Contracts of employment for fixed-terms have become common place in the workplace in this country, and, more and more, the Industrial Court is called upon to make pronouncements on the legal import of these contracts in the industrial relations context. The Court therefore takes judicial notice that, in Trinidad and Tobago, a number of persons are employed in the public and private sectors under what are often labeled as "fixed-term" contracts.

In the general sense, there are particularities of a fixed-term contract, such as, it is for a particular purpose which is discharged by performance, and also, that both parties end the arrangement at the end of the term of the stated contract. When the Court examines a contract, including those which has been labelled as "fixed-term", what is of paramount consideration, is the true legal nature of the employment relationship which exists between the parties and not the label which the parties may use to describe their relationship. It is therefore important for us to lift the veil or to remove the label which has been ascribed to this employment contract to determine the true nature of the relationship between the CPO and the Worker.

In Industrial Relations, when a Worker is employed on a bona fide fixed-term contract this type of employment is usually considered as "temporary" or "casual work". Employment of this type may happen for various reasons; there might be a need to fill a gap for someone who is absent or pregnant, there might be uncertainty about the duration of the job, or there might be a need for a short engagement for that position at that moment, among other things.

When we examine the evidence of the employment relationship between the parties in this Trade Dispute, we note that the Worker was initially employed on 14 September, 2004 on a three year contract and she continued to be employed on several successive contracts for varying periods with the Ministry. Throughout her employment with the Ministry, she performed the same functions and the same duties as she did in 2004. Some thirteen (13) years later, when this dispute was listed for hearing by the Court, the Worker was still employed at the Ministry where she was still performing the same duties and functions and the job continued to exist. The only difference, which is superficial, is that the job title has changed, the job is no longer referred to as School Clerical Officer as it was in 2010, instead it is now titled Business Operations Assistant. The parties agree that the job description, duties and functions of Business Operations Assistant are identical to that of School Clerical Officer, and that what has occurred was merely a name change.

This employment relationship has been labelled as a "fixed-term" contract by the CPO and the Ministry, even though the evidence is that the relationship, between the Worker, the CPO and the Ministry is for an indeterminate period. Is this a fixed-term contract?

It is uncontroverted that this Worker applied for maternity leave towards the end of her second three year contract. Simply put, the application was made in the sixth year of her employment with the CPO, in the latter part of a second three year contract, in what can only be considered an indeterminate employment relationship.

The CPO argued that it is contrary to its stated policy to grant maternity benefits to a Worker after a contract has expired. Essentially, the CPO's argument is that the right to maternity benefits ends with the contract, therefore if maternity leave is due after a contract comes to an end, that leave is disaggregated and benefits are paid only for the period which can be covered during the life of the contract.

In our view, it will render the protection which the Act is intended to provide, meaningless, if it can be subverted by the CPO by a mere policy; a policy, which appears to approach Maternity Protection for women who are on contract as a one size fits all approach instead of a case by case approach.

A worker who has been employed under successive contracts, and for whom this Court cannot determine a definite end date of employment, cannot be given the same consideration for leave benefits as, for example, a person who is employed on a very short fixed-term contract and who may not fulfill the conditionalities of Section (7) of the Act. While there may be rights for which the person on a very short contract is entitled; can an employer of a worker, who is employed on successive fixed-term contracts, be allowed to distinguish this type of employment arrangement from permanent employment, for the purpose of paying Maternity Benefits to someone who may be entitled to receive those benefits?

The uncontroverted evidence is that at the time of her maternity leave application in 2010, the Worker was employed continuously in the same job, where she performed the same duties and functions for six years in an indeterminate employment arrangement. In addition, the job description and all of the job functions remained the same throughout those six years...Is this a fixed-term contract of a three year duration, as submitted by the CPO, or is it that the CPO has attempted to deprive the Worker of her rights to maternity leave benefits from an ordinary contract of employment dressed up as a "fixed-term" contract? Has the CPO together with the Ministry deprived the Worker from receiving all of her maternity leave entitlement by the labelling of the relationship as a "fixed-term" contract?

The Act does not provide for a pregnant woman to receive a part or portion of the maternity leave to which she is entitled. This is not contemplated at all. The Act provides, that when a woman meets the requirements of Section 7, she shall proceed on maternity leave and she has the right to receive all the benefits and protection which are provided by the law even if, there is unfortunately, a miscarriage. There is absolutely no provision in law for an employer to disaggregate the thirteen (13) or fourteen (14) weeks leave entitlement which is due to a worker and to determine which portion of that leave the said worker shall receive. The CPO and the Ministry must operate within the confines of the law; they do not have the power to circumvent the provisions of the Act by a contract or any other legal arrangements.

We must point out, that the interpretation and the implementation of the provisions of the Act, as have been done in this case by the CPO, lead to absurdities and defy industrial relations commonsense. Industrial relations commonsense is the approach we use to resolve disputes at the Industrial Court. Industrial Relations commonsense demands that a worker who has a six (6) year employment history and who is pregnant, during the course of her employment, receives all of the respective benefits from the employer and the National Insurance Board. These are benefits to which she is entitled; her rights and her entitlement to those benefits cannot be disaggregated by the whim and fancy of an employer who chooses to label the employment relationship as "fixed-term".

We wish to state that it is very disturbing to this Court, that the CPO has labelled the employment relationship between the parties as "fixed-term" and has limited that relationship to only one contract for the purpose of determining the Worker's maternity leave entitlement. The duty and responsibility of the Industrial Court of Trinidad and Tobago, as provided by Section 10(3) (b) of the IRA, is to make decisions in accordance with "equity, good conscience and the substantial merits of the case before it having regard to the principles and practices of good industrial relations."

Equity in the workplace is not a theoretical construct. It means something. It means, in essence, that each Worker has the right to receive fair treatment and to have equal access to opportunities and benefits in the workplace. Equity and good conscience, in accordance to the IRA, demand that this Worker receives the same treatment as pregnant women who are permanently employed at the Ministry and indeed across the public sector in Trinidad and Tobago.

We find that it is contrary to the principles of equity and good conscience to disaggregate the maternity leave due to the Worker, and to pay to her a portion of that leave, especially at a period when she was vulnerable. We condemn this decision of the CPO in the strongest terms and reiterate that *"....the reasoning applied to the interpretation of social legislation; that is, that such legislation is to be seen as an instrument of social engineering and that the Court must not lose sight of its function to ensure that the intended beneficiaries of such social engineering are not deprived of their rights by reason of their relatively inferior bargaining strength. ....We must look beyond the veneer of the contract and expose to full view what in reality is a mere attempt at circumvention of the Act. ....A contract which seeks to take away from him such benefit must lead to infringement of the Act."*

The true purpose and intent of the Act have been vitiated by the policy approach which has been articulated by the CPO; a policy which is contrary, not only to the spirit of the Act, but also to the spirit of equity, good conscience and to the principles and practices of good industrial relations. These principles, which are contained in the IRA, are the bulwark against unfairness and injustice and they are among the fundamental canons of the practice of good industrial relations in this country." [66]

66 MPD No. 003 of 2012 Oilfields Workers' Trade Union and Ministry of Education and The Chief Personnel Officer.

Why it is Important to Examine the Nature of the Relationship between the Parties?

As can be seen from the cases, Courts examine the evidence to determine whether or not the employment contract between the parties is a genuine fixed-term contract. In so doing, the Courts have to discern

- whether the employee knew that he/she had been employed under a contract for service for a particular period and/or to do a specific job on a temporary basis;
- whether the nature of the initial employment relationship changed; or
- whether the employment is a contract of service and therefore it is permanent employment for an indeterminable period.

In some of the employment relationships which are examined by the Court, a person is employed on several successive contracts which span a number of years. This person is usually employed to do the same job, and to perform the same duties and functions for the entire period of the employment arrangement. Additionally, he/she may be employed on terms similar (if not identical) to his/her co-workers, in a job which continues to exist after the employment relationship has ended. Yet, the employer regards and labels this type of employment as "fixed-term" and does not consider the person to be a "worker" within the meaning of the IRA. There have been instances after the employment contract comes to an end, that only the most recent or current contract is regarded as the existing contractual arrangement between the parties, with little or no regard to the nature of the employment or the entire employment history, which as I said before, may span a number of years. This is evident from the facts of TD No. 21 of 2015 Banking, Insurance and General Workers Union and Tobago House of Assembly and also TD No. 384 of 2010 Oilfields Workers' Trade Union and Chief Personnel Officer Ministry of Education, mentioned before.

In my view, Courts have to strike a balance on the one hand to protect employers from unfounded and false claims of dismissals when there are genuine fixed-term contracts and on the other hand, to protect employees from dismissal from ordinary forms of employment which are labelled and dressed up as fixed-term contracts. This can only be done when the Court determines the true nature of the contractual relationship which exists between the parties.

When it has been determined that a contract did not end with the effluxion of time but it is indeed permanent employment which is disguised as a fixed-term contract, the Court removes the veil and the label which parties have ascribed to the relationship and applies the principles and practice of good industrial relations, prescribed by the IRA, to determine the fair and just resolution of the dispute, being ever mindful that each case is determined on its own particular set of facts and merits.

The following are two decisions from the Industrial Court of Antigua and Barbuda on the issue of employment contracts.

The Hon. Philip A. Pilgrim, President of the Industrial Court of Antigua and Barbuda in **Hyacinth Pestaina and Dickenson Bay Management Ltd (DBA Sandals Antigua)** held that the person was not an employee:-

> "Mrs. Pestaina and Sandals entered into an agreement or contract in writing (afterwards referred to as "the first contract") dated December 16, 1999. In the first contract Mrs. Pestaina agreed to be employed as Sandals Shop Manager. Either party was at liberty to terminate the first contract by giving to each other thirty (30) days notice in writing. Mrs. Pestaina trading as VISAGE, entered into a contract with Pinebrook Management Co. Ltd. Pinebrook is owned by Sandals. When Mrs. Pestaina entered into the second contract with Pinebrook, it was engaged in the operation of a hotel. It is named Grand Pineapple Beach Resort. Pineapple is located at the other end of the island 16 miles away. She could not decide to appoint someone else to perform her duties at Sandals. The first contract

was terminated by Sandals in a letter to Mrs. Pestaina dated June 05, 2007...A claim of unfair dismissal can only arise in circumstances where a "contract of service or apprenticeship" exists in accordance with Section 230 (2) of the Employment Rights Act (UK) 1996....in many areas of the law it is of fundamental importance to determine whether a worker is an employee or an independent contractor. In the fields of taxation and tort, this determination is important for a view to be formed of (a) vicarious liability and (b) assessment of income, respectively...In the area of employment law the Labour Code of Antigua and Barbuda confers upon employees only a number of statutory rights. These include a guaranteed pay, employment in conformity with the Labour Code, a statement of working conditions, a statement upon termination, certain leave privileges, maternity rights, holiday with pay, the right not to be refused employment because of membership or non-membership of a trade union, a safe system of work, statutory sick pay, and redundancy payment. It is only employees who are entitled to commence claims of unfair dismissal...whether or not the concept of 'mutuality of obligations' does exist in a particular case "it will usually be necessary to go on to the following 'tests for service' (i.e. employment status) which have evolved over many years, though with the obvious caveat that it is unlikely in most cases that any one will constitute 'a test' as such."- See Harvey op cit at paragraphs [22] to [27]...

The control test

....in Performing Right Society v Mitchell and Booker Ltd [1924] 1 KB 762, at page 768 McCardie J defined how the control test is to be used as follows:-

"...A master is one who not only prescribes to the workman the end of his work, but directs or at any moment may direct the means also, or, as it has been put, retains the power of controlling the work: see per Crompton J in Sadler v Henlock (1) 4 E & B, 570, 578."

Apart from control, one of the test or feature of an employment relationship is articulated by Denning L.J.:-

"The authors of Harvey op cit have posited at paragraph [50] that the integration test: "might be a significant factor where the individual started off as an independent contractor but ended up working full-time for one 'client', so that over the passage of time he has become indistinguishable from direct employees doing similar work."

The multi-factor test

"No one test on its own may be utilised to determine whether a worker has been employed as an employee or an independent contractor. The tests assist as useful general guides, but the modern approach is to examine the totality of the various elements which constitute the relationship between the parties."

The hiring of workers or workmen to assist in the execution of work for another person has been the subject of judicial interpretation. In the U.S. Silk case, both sets of drivers were held to be independent contractors. One of the factors which the Court took into consideration was that the drivers owned their own trucks. In addition to this factor however the major facts which the Court examined were "the total situation, including the risk undertaken, the control exercised, the opportunity for profit from sound management that marks these drivers-owners as independent contractors...A contract for services may exist even though "a substantial measure of control" is evident. It is worthy to state however that the control which existed in the Hitchcock case had essentially to do with "the conduct of the Post Office business" as opposed to the investment and risk. See Slynn J. in the Hitchcock case at page 108...similarly, in this case, the nature of the control

> which was exhibited by Sandals was related to its level of investment in the business between the two parties... simply put, Mrs Pestaina cannot successfully assert that she was an employee of Sandals and simultaneously state that she continued to be the employer of the three (3) persons who remained her employees. This would be an incongruous set of circumstances...I hold that Hyacinth Pestaina was employed by Sandals from December 16, 1999 to June 05, 2007 as an employee under a contract for services...In light of the findings, there is no need to determine these issues. The Employee's Reference is dismissed."[67]

In **Edwin Brown and Kings Casino Limited**, the Hon. Philip A. Pilgrim, President of the Industrial Court of Antigua and Barbuda examined the definition of contracts of service and contract for service:-

> "Mr. Brown obtained employment with Kings Casino as a security officer in or about March 1995. Kings Casino Limited operates a casino. It conducts its business at the Heritage Quay Shopping Centre. Mr. Brown's employment with the casino was also subject to an agreement between himself and the casino. This agreement is dated June 14, 2008. In summary that agreement portended that should Mr. Brown be 'caught gambling' while he was executing his duty as a security officer, he would be 'terminated immediately'. Due to certain circumstances which took place on August 22, 2008, it was the Employer's duty to suspend Mr. Brown from his position as security officer "until the matter and any concerns can be addressed by the owner..." It is Mr. Brown's evidence that he had a conversation with Mr. Fagalde. Based on this conversation and as the casino never called him after August 22, 2008 to provide any security service, he interpreted the

67 Reference No. 9 of 2008 Hyacinth Pestaina and Dickenson Bay Management Ltd. (DBA Sandals Antigua).

'suspension' contained in a letter dated August 23, 2008 by the casino to him as a letter of dismissal...The First Issue: Whether or not Edwin Brown was employed by Kings Casino Ltd. from in or about March 1995 to August 23, 2008 as an employee under a contract of service or pursuant to a contract for services?...The term "employee" is defined at Section A5 of the Antigua and Barbuda Labour Code as follows:-

> "... 'employee' means any person who enters into or works under... a contract with an employer, personally to perform any services or labour, whether the contract be oral or written, expressed or implied..."

In Charles Hunte and Life of Barbados (Civil Appeal No. 23 of 1990,) Byron, J. A. (as he then was) at page 3 of the Court of Appeal judgment stated inter alia as follows:-

> "...The wording of the (definition) does not highlight the distinction between contracts of service and contracts for services. But as a general principle contracts for service are not contracts of employment... The existence of a contract of employment or a contract of service or apprenticeship is a necessary and vital ingredient of a contract with an employer. It is the basis for the initiation of all References which deal with matters of unfair dismissal in this Court..."

In Ready Mixed Concrete (South East) Ltd. v Minister of Pensions and National Insurance [1968] 2 Q.B. 497 at page 515 Mac Kenna J. identified three conditions which are required to be present in a contract of service. He stated as follows:-

> "A contract of service exists if these three conditions are fulfilled:-
>
> (i) The servant agrees that, in consideration of a wage or other remuneration, he will provide his own work and skill in the performance of some service for his master.

(ii) He agrees, expressly or impliedly, that in the performance of that service he will be subject to the other's control in a sufficient degree to make that other master.

(iii) The other provisions of the contract are consistent with its being a contract of service...

As to (i). .....in all the circumstances of this case I hold that there existed between the two parties a contract for services. He was not unfairly dismissed...... There must be a wage or other remuneration. Otherwise there will be no consideration, and without consideration no contract of any kind. The servant must be obliged to provide his own work and skill. Freedom to do a job either by one's own hands or by another's is inconsistent with a contract of service, though a limited or occasional power of delegation may not be: see Atiyah's Vicarious Liability in the Law of Torts (1967), pp. 59-61 and the cases cited by him."

...The Court should have regard to Performing Right Society Ltd. v Michell and Booker Ltd. [1924] 1 K.B. 762. In this case Mr. Daniels cited what McCardie J stated at page 768 to the effect that a master is one who "retains the power of controlling the work...for several years certain tests have evolved which the Courts utilize to determine whether or not a contract of service does exist. The control test is one of those tests. The matter however does not depend solely upon the existence of the nature and extent of control...the law now recognises that a contract of employment involves mutual trust and confidence: see Mahmud v Bank of Credit and Commerce International S.A. [1997] I.C.R. 606: and, in particular, Lord Steyn at pages 620-622. The employee is obliged to use his best endeavours to ensure the efficient running of the employer's business. It connotes a requirement of personal service." [68]

68 Reference No. 7 of 2009 Edwin Brown and Kings Casino Limited.

It is noteworthy that although Antigua and Barbuda has a Labour Code, the approach of the Industrial Court of that country to the law on fixed-term contracts is very similar, if not identical, to the approaches of the Industrial Court in Trinidad and Tobago and the English courts. The Courts examine all the various elements which constitute the relationship between the parties, in order to determine whether or not it is a contract of service or a contract for service.

Chapter IV

LAYOFF

The global economic recession together with the Covid-19 pandemic have had a profound effect on the world of work and have triggered mass, unprecedented layoffs worldwide as companies move to downsize their workforces.

The unprecedented global reach and impact of the pandemic with its attendant economic devastation and damage to the labour market appear to be deep and long lasting. There are reports of permanent job losses and what has been described as a global shock as the world grapples with the long-lasting implications of fundamental changes in the world of work.

The ILO in its report for the last quarter of 2020 spoke of "the devastating losses in working hours caused by the COVID-19 pandemic have brought a 'massive' drop in labour income for workers around the world...

Global labour income is estimated to have declined by 10.7 per cent, or US$3.5 trillion, in the first three quarters of 2020, compared with the same period in 2019. This figure excludes income support provided through government measures.

The biggest drop was in lower-middle income countries, where the labour income losses reached 15.1 per cent, with the Americas the hardest hit region at 12.1 per cent." [69]

There is a temptation sometimes to put international labour standards aside and treat them as not important in times of crisis. It will do good to remember that the principles of fairness, equity and natural justice are principles on which the foundation our societies were built and which have assisted in stabilising our economies and countries over time.

This is the time, more than ever, where the adherence to proper labour standards assume even greater importance to minimise instability in the future and to safeguard the interests of all, in the world of work.

In Trinidad and Tobago, layoff is not defined or provided for in any statute, and many companies do not have policies which guide the procedure to be followed when a layoff is contemplated. Before the Retrenchment and Severance Benefits Act Chapter 88:13 (RSBA) [70] came into effect, Layoff articles/clauses were prominent in collective agreements. Since 1985, after the proclamation of the RSBA, there appears to be a shift in focus in collective bargaining and what has emerged is the inclusion of articles/clauses in collective agreements which address Retrenchment and Redundancy and less emphasis is placed on including articles/clauses which provide for layoff in collective agreements. As a result, Layoff articles/clauses are no longer prominent features in many of the collective agreements.

As stated before, the Covid-19 pandemic has created immense socio-economic hardship, this is particularly so among low income families. Global unemployment in 2021 is high and many businesses have resorted to layoff as a stopgap measure to assist with their financial woes.

69 https://www.ilo.org/global/about-the-ilo/newsroom/news/WCMS_755875/lang--en/index.htm last visited on 16th December, 2021

70 Retrenchment and Severance Benefits Act Chapter 88:13 of the Laws of Trinidad and Tobago.

When mass layoff is contemplated, as we are currently witnessing in this pandemic, it may be useful for companies to consider other strategies before resorting to layoff. Where possible, the parties (union, workers and management) can consider the reduction of the hours of work across the board, in order to spread the economic consequences of cost-reduction among all the workers instead of among a few. In this way, all the workers can bear the burden of the reduction of work-hours together.

This and other approaches to cost-reduction (such as identifying and eliminating wasteful practices) can only be achieved with genuine consultation among the social partners. It is also important when layoff is contemplated to ensure that the process which is adopted is not in violation with the provisions of the collective agreement or with the terms of an existing contract of employment.

Layoff in the Commonwealth Caribbean

A layoff is the temporary discharge of a worker or workers by an employer due to the unavailability of work. At common law, there is no right of an employer to layoff an employee without pay. Further, at common law an employer is not obliged to provide work for an employee to do provided that the employee receives his salary or wages. Thus, if an employer chooses to send an employee home on a layoff, the common law provides that such an employee is still an employee and must receive or continue to receive his wages or salary during the period of layoff.

Some Commonwealth Caribbean countries have statutes which make provision for layoff in the workplace. For example, in Barbados the Severance Payments Act Chapter 355A provides the following:-

> *"18. (1) Where an employee is employed under a contract on such terms and conditions that his remuneration thereunder depends on his being provided by the employer with work of the kind which he is employed to do, he shall for the purposes of this Act be taken to be laid off for any week in*

> *respect of which, by reason that the employer does not provide such work for him, he is not entitled to any remuneration under the contract."*

In June 2020, there was an amendment to this Act by the Government of Barbados (*Severance Payments (Amendment) Act, 2020*) in an effort to address some of the problems which were created by the Covid-19 pandemic. This amendment provides for severance payments for employees and states inter alia:-

> *"Temporary right to severance payment for lay-off or short-time*
>
> *6A (1) Where an employee has been laid off or kept on short-time*
>
> *(a) commencing at any time between the 1st day of March, 2020 and the 30th day of April, 2020 that employee will not be entitled to claim severance payment, unless he had been laid off or kept on short-time for 22 consecutive weeks; or*
>
> *(b) for a series of 18 or more weeks within a period of 24 weeks, then, if the employee, within 4 weeks after the relevant date, gives notice in writing to his employer indicating (in whatsoever terms) his intention to claim a severance payment in respect of the lay-off or short-time (in this section and section 7 referred to as "a notice of intention to claim") the employee is, subject to this section, entitled to a severance payment for being laid off or kept on short-time".*

In Guyana there is no expressed definition of "layoffs" in the Termination of Employment and Severance Pay Act Chapter 96:01 however that Act makes provisions for layoff and sets a limit of six weeks for a period of layoff. Section 14 of this Act provides inter alia:-

> *"14. (1) No employer shall layoff an employee except where the employer is empowered by this Act to*

terminate the employment of the employee because of redundancy under section 12.

(2) No layoff under subsection (1) shall exceed six weeks.

(3) Any employer who contravenes the provisions of this section shall be liable on summary conviction to a fine of fifteen thousand dollars."

In Jamaica, the Employment (Termination and Redundancy Payments) Act 1974 provides at Section 5A (3) and 5A (4) for redundancy payment:-

"5A (3) For the purposes of this section-

(a) an employee is laid off without pay if, other than on disciplinary grounds-

(i) he is laid off without pay in accordance with the terms of his employment; or

(ii) the circumstances of his employment are changed so that for some period he receives no pay pending a decision by his employer to reinstitute previous, or similar circumstances of employment; and

(b) a person may, subject to regulations, be regarded, during any period, as laid off without pay notwithstanding that during that period he receives some pay or is engaged to work for limited times only.

5A (4) Regulations may make provision for-

(a) the form of notice to be given for the purposes of subsection (1);

(b) determining the extent (if any) to which periods of lay-off during which an employee receives some pay, or is engaged to work for limited times only, may be regarded, for the purposes of this section, as a period of lay-off without pay;

> (c) *resolving any doubt or dispute as to the date on which layoff commences for the purposes of this Act."*

In Trinidad and Tobago there are no provisions for layoff in any statute, as I stated in **Steel Workers' Union of Trinidad and Tobago and ArcelorMittal Point Lisas Limited**:-

> "Layoff in times of depressed prices and economic challenges has been a strategy in our industrial relations culture and practice for decades and the procedure governing layoff is a usually included term in many collective agreements in this country. [71] A layoff in fact is a temporary suspension of an employee's contract of employment at the employer's instigation due to no fault or misconduct by the employee with the intention that the employee resumes the contract when the situation causing the layoff has abated. It is less drastic than termination for redundancy. However, the legal difficulty which the employer faces is that the employer has no inherent right to suspend a worker and fail to pay wages due by means of a layoff because of a redundancy situation [72] unless it is an express term of the contract of employment or incorporated by way of a Collective Agreement pursuant to Section 47(2) of the IRA, or implied using the regular principles of the law of contract or the custom of the particular trade or industry. This is well-established principle in law which this Court has recognized. Moreover, even if there is such a right, the implied duty of respect, trust and confidence which an employer owes to the employee requires reasonable notice of such an action even if such notice was not stipulated in the Collective Agreement.

71 I.C.A. No. 9 of 1986 Transport and Industrial Workers' Union v Consolidated Appliances Limited.

72 TD No. 267 of 2012 Communication Workers' Union v Home Construction Limited.

In the Company's evidence the term layoff is used interchangeably with redundancy. So there is no question from all of the evidence that the Company was attempting to deal with the issue of surplus labour due to financial challenges.

The IRA is silent on the term "layoff" and the Collective Agreement between the parties is also silent on the issue of "layoff". In Trinidad and Tobago, the Retrenchment and Severance Benefits Act, Chap. 88:13 (RSBA) is the legislation which provides a structure and framework for redundancy or retrenchment at the workplace, unlike the comparable legislation in other jurisdiction such as the United Kingdom and some Commonwealth Caribbean states. This Act does not provide for "layoff". Instead it defines retrenchment as "termination of employment of the worker at the initiative of the employer for reason of redundancy", and sets out the guideline which should be adopted if there is redundancy or retrenchment. It is the absence of any statutory provisions or scheme governing layoffs, it may be useful when there is collective bargaining for parties to consider always incorporating a provision of layoff in their collective agreement.

The parties in this case seem to accept that the Company had the right to layoff in a redundancy situation or at least the assertion by the Company that it had such a right is not contested by the Union. In our view, regardless of whether or not the Company has the right to lay off its workers, since it is the Company that is initiating the layoff, it is only fair and equitable that the spotlight be on whether the Company acted in accordance with the principles and practices of good industrial relations and the duty in respect of trust and confidence in exercising what it considers to be its right. This is especially so in this case where the Collective Agreement made no provision for layoff or the procedures attendant thereto.

In the absence of such provisions, this Court is guided by the accepted procedures followed in similar cases that have come before it. Also, since this was akin to a redundancy situation, and we note that the Company has put its case to us on this footing, using layoff almost synonymously with retrenchment, the guidance provided both by the RSBA, and the decisions of this Court, give general directions on how the parties ought to conduct themselves in arriving at the standards which governs good industrial relations practice.

The most significant procedural considerations in the RSBA are formal detailed notice of the proposed action, the date of the proposed action and the criteria used in the selection of the workers to be affected and significantly, prior to giving formal notice, enter into consultation with the RMU with a view to exploring the possibility of averting, reducing or mitigating the effects of the proposed action. It is within this understanding that the statement of His Honour Mr. Addison Khan, former President of the Industrial Court, should be understood when he opined:-

> "The practice of a temporary layoff is well recognized in industrial relations practice. A temporary layoff is a remedy which may be utilized by an employer to obtain relief where circumstances beyond his control warrant its implementation. It is a right which an employer may use only when the circumstances demand it. It must not be abused or be as a result of a whimsical decision. It must be required by the circumstances which must be beyond the control of the employer and not of his own making." [73]

73 I.C.A No. 9 of 1986 Transport and Industrial Workers' Union and Consolidated Appliances Limited.

> We also agree with the dicta of His Honour Mr. C.S.E. Beckles where he stated:-
>
> > "Colin Bourne, the learned author of the texts: "Redundancy Law and Practice" – Butterworths 1983 – in discussing the question of lay off defines it thus "An employee may be said to be laid off when he is not offered work for a temporary period". And our own Court has stated in IRO 23/87 – TIWU v Bata Limited, 'It is a well established practice... that the employer is entitled to lay off temporarily the necessary number of workers where in the course of business circumstances arise which make this necessary." [74]
>
> The gravamen of the Union's complaint under this provision is that, as the RMU, it was not consulted on the issue of layoff before the actual day on which the layoff was implemented, and; it was not given the opportunity to speak to its members in relation to the proposed layoff. It also complains about the fact that the Company bypassed the Union and went directly to the workers with the vacation leave plan that the Union had rejected and in so doing failed to give recognition of the Union as the RMU." [75]

In the absence of legislation to address layoff in Trinidad and Tobago, it is extremely important when the issue of layoff arises in the workplace that management holds consultative talks with the Union (if there is a RMU in the establishment) or has consultations with workers with a view to effecting a smooth layoff exercise which will lend to a less acrimonious relationship in the workplace. As I stated:-

> "In our view, consultation with a RMU is an integral part of the procedural duty of employers where redundancy or layoff is contemplated. This consultation must be fair and

74 TD No. 99 of 1990 Communication Workers Union and J.N. Harriman and Co. Limited.

75 Complaint No. GSD - IRO 031 of 2015 Steel Workers' Union of Trinidad and Tobago and ArcelorMittal Point Lisas Limited.

> adequate to allow the RMU the opportunity to deliberate and to respond to what has been contemplated by the Company. The level of consultation which is required with the Union can be no less than the type of consultation which is contemplated in redundancy and retrenchment cases as provided by the RSBA. It must be pointed out that in a layoff, it is the Company who benefits by not having either to pay wages or to pay severance benefits. The only hope for the laid off worker is re-employment." [76]

Layoff Clauses

I also wish to encourage parties to include layoff clauses in collective agreements (where possible and where needed). In Trinidad and Tobago, collective agreements are legally binding on the parties and they can go a long way to guide the approach to be adopted when a situation occurs which requires a reduction of the workforce. In organisations where there is no RMU, particularly in those which are engaged in seasonal employment, there may be a need to consider the implementation of a stated layoff policy, which can be communicated to each individual worker at the beginning of his/her employment.

The following are two samples of layoff clauses in collective agreements of various bargaining units of which National Union of Government and Federated Workers is the Recognised Majority Union. I do hope these two samples can serve as a guide to persons who may wish to include layoff in their policies or in their collective agreements. They may also guide those who wish to make temporary arrangements to reduce staff.

> **CLAUSE 1**
>
> "Article – Redundancy, Severance pay and new technology:-
>
> An employee who would otherwise qualify for severance pay under the terms of this agreement, shall not be entitled to severance pay where:-

76 Ibid.

i. He/she is temporarily laid off as a result of a reduction of operations; provided that the period of layoff shall not exceed five (5) weeks, and that at the end of this period, if the employee concerned is still laid off, he has the right to severance pay at the appropriate rate; but the worker may, with the approval of Union make agreement with the employer not to claim severance pay for a further specified period of time."

CLAUSE 2

"Temporary Shut Down Under the Vacation Leave Clause

(a) Due to the necessity of the Company having to close down most of its operations annually for about four (4) weeks, workers who will not be required to work will take their annual vacation during this period.

(b) A worker who would like to have his leave other than at the shutdown period can apply for leave and the Company would decide in its usual discretion whether it is convenient for the leave to be granted at the requested time. Assuming that it is convenient, the worker would be granted leave with the clear understanding that he would not be guaranteed work at the normal shut-down period. If, however, work is available at shut-down time, work would be offered to the worker.

(c) Workers who are required to work during the shut-down period will take their leave on a schedule of vacation leave prepared by January 15 of each year and which will take into account dates selected by the workers as well as the exigencies of the service of the Company."

The layoff clauses which I have included are by no means prescribed models, nor are they exhaustive, but I believe that they can help to fashion a workplace policy on layoff.

Some Other Decisions of the Industrial Court of Trinidad and Tobago

In **Trinidad Lake Asphalt Company Ltd and Contractors and General Workers Trade Union** H H Bramble, Vice President on the issue of layoff stated inter alia:-

> "The Union claimed that it was usual for the Company to discuss the position with them before putting a decision to layoff into effect. This is good industrial relations practice as it would give the Union an opportunity to eke out the best term for its members. For example, the parties could explore the question of alternative employment for some workers or a shortened work-week. In this case the Union says that it was not consulted with reference to the layoff from January, 1976. In its letter of November 20, 1975 the Company informed the Union that it would be forced to close down its operations for a while if it did not receive orders amounting to 10,000 to 15,000 tons. Discussions were held and the Union did not accept the Company's proposals for a shortened work-week. An order of some substance – not near the above figures – was received before these proposals could be put into effect and as soon as it was filled the Company gave two days written notice of a layoff without any further discussions with the Union. We are of the view that there should have been further discussions between the parties.
>
> Discussion is a prerequisite to the Company's exercising its discretion to suspend operations but not an absolute bar. Any suspension of operations is a variation of the contract of employment and we do not hold that the Company has an absolute right to do this in spite of the wide discretion that can be implied in the guarantee clause. It has been established that the discretion to suspend was always preceded by discussions on the matter. The Union is not in a position to say "no layoff" but in the interest of good industrial relations must be given an opportunity to put its views on the different aspects to the Company, discuss

> them and make suggestions to avoid or mitigate the layoff... If there is no agreement the Company would be justified in instituting it only if it could show that that course of action was reasonable when all the facts were taken into consideration.
>
> What is of importance is whether reasonable notice of the layoff was given. It is unfortunate that in an industry where there is likely to be a layoff at times the Collective Agreement made no direct reference to it; it is only implied in the guarantee clause. It is usual in such agreements to specify the period of notice required in suspension of work for varying periods." [77]

In **John Dickinson & Co. Ltd and Transport and Industrial Workers' Union,** I agree with H H Bramble in his dicta which addressed the issue of layoff and redundancy. He held:-

> "In Industrial Relations temporary layoff has a different meaning from redundancy. In a temporary layoff situation the fixed or probable period of such layoff should also be stated. According to the Dictionary of Industrial Relations by Harold S. Roberts: – 'Temporary Layoff: – A separation from employment at the instigation of the employer but without fault on the employee's part usually of a temporary nature.' According to Rex Nettleford in his 'Trade Union and Industrial Relations Terms':- Redundance: is the end product of retrenchment. It refers to workers who become excessive for such causes as mechanization, reorganization, etc. Retrenchment: Permanent loss of employment brought about by the introduction of economics, e.g. automation, mechanization, reorganization, etc....We interpret the term "to warrant a reduction in the Labour Force" in Section 2 of the Article to mean a permanent reduction in the Labour force due to redundancy." [78]

77 TD No. 226 of 1976 Trinidad Lake Asphalt Company Ltd and Contractors' and General Workers' Trade Union.

78 I.I.A. No. 25 of 1978 John Dickinson & Co. Ltd and Transport and Industrial Workers' Union.

In **Beatrix Limited and the Union of Commercial and Industrial Workers**, H H Ramchand in his dicta considered the provisions of an Article in the collective agreement and held:-

> "We find that in accordance with the provisions of Article 13(1) dealing with severance payment reproduced above the workers who were laid off when the Union made its application to the Court under Section 16(2) were entitled to receive their Severance Benefits since they were laid off for more than three months. We also find that the remaining workers who were laid off by the Company on 29th March 1982 all qualify under Article 13(1) to receive their Severance Benefits since they have also been laid off for more than three months." [79]

Additionally, in **Transport and Industrial Workers' Union and Consolidated Appliances Limited**, H H Khan examined the provisions of an article in a collective agreement and held:-

> "Article 36 is of course, very clumsily worded and is ambiguous. It is the duty of the Court nevertheless to endeavour to make some sense of it. Firstly, it appears from Article 36 that it is a condition precedent to any temporary lay-off of workers, in the event conditions warranting such temporary lay-off arise, that the Company must discuss the matter with the Union before laying-off the workers. Secondly, in the event of breakdown electrical outages, shortage of gas, flood or fire, workers shall be guaranteed wages on the basis stated in Section 2 of Article 36. Thirdly, in the event that such conditions (i.e. the specific conditions enumerated in Section 2) continue for more than two (2) continuous days, then the Company may temporarily lay-off workers. In my opinion, this is the only sensible interpretation. The terms and conditions of a collective agreement which has been duly registered pursuant to and in accordance with the Act, is, during its continuance, binding on the parties

79 TD No. 94 of 1982 and I.I.A. No. 22 of 1982 (consolidated) Beatrix Limited and Union of Commercial and Industrial Workers.

to it. It is recognised, however, that a registered collective agreement is framed against the background of what has been described and known as the principles of good industrial relations practice. The Act expressly enjoins the Court in matters before it to 'act in accordance with equity, good conscience, and the substantial merits of the case before it, having regard to the principles and practices of good industrial relations.' The practice of a temporary lay-off is well recognised in industrial relations practice. A temporary lay-off is a remedy which may be utilised by an employer to obtain relief where circumstances beyond his control warrant its implementation. It is a right which an employer may use only when the circumstances demand it, it must not be abused or be as a result of a whimsical decision. It must be required by the circumstances which must be beyond the control of the employer and not of his own making.

In a judgment of this Court in IROs Nos. 23 & 24 of 1987 between Transport and Industrial Workers' Union and Bata Trinidad and Tobago Limited, which was delivered on 9th July, 1990, the Court discussed the nature of a temporary lay-off. The Court stated in that case:-

> "It is only in extremely rare instances that the terms relating to hours of employment in a collective agreement provide a guarantee that the workers will be provided work during these hours. Apart from these instances collective agreements prescribe merely what the hours of work or the normal or regular hours of work shall be. It is well established practice in these cases that the employer is entitled to lay-off temporarily the necessary number of workers where in the course of business, circumstances arise which make this necessary. Many collective agreements make provisions, more or less detailed, for such lay-off. In the instant matter, as we have seen, the collective agreement for the 1981 – 1983 period recognised this right to lay-off in Sections 1 and 7 of Article 17

and the parties had executed an agreement that these provisions should continue in the succeeding 1984 – 1986 collective agreement. The traditional method of lay-off has been to lay-off the requisite number of workers for a continuous period. In recent times there have been instances of temporary reductions in the labour force being effected by lay-off of the entire workforce for one day at a time. For instance if a reduction of the workforce by twenty (20) per cent becomes necessary the whole labour force is laid off over a period of time for one day each week, that is, twenty (20) per cent of the normal work time of five (5) days per week, instead of twenty (20) per cent of them being laid off continuously during the period. Thus the burden of loss of work is shared equitably by all instead of eighty (80) per cent working full time and twenty (20) per cent having no work at all. Under modern methods of production it is not always altogether feasible to apply the traditional method of lay-off. Other factors may also operate against it. In the instant matter, for example, the Company pointed out to the Union that because of the wide geographical spread of the bargaining unit comprised as it was of a number of small outlets from Tobago to Point Fortin in Trinidad, the traditional method would not be feasible under the applicable industrial relations principle of 'last in, first out'."

H H Khan continued:-

"In my opinion, however an employer cannot continue a temporary lay-off indefinitely. The principles of good industrial relations practice require the expeditious determination of matters of industrial relations. Workers should not be subjected to inordinately long periods of unemployment or reduced wages because of the temporary lay-off. The use of the word 'temporary' means that the lay-off would only last for a time. In my experience, temporary lay-off usually last for approximately three (3) months. In my opinion, unless the parties agree on a longer period for

> a temporary lay-off in a registered collective agreement, or unless there are exceptional circumstances, no temporary lay-off should exceed three (3) months in accordance with the principles of good industrial relations practice." [80]

The impact of the Covid-19 pandemic on the labour market globally puts the issue of internal workplace policies and arrangements for layoffs centre stage, as more and more businesses have been impacted by the measures which have been introduced by the State to contain the spread of the pandemic. I hope that the jurisprudence of the Industrial Court of Trinidad and Tobago and that of the Commonwealth Caribbean territories on layoffs (and also the layoff clauses), can serve as a guide to employers who do not have layoff policies in their handbooks or in collective agreements; and who may be contemplating new approaches (including remote work and layoff) to save their businesses.

Moreover, as we make adjustments in the workplace to treat with the new paradigm which has been created for the most part by the global economic recession and the Covid-19 pandemic, the cooperation, consultation and collaboration of the social partners, including tripartite discussions, are key to maintaining order and stability in the labour market. As I stated in September 2020:-

> "Social dialogue is key to the adjustment which the workplace has to make during and after this pandemic. I cannot overstate how important is a climate of robust discussions, genuine consultations and compromise, built through social dialogue for the effective implementation of measures to address this pandemic and its impact on the labour market. A commitment of employers and trade unions to adjust to new and necessary workplace policy measures, and to do so in a spirit of respect and compromise, is important for the survival of businesses, the saving of lives and the saving of jobs." [81]

80 I.C.A No. 9 of 1986 Transport and Industrial Workers' Union and Consolidated Appliances Limited.

81 Address by Her Honour Mrs. Deborah Thomas-Felix, Special Sitting for the Opening of the Industrial Court 2020/2021 Law Term.

The Covid-19 pandemic has provided the opportunity for governments, employers, trade unions and workers alike, to ensure that the principles and practices of good industrial relations, and the international labour standards which govern layoff and work in general, are promoted and applied. As we look at the future of work when this Covid-19 pandemic is over, and consider how we regenerate work and the work-space globally, we will have to embrace the transformative changes in the modalities of work with continued re-skilling, re-training and digitisation in the workplace. We may also have to address digitisation gaps in the short term and the vulnerabilities of many workers in various sectors, as we move forward.

In summary, it is important to bear in mind that a layoff is not a retrenchment. Layoff, unlike retrenchment, is temporary in nature and "the fixed or probable period" of a layoff should be stated. It will also lend to the smooth management of business – especially those engaged in seasonal or temporary work – to include layoff clauses in collective agreements and in workplace policies.

Chapter V

RETRENCHMENT

The main legislation on retrenchment in Trinidad and Tobago is the Retrenchment and Severance Benefit Act (RSBA).

This Act outlines the procedure which is to be adopted when there is a redundancy and it also provides for severance payments to workers. However, one must always bear in mind that the IRA is the parent legislation on Industrial Relations law, and it contains the overarching principles for the effective management of workplace related issues, namely, equity, good conscience and the principles and practice of good industrial relations.

The RSBA at Section 2 defines redundancy and retrenchment as follows:-

> *"Redundancy" means the existence of surplus labour in an undertaking for whatever cause and*
>
> *"Retrenchment" is defined as the termination of employment of a worker at the initiative of an employer for the reason of redundancy*

When an employer proposes to retrench workers, the following legal requirements stated at Sections 4–8 of the RSBA are to be observed as part of the process:-

"4.(1) *Where an employer proposes to terminates the services of five or more workers for the reason of redundancy he shall give formal notice of termination in writing to each involved worker, to the recognised majority union and to the Minister.*

(2) *The notice shall state–*

(a) *the names and classifications of the involved workers;*

(b) *the length of service and current wage rates of the involved workers;*

(c) *the reasons for the redundancy;*

(d) *the proposed date of the termination of employment;*

(e) *the criteria used in the selection of the workers to be retrenched;*

(f) *any other relevant information*

(3) *Where notice of retrenchment given by an employer to fewer than five involved workers is followed by notice of retrenchment to any other worker within the time period of the previous notice to the other workers, all workers receiving such notice shall be counted together in determining the number of workers to whom notice has been given for the purposes of this section.*

5. *Notwithstanding section 4, an employer may, prior to the giving of formal notice in writing of retrenchment, enter into consultation with the recognised majority union with a view to exploring the possibility of averting, reducing or mitigating the effects of the proposed retrenchment.*

> 6. *Subject to section 7, the minimum period of formal notice required by section 4 shall be forty-five days before the proposed date of retrenchment.*
>
> 7. *Where, due to unforeseen circumstances it is not practicable for an employer to comply with the requirements of section 6 with respect to formal notice, he shall give the maximum notice that he can reasonably be expected to give in the circumstances and the onus shall be on him to prove that the circumstances which prevented him from complying with section 6 were indeed unforeseen.*
>
> 8.(1) *Within seven days of receipt of the notice from the employer, the recognised majority union shall reply in writing copied to the Minister, stating its position regarding the proposed retrenchment and giving reasons for its objections, if any, to the action proposed by the employer.*
>
> (2) *Where the recognised majority union fails to reply in accordance with this section, the employer may proceed to effect the retrenchment in accordance with the notice given after notifying the Union and the Minister of his intention so to do."*

Further, Section 23 of the RSBA provides:-

> *"23.(1) A dispute arising out of a retrenchment issue including-*
>
> *(a) dispute which alleges unfair dismissal;*
>
> *(b) a difference of opinion as to the reasonableness or otherwise of any action taken or not taken by an employer or a worker; or*
>
> *(c) a dispute as to what is reasonably comparable in respect of a terminal benefit scheme, may be reported to the Minister as a trade dispute and shall be dealt which as such under the Industrial Relations Act."*

The term retrenchment is defined in **Commercial Finance Co Ltd (in liquidation) v Ramsingh-Mahabir** by the Privy Council as:-

> "'Retrenchment' means termination for the reason of redundancy, and 'redundancy' means the existence of surplus labour in an undertaking for whatever cause. It does not apply to the termination of employment simply because the business has ceased to exist. Retrenchment contemplates that the business will continue in existence but that there are too many workers for the purposes of the business so that some have to be made redundant. Moreover, termination of a worker's employment has to be at the initiative of the employer. Termination by operation of law, following a compulsory winding up..., is not a termination at the initiative of the employer." [82]

Retrenchment is Never Due to the Fault or Misconduct of a Worker

One must always bear in mind that the retrenchment is never due to the fault or misconduct of a worker, instead it is mainly due to the financial and other economic constraints proffered by the Employer. The prospects of retrenchment and the uncertainty of the future can be a very demoralising and frightening experience. It is therefore very important that employees receive adequate notice of an impending retrenchment. Moreover, the period of notice of retrenchment is meant to provide the worker with the opportunity to prepare for his/her future, and to adjust to the new situation at work, among other things. This is also an opportunity for a Company to use that period of notice, to see if there are other areas within the organisation where the worker can secure alternative employment, in an effort to mitigate and/or to reduce the impact of the proposed retrenchment.

82 (1994) 45 WIR 447.

Consultation and Notice

Sections 5, 6 and 7 of the RSBA provide for an employer to give notice in writing of a proposed retrenchment to the worker, a recognised majority union and to the Minister of Labour. I cannot overstate the importance of giving notice to individual workers and to the RMU when a retrenchment is contemplated. It is equally important to "hold talks" with the Union (if there is one) to explore other possibilities to avoid retrenchment. Consultation and notice are critical elements to the retrenchment process and they are key to the principles and practice of good industrial relations. In instances where these two elements are absent, the Court may hold that the retrenchment process is not in accord with the laws and with the principles and practice of good industrial relations, and can deem the retrenchment to be a dismissal which is *"harsh and oppressive."*

In **Jamaica Flour Mills Limited** three workers were dismissed on the grounds of redundancy, without any previous communication or any notice that they were to be made redundant. The Industrial Dispute Tribunal of Jamaica, while not questioning the redundancy, held that the dismissal was "unjustifiable" and ordered reinstatement and stated that:-

> "it was unfair, unreasonable and unconscionable for the Company to effect the dismissals in the way that it did. It showed very little if any concern for the dignity and human feeling of the workers. This is indeed aggravated when one considers their years of service involved." [83]

This decision was upheld by the Court of Appeal of Jamaica and the Privy Council.

83 Privy Council Appeal No. 69 of 2003 Jamaica Flour Mills Ltd v The Industrial Disputes Tribunal and National Workers Union [2005] UKPC 16.

In **Banking, Insurance and General Workers Union and Public Services Association** I emphasised that:-

> "Fair consultation requires (the employer) to hold talks with the Union when the proposals for retrenchment are at a formative stage. Fair consultation also requires that the Union receives adequate information from (the employer) for it to address and respond if necessary." [84]

This point was further reiterated in **Steel Workers' Union of Trinidad and Tobago and ArcelorMittal Point Lisas Limited**:-

> "In our view, consultation with a RMU is an integral part of the procedural duty of employers where redundancy or layoff is contemplated. This consultation must be fair and adequate to allow the RMU the opportunity to deliberate and to respond to what has been contemplated by the Company. The level of consultation which is required with the Union can be no less than the type of consultation which is contemplated in redundancy and retrenchment cases as provided by the RSBA. It must be pointed out that in a layoff, it is the Company who benefits by not having either to pay wages or to pay severance benefits. The only hope for the laid off worker is re-employment.
>
> We hold therefore that the procedures which are provided in the RSBA should serve as a guideline for what constitutes good industrial relations in instances of layoff, redundancy and retrenchment.
>
> It is our finding that the Company failed to treat with the Union in good faith for the purpose of collective bargaining when it did not give the Union the opportunity to deliberate and to respond to its proposal which was raised for the very first time at the meeting on 7th December. Even when the Union requested a meeting after the layoff was put into effect, the Company refused to meet with the

84 TD Nos. 244 & 245 of 2004 Banking, Insurance and General Workers Union and Public Services Association.

> Union, giving it no option but to resort to the procedures under the IRA and the instant proceedings." [85]

In **Communication Workers' Union and Front Row Limited**, H H Ramparas examined the issue of the requirement to provide formal notice of retrenchment when such a notice was posted on a Notice Board:-

> "From the facts and evidence, the only issue that arises for determination in this dispute is whether the Employer's posting of notice on the notice board complied with the provisions of Sections 4 and 6 of the Retrenchment and Severance Benefits Act (RSBA) and the principles of good industrial relations practice. Clearly it is a requirement of the RSBA that formal notice of termination in writing, must be given to each worker where five or more workers are terminated and a minimum period of forty five days' notice is necessary.
>
> Thus failure to give formal notice is a breach of the law and the principles of good industrial relations practice....M.A. de La Bastide C.J. expressed the importance of notice in the Claude Albert case in this way. He stated that:-
>
> > "Notice is intended to provide the employee with the opportunity to adjust to the loss of his job, primarily by finding another one. Payment in lieu of notice compensates the employee for loss of that opportunity, it provides a sort of financial buffer to tide him over." [86]
>
> On the totality of the evidence we are satisfied that the retrenchment of the worker was genuine and the Employer acted reasonably and in accordance with the principles of good industrial relations practice. Notwithstanding this, we find that the Employer failed to comply with the

85 Complaint No. IRO 031 Of 2015 Steel Workers' Union of Trinidad and Tobago and Arcelormittal Point Lisas Limited.

86 Civil Appeal No. 37 of 2000 Claude Albert and Alston's Building Enterprise Limited.

> requirement of notice as required by the Act. A notice posted on a notice board was definitely not formal notice as stipulated in section 4." [87]

In **Oilfields Workers' Trade Union and Offshore Atlantic Limited,** H H Seale considered sections 6 and 7 of the RSBA with respect to maximum notice to be given in terms of redundancy:-

> "Section 7 RSBA - Where, due to unforeseen circumstances it is not practicable for an employer to comply with the requirements of section 6 with respect to formal notice, he shall give the maximum notice that he can reasonably be expected to give in the circumstances and the onus shall be on him to prove that the circumstances which prevented him from complying with section 6 were indeed unforeseen. However, the Company breached section 7 of the Act by failing to give the maximum notice that it could reasonably be expected to give in the circumstances. It would appear from the testimony of Miller that the Company was concerned about the reaction of the Workers while receiving such news when out to sea (it seemed more from a point of view of sabotage than from their psychological well - being) which is not a trivial matter.
>
> However, such an excuse even if the Court were to accept it as it relates to the Workers, and I do not, cannot hold for informing the Union as is required by section 4 (1). Section 7 is clear and the construction to which it lends itself is that the only reason that should preclude an employer giving the notice required under section 6 is that of unforeseen circumstances, not operational requirements, nor fearful imaginings. I hold that the Company did not give the Workers or the Union the maximum notice that it could reasonably have been expected to give. The one day and less than one day notice given was unreasonable.

87 TD No. 163 of 2005 Communication Workers' Union and Front Row Limited.

> By failing to give the maximum notice that was practicable and in selecting the Workers for retrenchment other than in keeping with the Memorandum of Agreement, its actions were harsh and oppressive and not in accordance with principles of good industrial relations practice." [88]

In **Oilfields Workers' Trade Union and Trinidad Cement Limited,** the main issue of contention before the Court in this IRO was that the retrenchment notices which the Company served on sixteen workers did not contain any period of formal notice. The following is part of my reasoning:-

> "The Union contended that, Contrary to Sections 6 and 7 of the Retrenchment and Severance Benefit Act, Chapter 88:13 and the provisions of the respective Collective Agreements, the Company did not give any period of formal notice which is fifty (50) days in the respective Collective Agreements.
>
> The Company in response argued that, Section 17 of the RSBA allows for the parties, by mutual consent, to adopt a procedure other than that in the RSBA. The Company points to the Notice of Termination Clause of Article 21(2) contained the Collective Agreement between the parties which states as follows:-
>
>> "If the services of a worker are terminated on the grounds of redundancy after not less than one year's continuous service with the Company, he/she shall be entitled to (50) fifty days' notice or (50) fifty days full pay in lieu thereof."
>
> The Company further argues that this Clause was adopted in accordance with the provisions of Section 17 of the RSBA and allows for the Company to retrench workers without giving any notice.
>
> In other words, there might be an unforeseen event or circumstance which has arisen, which makes it impossible

88 TD Nos.15-19 of 2009 (S) Oilfields Workers' Trade Union and Offshore Atlantic Limited.

or impracticable for an employer to give the requisite forty-five (45) days' notice, in those circumstances, the employer can give notice for a period of less than forty-five (45) days and of course explain the nature of the unforeseen event. The RSBA does not have a provision whereby parties can consent, through the collective bargaining process, for no notice to be given to workers or to any term which violates the provisions of the RSBA and IRA. Indeed, it is settled law, that where there are clauses in consent agreements which are unlawful and contrary to law and public policy; such clauses render the Agreement or the term in the Agreement (in this case a provision in the Collective Agreement) void.

The Parliament of Trinidad and Tobago, by virtue of Section 6 of the RSBA, has outlined the minimum standard of notice which can be given to a worker when there is a retrenchment. This Section does not speak to a situation of no notice. Indeed, Section 17 requires that when parties adopt a "procedure other than that prescribed" that a period of notice is stipulated. Section 17 does not provide for no notice. It stands to reason therefore, that the minimum notice outlined at Section 6 can be increased but the requirement for notice cannot be removed through collective bargaining by the parties.

It is trite law that legislation enacted by the Parliament (IRA and RSBA) cannot be negotiated, altered or waived during the collective bargaining process unless the legislation specifically provides for such alteration, negotiation or waiver. It is erroneous therefore for parties to believe, that by the mere insertion of a clause to a collective agreement of a provision for no notice which states "if the services of a worker are terminated on the grounds of redundancy ...., he/she shall be entitled to 50 days' notice or 50 days full pay in lieu thereof", that in so doing they have adopted a "procedure other than that provided", by the RSBA.

Collective bargaining has to be done within the confines of the law; what the parties have done is to substantially and materially alter the provisions of the RSBA through the collective bargaining process, contrary to law.

Does the RSBA provide for an automatic waiver of notice?

In our view that the RSBA does not contemplate an automatic waiver of notice. Moreover, the principle of "pay in lieu of notice" is not provided for in the RSBA itself. Instead, it is a principle of good industrial relations which is usually invoked when for good and proper reason an employer is unable to provide the requisite notice required by the terms of employment or by the stipulated law. Therefore, employers cannot inform workers that they have elected not to provide a period of notice and that they have chosen instead to "pay in lieu" of notice. Moreover, employers are duty bound, in law and in the practice of good industrial relations, to prove that there are unforeseen circumstances and show that those unforeseen circumstances are of such a nature that it is impractical or impossible to comply with the requirements for a minimum period of notice.

The question of providing **no** notice whatsoever to workers is not a provision of the legislation. Even if the notice which can be provided is below the minimum statutory standard of notice, notice is required, save in circumstances we have mentioned before. We remind parties, that a proper and genuine reason must be given for not meeting requirements of the forty five (45) days minimum standard of formal notice. We emphasise that to terminate workers with immediate effect is in total violation of what a retrenchment exercise is about and also contrary to the practice of good industrial relations."[89]

89 Complaint No. IRO 36 of 2018 Oilfields Workers' Trade Union and Trinidad Cement Limited.

The LIFO Principle and Retrenchment

The principles and practice of good industrial relations and the relevant laws must always be adhered to when there is redundancy or retrenchment. Thus, in addition to ascertaining whether the company acted reasonably in selecting an employee to be retrenched, the Court will also seek to determine whether the selection method/ process which was adopted by the employer was reasonable in accordance with the practice of good industrial relations.

LIFO or Last in First Out is a method of selection for redundancy or retrenchment purpose. This method, when used, selects the employee with the least amount of service first for retrenchment whilst those with a longer service time, namely those who came into the company first, are selected last. LIFO is not the only criteria used for retrenchment, it is usually used alongside other criterion. A very common industrial relations expression "first in last out all other things being equal" captures the LIFO and the selection process for retrenchment.

In **BL Cars Ltd. vs. Lewis** the Employment Appeal Tribunal (EAT) of England in construing a provision on the selection process under English law held that:-

> "The question that falls to be asked in determining whether an employee was unfairly selected for redundancy is "Was the selection one which were adopted and whether the employers have demonstrated that they fairly applied those criteria to this redundancy?" In the normal case of a large employer, that would usually involve the employers showing that in relation to his length of service, his job and his skills with those others who might be made redundant. In the ordinary case, though not invariable, that would involve evidence from the person who made the selection indicating that the rating of each person who might be made redundant had been made and that as a result it emerged fairly and genuinely that the employee was one of those who rated worst under those heads." [90]

90 [1983] IRLR 58.

In **Transport and Industrial Workers' Union and Public Transport Service Corporation** H H Elcock held that:-

> "The application of the LIFO principle is a right which every worker enjoys in respect of retrenchment and which prevents him from being unfairly retrenched....There can be no doubt that LIFO is the single most objective criterion used in redundancy. It goes without saying, therefore, that as a matter of comity and in the interests of orderly and good industrial relations, it is undesirable for us to depart from that principle, without justification. Accordingly, the employer bears the burden of proving, on the balance of probabilities, two issues: firstly why the skill, ability and merit factors were given greater weight (or all weight) than the seniority factor in retaining less senior employee in the same position. Secondly, the employer must demonstrate that the less senior employee retained, has a clear advantage over each of the retrenched workers on the basis of skill, ability and merit." [91]

In **Seamen and Waterfront Workers Trade Union and Port Authority of Trinidad and Tobago,** H H Elcock also asserted that:-

> "It is now well and truly established that the LIFO principle is one of the principles of good industrial relations practices, and this was taken for granted by both parties to this dispute. It was also common ground between them that this principle must of necessity be subject to the proviso "ALL OTHER THINGS BEING EQUAL"." [92]

91 TD Nos. 23 and 24 of 1990 Transport and Industrial Workers' Union and Public Transport Service Corporation.

92 TD No. 119 of 1993 Seamen and Waterfront Workers Trade Union and Port Authority of Trinidad and Tobago.

In **Banking, Insurance and General Workers Union and Public Services Association,** I held that:-

> "The Association has stated that it had adopted the principle of "last in first out all things being equal." Therefore, it is duty bound to apply the said principle in a fair and equitable manner. It is not in dispute that the workers had unblemished work records with the Association and that they were qualified and capable of performing the duties and functions of their juniors who were retained by the Association. Apart from seniority there is no other evidence to suggest that all things were not equal...We find that the Association has failed to show that the criterion which was used to select the clerks for dismissal was equally applied to the other employees who held positions similar to those held by the workers and who have not been dismissed. From the list of employees in the establishment, which have been supplied by the Association to the Court, it is clear that there are several employees with comparable positions who are junior to three of the workers who were retrenched. The Association has therefore acted in contravention of the aforementioned principle when it retrenched workers who had more years of service instead of junior employees." [93]

Alternative Employment within the Structure of the Organisation

As a matter of good industrial relations, an employer should make reasonable and genuine efforts to look for alternative employment within the business establishment before effecting the retrenchment of a worker.

93 TD No 244 & 245 of 2004 Banking, Insurance and General Workers Union and Public Services Association.

In **Banking, Insurance and General Workers Union and Public Services Association,** I discussed alternative employment within the structure of the organisation as an important principle:-

> "We also find that the (employer) failed to make reasonable efforts to look for alternative employment within the structure of the organization for the workers before they were retrenched even though they were employed for a significant number of years. This is contrary to good industrial relations practice." [94]

In the case of **Contractor and General Workers Trade Union and Tucker Energy Services Limited**, I examined the procedure which was adopted by the Company and held that:-

> "A company in the practice of good industrial relations must show that a fair and reasonable system and criterion is adopted to assist in determining which workers should be retrenched and who must stay if it is retrenching workers. Also that such an exercise is within the confines of the law. In the instant case, there was no evidence of consultation with the Union and workers were not informed of the impending retrenchment... Additionally, there is no evidence that the Company considered suitable alternative employment for the workers within the organisation. There is no evidence of notice to the Minister of Labour and Small and Micro Enterprise Development." [95]

In **Southern Drilling Contractors Limited and Oilfields Workers' Trade Union** Vice-President H H Braithwaite (as he then was), examined the LIFO principle and stated:-

> "This dispute is over a claim made by Wilfred Henry on Southern Drilling Contractors Limited (hereinafter called "the Company") to be paid severance pay under the

94 Ibid.

95 TD No. 331 of 2013 and TD No. 57 of 2008 (consolidated) Contractor and General Workers Trade Union and Tucker Energy Services Limited.

provisions of Article 19 (2) of an industrial agreement subsisting between the Company and the Oilfields Workers' Trade Union (hereinafter called "the Union").

Under this Article it is provided that, in the event that it becomes necessary for the Company to terminate the services of a permanent employee with more than one year's service on account of redundancy the Company shall make a severance payment in accordance with a prescribed scale.

The Company however considered that in carrying out the retrenchment it was under an obligation by the terms of the industrial agreement to apply the principle of "last come first go", by offering alternative employment where possible to the more senior employees in preference to the less senior. This principle had in fact been applied to Henry on the occasion of an earlier retrenchment in 1965.

Against the prospect of retrenchment therefore the acceptance of such an offer must as a matter of fairness and in conformity with good industrial relations practice be held to be contingent upon the workman's ability and capacity to perform it satisfactorily.

Accordingly, if it transpired within a short or reasonable time after accepting such an offer that the workman could not so perform the duties of the alternative job which he accepted and was forced into the position of having to resign on that account, then his employer would not escape his obligation to meet the severance benefits that became payable when the substantive job in which the workman was employed became redundant." [96]

96 TD No. 196 of 1967 Southern Drilling Contractors Limited and Oilfields Workers' Trade Union.

Dismissal under the Guise of Retrenchment

The Antigua and Barbuda Labour Code proviso to s.C60 (1) provides that a dismissal may be deemed to be unfair if there is no factual basis for the claimed redundancy.

In **Antigua Village Condo Corporation v Watt AG 1994 CA 2**, the Eastern Caribbean Court of Appeal upheld the finding of the Industrial Court of Antigua and Barbuda and held that since redundancy was the reason assigned by the employer for the employee's dismissal, for which there was no factual basis, in that the tasks which the respondent was employed to perform continued to exist, the Industrial Court was justified in concluding that the dismissal of the respondent was unfair.

The Bahamas Employment Act (No. 27 of 2001) at section 37 provides that a dismissal for redundancy is unfair if the circumstances constituting the redundancy applied equally to one or more employees who held similar positions similar, and who have not been dismissed.

In **Neely v Credit Suisse Trust Ltd BS 2009 SC 12**, the Supreme Court of Bahamas ruled that there was no redundancy where the requirement for employees, not necessarily the work, has ceased or diminished or was expected to cease or diminish.

In **Communication Workers' Union and Maibrol Insurance Brokers Limited**, H H Ramrekersingh held that:-

> "The Company has patently failed to establish that the worker was surplus to its requirements. The alleged reorganization appears to have been nothing more than a transparent ruse to terminate the services of the worker for reasons known only to the top management of the Company." [97]

97 TD No. 314 of 2004 Communication Workers' Union and Maibrol Insurance Brokers Limited.

In **Banking, Insurance and General Workers Union and Public Services Association**, I ruled that the dismissal was disguised as retrenchment and affirmed that fair consultation is vital in the retrenchment process:-

> "It is an integral part of good industrial relations practice for employers to have consultation with recognized trade unions in cases where retrenchment is considered. That consultation, within the meaning of the Retrenchment and Severance Benefits Act, must be fair and adequate... Sections 4 and 5 of the said Act are obvious safeguards to prevent employers from using the selection of retrenchment as a backdoor device for dismissing workers for unjust reasons.
>
> The framers of the Act could not possibly have contemplated consultation to be a mere letter from an employer informing a union of a retrenchment after the entire exercise has been completed. This cannot by any measure be fair and adequate consultation or proper notice. From the evidence it is clear that the Association in the instant dispute failed to have proper consultation with the Union." [98]

In **Banking, Insurance and General Workers Union and Royal Bank Trinidad and Tobago Limited**, H H George- Marcelle asserted:-

> "Notwithstanding, Section 4 an employer may prior to the giving of formal notice in writing of retrenchment, enter into consultation with the recognised majority Union with a view to exploring the possibility of averting, reducing or mitigating the effects of the proposed retrenchment.
>
> Secondly, ILO Convention 158 - Termination of Employment Article 13 of the Convention requires that an employer contemplating terminations for reasons of an economic technological, structural or similar nature,

98 TD No 244 & 245 of 2004 Banking, Insurance and General Workers Union and Public Services Association.

> the Worker's representatives be consulted as early as possible, on measures to be taken to avert or to minimize the terminations and measures to mitigate the adverse effects of any termination of the Workers concerned such as finding alternative employment.
>
> In August 2005, the International Finance Corporation's Good Practice Note on Managing Retrenchment, stressed the importance of consultations to both the development and the implementation of a retrenchment plan. The Good Practice Note states that "without consultation, companies run the risk of not only getting key decisions wrong, but also of breaching legal rules; and collective agreements and alienating Workers and the community. Workers can often provide important insights and propose alternative ways for carrying out the process to minimize impact on the workforce and the broader community". International Finance Corporation of the World Bank Group, "Good Practice Note-Managing Retrenchment", August 2005." [99]

In **Contractor and General Workers Trade Union and Tucker Energy Services Limited**, I ruled that the workers in this dispute were summarily dismissed and were not retrenched as the Company asserted. I stated the following:-

> "The dicta in Grundy (Teddington) Ltd v Plumier (1983) ICR 367 are also instructive when it was noted that:-
>
> > "In the particular sphere of redundancy, good industrial practice in the ordinary case requires consultation with the redundant employee so that the employee may find out whether the needs of the business can be met in some other way than by dismissal and, if not, what other step the employer can take to ameliorate the blow to the employee."

99 TD No. 348 of 2014 between Banking, Insurance and General Workers Union and Royal Bank Trinidad and Tobago Limited.

> We note that the letter of retrenchment to the aggrieved workers is dated the same day the said workers are required to exit from the establishment. We reject the Company's evidence that there was in fact a retrenchment of some one hundred (100) workers from the Company. We accept the workers' evidence that they were summarily dismissed by the Company and they were not afforded an opportunity to be heard." [100]

The dicta of H H Mahabir in **Oilfields Workers' Trade Union and Trinidad and Tobago National Petroleum Company Limited** is also instructive on the issue of whether there existed redundancy or whether it was in fact a dismissal:-

> "His statement addressed the issue of the company's proposed restructuring and Barrow's negative conduct and, is indicative to us, that it was a ground for his selection for dismissal. But redundancy, by its very definition, is considered a non-fault dismissal, where the employee is not to be blamed for their job loss. Neither their conduct nor their capacity is an issue. It is simply that in the circumstances the employer faces, the employee is considered to be surplus to the needs of the business...In summary we find that National Petroleum failed to demonstrate its transparency and good faith in the implementation of its decision to retrench the former employees.
>
> Singling out an employee for separation is a hard blow with far reaching pecuniary and non-pecuniary damage taken into consideration factors such as long years of devoted service and efficient job performance...On the findings of fact, we find that this was a simple retrenchment scheme which went wrong because the Company failed to abide by the rules prescribed by law, settled jurisprudence and the principles of good industrial relations practice.

100 TD No. 331 of 2013 and TD No. 57 of 2008 (consolidated) Contractor and General Workers Trade Union and Tucker Energy Services Limited.

> Therefore, the dismissals of the workers were not by reason of redundancy. In other words, we find neither direct connection of the workers' dismissals to the redundancy situation in February 2000 nor procedural connection. Accordingly, the workers had been dismissed in circumstances that were harsh and oppressive and not in accordance with the principles of good industrial relations practice." [101]

H H Soverall examined the principles which are associated with redundancy in **Seamen and Waterfront Workers Trade Union and West Indian Tobacco Company Limited**. The following is a part of that judgment:-

> "In the judgment in Trade Dispute No. 93 of 2002 between OWTU and PCS Nitrogen, the Court identified the following events as crucial in dismissing a worker on the ground of redundancy:-
>
> - Surplus labour to the requirements of the Employer;
> - Failing to ascertain whether instead of dismissing for redundancy, offer alternative rather than hire contract employees;
> - Failure to retrain to fill other positions based on ability of other workers;
> - LIFO principle – selection for dismissal;
> - Failure to give warning of redundancy so employees can take early steps to inform themselves of relevant facts and consider alternative solutions or employment; and
> - Failure to consult
>
> Each event on its own accord is sufficient and can give rise to an invalidation of or nullifying a retrenchment. There is, therefore no need to prove all since a breach of one is

101 TD No 43 of 2001 Oilfields Workers' Trade Union and Trinidad and Tobago National Petroleum Company Limited.

> sufficient to overturn a retrenchment and in so doing, may be deemed an unfair dismissal." [102]

In **Government Industrial and General Workers Union and Laughlin & De Gannes Limited**, H H Daniel examined some of the fundamental principles which should be considered before a retrenchment is effected:-

> "On June 25th, 2008, upon completion of the worker's evaluation, her supervisor commented on the worker's performance by stating "Performance exceeded expectation in all significant areas and met exceptional in all others." On 21st September, 2012 the Company wrote the worker informing her that effective 1st October, 2012, she is to report to the Company's Champs Fleurs Branch, the reason given was that her knowledge and experience will aid the development of the Branch. On 30th June, 2015, the Company wrote the worker indicating due to poor performance of the Branch, the Company decided to close its branch, and therefore the worker's position would become redundant, which has resulted in the worker being terminated from her job effective 31st January, 2015...
>
> There needs to be a greater appreciation to the reality that a worker as in this instance, who would have spent many years of uninterrupted service in an organisation, would have earned an equitable and proprietary attachment and interest therein. If the equation that gives rise to the creation of a product or service is the fusion of capital and labour, then it stands to reason that a worker cannot be viewed and treated as mere cog or adjunct; that he or she is a mere object without feelings or emotions. There is no evidence before this Court, if any justifiable reason(s) advanced for therein being a redundancy herein. Consequently, the Court found as a fact that there is no evidence from which the Court can accept as a fact that

102 RSBD No. 10 of 2008 Seamen and Waterfront Workers Trade Union and West Indian Tobacco Company Limited.

there was a genuine redundancy. Notwithstanding the above findings as a fact, that there was not a genuine redundancy, the Company contended that it acted procedurally correct and adhered to the prerequisite of a proper retrenchment for the record and to add to the jurisprudence in this area the Court will still examine this issue. One of the fundamental pillars of a proper retrenchment is consultation. Was there consultation herein? The Company argued there was no consultation and advanced as their reason, security concerns. It begs the questions, security for what, for whom, where, how? It is not the duty of the Court to speculate what are these security concerns, if there are any at all. Further, whether they are genuine or not, ought they not to be specified upon. For these reasons, we find as a fact that there was an absence of consultation.

A second requirement, procedurally is whether the Company would have explored suitable and alternative opportunities for the worker within the Organisation. The Company merely stated there was not a similar position within its fold. This would not by itself meet the interest of the Act, in any event, there is no evidence that an alternative job was sought or offered to the worker; be it lesser or greater salary. The Court found as a fact that the Company did not, or at the very least, provide any evidence that they sought alternative employment for the worker.

The third prerequisite for a proper retrenchment is not just notice, but sufficient notice be given to a worker. There is no proper reason advanced by the Company as to why the worker was not afforded proper notice. An employer must be mindful that Notice in a redundancy process is for the benefit of both employer and employee. It affords a worker a grace period not only to seek within the Company but also outside the Company for alternative employment. There can be few things as impacting on a human being

> in a more distressing manner than to dress for work and being told that it would be his or her last day. How can one detach emotionally or otherwise, years of attachment in two to five minutes it may take to read a dismissal letter. A Company must act more humane, simply because a worker is a human being. For these reasons, we are satisfied that the Company breached the requirements of a proper retrenchment.
>
> DECISION
>
> In all the circumstances and based on the totality of the evidence herein, the Court is satisfied that there is no evidence to justify the retrenchment of the worker herein. We find the case for the Union to be credible and in accordance with Section 10(5) of the Act, we hold that the retrenchment of the worker herein was effected in circumstances that were harsh and oppressive and devoid of the elements of natural justice and of the principles of good industrial relations practices." [103]

Vacation Leave and Retrenchment

In **National Workers Union and Kee-Chanona Limited**, H H Seale addressed the issue of whether accrued Vacation Leave can be merged into the period of statutory notice for Retrenchment:-

> "In Oilfields Workers' Trade Union and Automotive Components in which the Court among other things, considered the question of the concurrence of vacation leave and the notice period in a situation of retrenchment. In that case, the Court asked the question"...could the employer by fiat, effect a merger of the Worker's accrued vacation leave into his redundancy notice?" The Court's answer was "We think not." However, the Court in using

103 RSBD No. 04 of 2017 Government Industrial and General Workers Union and Laughlin & De Gannes Limited.

> an analogy between accrued vacation leave and a profit sharing scheme stated and I agree that:-
>
> > "in bringing to account the entitlement to accrued leave the employer must give effect to it separate from both the severance benefits contemplated in Section 18 of the Retrenchment and Severance Benefits Act 1985 and the period of notice prescribed by Section 6 of that Act...In our view accrued vacation leave and period of statutory notice do not comingle. They collide."
>
> It is well to remember also that by section 23(2) of the RSBA a claim against an employer for unpaid severance benefits is deemed to be a trade dispute and in determining trade disputes this Court is enjoined to do so in keeping with the principles of good industrial relations practice. The Court finds that to allow the period of notice under the RSBA and the vacation leave earned pursuant to the Worker's contract of employment to run concurrently, especially where the Employer proposes to do so retroactively, would be contrary to the principles of good industrial relations practice. I hold that the period of notice and the vacation leave are to be treated separately."[104]

Steel Workers' Union of Trinidad and Tobago and ArcelorMittal Point Lisas Limited, I also addressed issues with respect to vacation leave:-

> "In order to fully grasp the significance of the acts or omissions of the parties, it is necessary to first place in its legal context the proposed alternative placing workers on vacation leave or laying off workers that the Company presented to the Union in relation to its financial situation. These options must not only be viewed in the context of collective bargaining and industrial relations principles which are laid down in the IRA, but also the managerial prerogative rights of the employer and the

104 RSBD No. 22 of 2009 National Workers Union and Kee-Chanona Limited.

legal contractual rights of the individual worker. In an attempt to address its financial woes, the Company made a vacation leave proposal which was inconsistent with the Collective Agreement. This in fact was that the workers would proceed on leave en masse and at the instigation of the Company rather than on the application of the individual worker.

Vacation leave is the individual contractual right of each worker who is entitled to indicate when he or she wishes to take such leave, of course, by an arrangement consequent to the Company, as the Collective Agreement provided. The difficulty which the Company faced was that no provision of the Collective Agreement gave it the exclusive right to decide when a worker goes on leave. This necessarily had to be by agreement or by waiver of right.

We find the case of Duncan v Attorney General for Grenada illuminating of the nature of the right to leave. In that case, the Eastern Caribbean Court of Appeal addressed the issue of leave entitlement in an employment relationship. While that case concerned a public officer, the statements of Byron CJ (Ag), as he then was, is very instructive to the complaint before us. Therein, the officer was told to go on leave to facilitate the 'reorganization' of the Ministry. In addressing the legality of this action, the learned Acting Chief Justice said:-

> "The Staff Orders categorise a variety of types of leave. These include "departmental leave"; "leave on the ground of urgent private affairs"; "overseas leave"; "leave prior to retirement"; "leave prior to resignation"; "vacation leave"; "sick leave". There is provision for the grant of leave to facilitate improvements in the organisation of a department or Ministry. An allegation that one's absence from work is necessary for making improvements in the workplace is a serious complaint about one's ability or attitude. Requiring an officer to be absent from work for that purpose is

> not for his benefit. It implies dissatisfaction with the officer. In my view it cannot be leave." [105]

We note that the vacation leave proposal made by the Company was itself part of a temporary workforce reorganization, not as a complaint against the workers, but to meet the dire financial situation faced by the Company. We agree with the Eastern Caribbean Court of Appeal that leave is the contractual right and privilege for the benefit of the worker not the employer and we use this as the starting point. The Court said:-

> "This argument highlighted the difficulty of the respondent, because it conceded the essential fact that the appellant's absence from work was required to facilitate the reorganization of the Ministry. This leads to the important question of whether an absence from work for that purpose is leave. What therefore is leave? What is Leave? The Concise Oxford Dictionary 8th edition, describes "Leave" as "Permission to be absent from duty." The Staff Orders regulate the circumstances and procedure for the grant of leave. The context of these orders clearly indicate that leave is a privilege for which the public servant becomes eligible as an incident of his employment. It is for the benefit of the worker."

A similar situation exists in relation to the Collective Agreement in this case. Therefore, to use the workers' contractual legal right to vacation leave as a strategy to assist the Company in its operations, which, albeit is in a dire economic circumstances, demanded not only consultation but also consent of the workers to waive their legal rights. In addition, we find that the Union was not unreasonable in indicating this when it informed the Company that its consultant and its attorney had advised that the proposal of the Company was in violation

105 Civil Appeal No. 13 of 1997 Duncan v Attorney General decided December 8, 1977 (unreported).

> of the Collective Agreement. This, as we said before, is the starting point of negotiations and was not really an insurmountable impasse.
>
> We take note of the Company's own evidence that the Union did not object to the Company taking the initiative to send workers on leave who had accumulated vacation leave, with the lone proviso that such an action be in conformity with the Collective Agreement. Indeed, the principles and practices of good industrial relations supported this concession and conversely it dictated that the response of the Company should have been to continue negotiations with the Union as RMU of the workers, not to hold the threat of layoff of all workers over the Union's head like the Sword of Damocles." [106]

H H Mahabir in **Oilfields Workers' Trade Union and Trinidad and Tobago National Petroleum Marketing Company Limited** reasoned that there are some essential procedural requirements in law and in the practice of good industrial relations when an organisation is engaged in restructuring or is undertaking a redundancy exercise:-

> "The employer must ensure that they follow the procedures set out in the RSBA and engage in behaviours that are consistent with the principles of good industrial relations practice. These include: consultation, the consideration of alternatives and a fair selection process. Furthermore, for the redundancy process to be considered procedurally fair, then all actions taken must meet the principles of natural justice, including a decision free from bias and predetermination.(See Mitchell, D. 1992 – "The burgeoning of fairness in the law in relation to redundancy." Auckland University Law Review 897 -930.)" [107]

106 Complaint No. IRO 031 of 2015 between Steel Workers' Union of Trinidad and Tobago and Arcelormittal Point Lisas Limited.

107 TD No 43 of 2001 between Oilfields Workers' Trade Union and Trinidad and Tobago National Petroleum Company Limited.

As I conclude the discussion on this Chapter, I wish to reiterate, that for many workers the loss of a job, due to no fault of their own, can have dire financial consequences and a debilitating effect on their lives. It is therefore critical that there be adherence to the laws, the principles of fairness and the principles and practice of good industrial relations before an exercise of reduction or reorganisation of the workforce is implemented. The provisions of Article 13 of ILO Convention 158 which, together with national law, can serve as a useful guide for employers and trade unions when redundancy is identified and the retrenchment of workers is contemplated.

Article 13 Termination of Employment Convention No. 158

1. When the employer contemplates terminations for reasons of an economic, technological, structural or similar nature, the employer shall:-

   (a) provide the workers' representatives concerned in good time with relevant information including the reasons for the terminations contemplated, the number and categories of workers likely to be affected and the period over which the terminations are intended to be carried out;

   (b) give, in accordance with national law and practice, the workers' representatives concerned, as early as possible, an opportunity for consultation on measures to be taken to avert or to minimise the terminations and measures to mitigate the adverse effects of any terminations on the workers concerned such as finding alternative employment. [108]

108 ILO Article 13 Termination of Employment Convention No. 158.

Chapter VI

Dismissal/Termination

Progressive Discipline

"Employment may, in general, be terminated at common law either by dismissal or by resignation. If it is terminated by dismissal, that dismissal may at common law be either lawful or wrongful; and a dismissal, whether lawful or wrongful, may be challenged as being unfair by statute."

Halsbury Laws of England, Fifth Edition.[109]

In the practice of industrial relations there is a disciplinary process at the workplace which is usually adhered to by employers. This process, which is called progressive discipline, provides an employee with the opportunity to change behaviours and for the business to maintain standards of performance and conduct; and is accepted as a practice of good industrial relations. Progressive discipline is really a hierarchical method of discipline and procedures which progresses from one stage to the next, with each stage increasing in severity when there is a repeat of workplace violations. It is usually broken down into stages:-

109 Halsbury's Laws (5th Edition, 2009) Vol. 40, para 679.

- verbal warning
- written warning
- suspension
- the ultimate punishment, dismissal

It is noteworthy that this disciplinary process, does do not prevent an employer from summarily dismissing a worker if there are exceptional circumstances which warrant the use of that type of discipline.

In **Banking, Insurance and General Workers Union and Kemicals Worldwide (T&T) Limited**, I considered the principle of progressive discipline:-

> "The worker was employed in April 2005 as a sale representative with the Company... during the course of her employment she was promoted to Senior Sales Representative, a position she held at the time of her dismissal. On the 13th March, 2007 the worker was summoned to the office of the Managing Director, there she was handed a letter of dismissal...The Company's case is that when the worker assumed duty in 2005 her salary was below the threshold to be liable for income tax payments. Sometime after the Company made a request that the worker submits her Board of Inland Revenue (B.I.R.) number for its records, she failed to do so. Despite several other requests the worker did not submit the said B.I.R, number to the Company.
>
> The main issues to be considered by the Court are:-
>
> 1) whether the Company's claims of "loss of confidence" is justified in these circumstances;
>
> 2) whether the ultimate punishment of dismissal was justified;
>
> There is no evidence to suggest that over the course of the Worker's employment that any form of disciplinary action was taken against her for failure to provide the

Company with her B.I.R. number. Despite the fact that the Worker did not comply with that request she was promoted to Senior Sales Representative and at one time she was the person in charge of the administrative staff of the Company.

There is no evidence that the Company conducted an investigation into the matter after it received the worker's correspondence of the 8th March, 2008, nor did it hold any form of discussion with the worker on the issue. Instead the Company terminated the worker's services on the grounds of loss of confidence. The general principle of good industrial relations requires that employers use a system of progressive discipline in cases of misconduct by workers. Dismissal is at the very end of the range of disciplinary actions which are available to employers and ought to only be used when it is absolutely necessary or in instances where there is an exception to the general principle. In our view there are no exceptional circumstances in this trade dispute which warranted the deviation from this general principle.

We find on the evidence that the Company has failed to consider the established standards of progressive discipline when a decision was taken to discipline the worker; standards which are indeed very relevant in the given circumstances. We further find that the worker was not given the opportunity to be heard in accordance with the principles of natural justice. Thus on the totality of the evidence, the Court rules that the punishment which has been meted out by the Company to this worker was unjustified and unwarranted in the circumstances.

The worker's dismissal was harsh, oppressive and not in keeping with good Industrial Relations practices. The Company is hereby ordered to pay to the worker compensation and damages."[110]

110 TD No. 93 of 2008 Banking, Insurance and General Workers Union and Kemicals Worldwide (T&T) Limited.

In **Banking, Insurance and General Workers Union and Smith Robertson and Company Limited**, H H Stroude considered two issues related to progressive discipline and stated:-

> "Was the principle of Progressive Discipline applied prior to the termination of the Worker?
>
> Was the Worker's conduct such that the principle itself was not applicable?
>
> The Worker began her career at the Company in December 2011 when she was hired as a Selector with the Company. At that time the Worker was a single parent raising several children with little or no assistance. From 2013 onwards the Worker began receiving a number of warning letters which spoke to her progressively excessive tardiness and high absenteeism rate. These letters exhibited by both parties, highlighted the negative effect her absence had on the Company's operations and sought her improvement in respect of the same.
>
> Her final admission was that she knew her absences were looking bad on her part and when she received the warning letters, she understood them and signed. However, the Worker was never suspended and thus the principle of progressive discipline had not been applied... the concept of progressive discipline is not to be found in any of the Laws of Trinidad and Tobago. In fact, the Industrial Relations Act of Trinidad and Tobago Chapter 88:01 makes no reference to the principle. Although not new to good industrial relations practice, the principle itself seems to have evolved out of a number of labour disputes and collective bargaining practices in the United States. It is found mainly as a concept in Human Resource Management and envisions penalties which increase in severity for each infraction committed by the employee. Its application to the disciplinary process therefore adds to transparency and provides the Worker a fair opportunity

for improvement prior to the imposition of the ultimate sanction of dismissal.

Thus, the expected progression for a recalcitrant employee will be:-

1) Oral warnings 2) Written warnings 3) Suspension 4) Termination.

The Industrial Court has therefore recognized the application of progressive discipline as best practice for employers when deficiencies exist in the services these employees provide. The judgments on the principle disclose one common thread, namely that failure to follow each and every step in the process is not necessarily fatal to the employer, but rather each case is to be determined on its own merits...having heard the evidence, we find that the Company was extremely sympathetic and accommodating to the Worker, she was given many opportunities to improve over the years and she grasped at none.

In the end, she was also given the opportunity to be heard alongside her Union Representative. Her dismissal came not like a thief in the night as she parried her family challenges as both sword and a shield. The Company Handbook spoke of using the steps of Progressive Discipline according to the merits of the case and it is on the merits of the case that we find the actions of the Company reasonable and foreseeable in light of the numerous warnings and the Worker's chronic absenteeism. In light of the foregoing, this matter is dismissed." [111]

111 TD No. 509 of 2017 Banking, Insurance and General Workers Union and Smith Robertson and Company Limited.

The Law on Dismissal/Termination

A dismissal, in simple terms, is the termination of the employment of an employee by an employer against the will of the employee. Dismissals/Terminations are commonly referred to as "firings". A decision to terminate the services of a worker can be made for a variety of reasons, and is considered to be made due to the fault or conduct of the employee, as opposed to layoff or retrenchment which is not due to the fault of the employee but due to the employer's action.

In Labour Law and in the practice of good Industrial Relations, a dismissal is considered to be the ultimate disciplinary sanction which should only be imposed as a measure of last resort. Therefore an employer bears the evidentiary burden of:-

1. proving that he/she had just cause to terminate the employee; and
2. proving that the termination was done in accordance with the principles and practice of good industrial relations.

A dismissal is such an extreme measure of discipline, that an employer must establish that the employee's misconduct is serious enough to amount to a repudiation of the contract, and that dismissal is the suitable disciplinary measure to be adopted.

Equity, Good Conscience and the Substantial Merits of the Case

It is notable that England and some Commonwealth territories, including the Bahamas, have a concept in law known as "Unfair Dismissal" which places a duty on the employer to show, at the time of a dismissal, he had not acted in circumstances which had been deemed to be unfair by statute.

The Bahamas Employment Act No. 27 of 2001 at Section 35 provides, inter alia, that the question of whether the dismissal of the employee was unfair shall be determined in accordance with the **substantial merits of the case**.

The Employment Protection (Consolidation) Act 1978 of England provides at section 57(3):-

> *"the determination of the question whether the dismissal was fair or unfair, having regard to the reason shown by the employer, shall depend on whether the employer can satisfy the tribunal that in the circumstances having regard to* ***equity and the substantial merits*** *of the case he acted reasonably in treating it as a sufficient reason for dismissing the employee."*

It appears that the test for unfair dismissal under English law is wider than the test in the law of the Bahamas. **"Equity"** together with **"the substantial merits of the case"** is considered by the English Courts, whereas in the Bahamas only **"the substantial merits of the case"** is taken into consideration when there is a determination on whether a dismissal is fair or unfair..

The IRA of Trinidad and Tobago goes even further and provides at section 10(3)(b):-

> *"Notwithstanding anything in this Act or in any other rule of law to the contrary, the Court in the exercise of its powers shall – (b) act in accordance with* ***equity, good conscience and the substantial merits of the case before it, having regard to the principles and practices of good industrial relations.****"*

Thus, the powers which are conferred by Parliament to the Industrial Court of Trinidad and Tobago under the IRA to adjudicate upon cases, appear to be much broader than both the Bahamas and the English legislation. In addition to **equity and the substantial merits of the case** as provided in the English legislation, the Industrial Court looks at "**good conscience**". The Court must also have "**regard to the principles and practices of good industrial relations**".

Further, the Industrial Court of Trinidad and Tobago, pursuant to sections 10(5) and (6) of the IRA, can determine whether a dismissal is "*harsh and oppressive or not in accordance with the principles of good industrial relations practice*".

These sections provide:-

> *10 (5) An order under subsection (4) may be made where, in the opinion of the Court, a worker has been dismissed in circumstances that are* **harsh and oppressive or not in accordance with the principles of good industrial relations practice;** *and in the case of an order for compensation or damages, the Court in making an assessment thereon shall not be bound to follow any rule of law for the assessment of compensation or damages and the Court may make an assessment that is in its opinion fair and appropriate.*
>
> *10 (6) The opinion of the Court as to whether a worker has been dismissed in circumstances that are* **harsh and oppressive or not in accordance with the principles of good industrial relations practice** *and any order for compensation or damages including the assessment thereof made pursuant to subsection (5) shall not be challenged, appealed against, reviewed, quashed or called in question in any Court on any account whatever.* [112]

As a result of these provisions, the Industrial Court has broad jurisdiction to resolve disputes (including dismissals) in a simple, informal, practical manner using *"industrial relations common sense"* to determine if a decision is fair, just and in accordance with the principles of *"equity, good conscience and the substantial merits of the case before it"*; and also *"having regard to the principles and practice of good industrial relations"*. This broad jurisdiction of the Court has been elucidated in many judgments of the Court of Appeal in Trinidad and Tobago and the Privy Council such as the dicta in Chief Personnel Officer v Amalgamated Workers Union. [113]

---

112 Industrial Relations Act Chapter 88:01 of the Laws of Trinidad and Tobago.

113 Privy Council Appeal No. 0081 of 2015 Chief Personnel Officer v Amalgamated Workers Union [2020] UKPC 17.

In **UCATT vs. Brain,** the Court of Appeal of England in construing the provisions of the English legislation namely "having regard to equity and the substantial merits of the case" held:-

> "Whether someone acted reasonably is always a pure question of fact, so long as the Tribunal deciding the issue correctly directs itself on the matters which should and should not be taken into account. But where Parliament has directed a Tribunal to have regard to equity – and that, of course, means common fairness and not a particular branch of law – and to the substantial merits of the case, the Tribunal's duty is really very plain. It has to look at the question in the round and without regard to the lawyer's technicalities. It has to look at it in an employment and industrial relations context and not in the context of the Temple and Chancery Lane. It should, therefore, be very rare for any decision of an Industrial Tribunal under this section to give rise to any question of law. And this is quite plainly what Parliament intended." [114]

In **Oilfields Workers' Trade Union and Ministry of Education and the Chief Personnel Officer**, I examined the provisions of the IRA in particular the provisions of section 10(3)(b) and stated that:-

> "Equity in the workplace is not a theoretical construct. It means something. It means, in essence, that each Worker has the right to receive fair treatment and to have equal access to opportunities and benefits in the workplace. Equity and good conscience, in accordance to the IRA, demand that this Worker receives the same treatment as pregnant women who are permanently employed at the Ministry and indeed across the public sector in Trinidad and Tobago." [115]

114 (1981) IRLR 225.

115 MPD No. 003 of 2012 Oilfields Workers' Trade Union and Ministry of Education and the Chief Personnel Officer.

In the dicta of **Banking, Insurance and General Workers Union and Tobago House of Assembly**, with respect to the provisions of sections 10(3), 10(5) and 10(6), I stated that:-

> "It is neither fair, nor just and it is certainly not in the interest of the Worker who is the person immediately concerned or the community as a whole, or in accord with equity, good conscience and the principles and practices of good industrial relations, to paraphrase the words of the statute, for an employer to deprive a Worker of the protection of the law by the colourable device of successive renewal of a fixed term contract over a period of years.
>
> Even if we did not take this position in relation to the amenability of fixed-term contracts to the jurisdiction of this Court, we hold that we are not constrained by the label placed by the parties on the contractual relationship. This is only one consideration. What is important is the reality of the course of dealings between the parties and the principles and practices of good industrial relations in general. This is the overriding consideration to come to an understanding of the true legal nature of the relationship."[116]

The Right to Be Heard

A key principle of dismissal, in the industrial relations context, is for an employee to be afforded the opportunity to be heard on an issue before any disciplinary measures are imposed. This principle, along with the principle of natural justice, places a duty of fairness and impartiality on employers when they are deciding whether or not to dismiss workers.

116 TD No. 21 of 2015 Banking, Insurance and General Workers Union and Tobago House of Assembly. This decision was appealed and upheld by the Court of Appeal.

H H Tull made a Biblical reference in the dicta in the **Oilfields Workers' Trade Union and Trinmar Limited** to explain the importance of giving an employee the opportunity to be heard. He said:-

> "When Cain killed Abel, no less a person than the Lord God Almighty himself condescended to ask Cain "why have you done this terrible thing?" By asking this question, he gave Cain the opportunity to offer an explanation for his action before punishing him. Cain offered no such explanation but made a stirring plea in mitigation of the penalty imposed on him by telling the Lord; "This punishment is too harsh for me!" The record shows that Cain succeeded in obtaining an alteration of the terms of the original sentence. (Genesis 4:9-18)" [117]

While I may not be similarly gifted with the ability to translate biblical legend into legalese, I too, have always emphasised and more accurately, championed the principle of audi alteram partem that lies at the core of natural justice and forms a cornerstone in our practice of good industrial relations.

> "The audi alteram partem principle is a well-known, integral and a very important principle in the practice of industrial relations. This principle and the principles of natural justice place a duty of impartiality and fairness on decision makers at the work place. The right to a fair hearing is a fundamental right for all workers; decision makers therefore have a duty and obligation to be independent and unbiased when they hold disciplinary hearings into the conduct of workers. The audi alteram partem principle and the principles of natural justice are universal principles which aver that a Worker who is accused of misconduct at the work place has the right to be heard and the right to a fair hearing. Impartiality and fairness are bulwarks of the disciplinary process in Industrial Relations, the failure to

117 TD No. 12 of 1994 the Oilfields Workers' Trade Union and Trinmar Limited.

> adhere to these principles tantamount to conduct which is harsh and oppressive and conduct [sic] and in breach of the principles and practice of good industrial relations." [118]

When you, the reader, examine the cases it may not escape you that all Courts insist that the audi alteram partem principle is adhered to by decision makers. This principle together with the rules of natural justice is so fundamental to the practice of good industrial relations that they are emphasised in many of the judgments of the Industrial Court of Trinidad and Tobago. The failure to adhere to these principles can be deemed to be conduct which is *harsh and oppressive and in breach of the principles and practice of good industrial relations.*

In the case of **The Marketing Board and the Civil Service Association**, which is the second Trade Dispute to be filed after the Industrial Court of Trinidad and Tobago opened its doors in 1965, Sir Isaac Hyatali, President, in his dicta elucidated on the principle that a worker should be afforded an opportunity to be heard before an employer proceeds with a dismissal:-

> "These rules (i.e. the rules of natural justice) however are part of the common law and were formulated to ensure that tribunals invested with judicial or quasi-judicial functions should not, among other things, condemn or punish a man unless he had an opportunity of answering what is alleged against him.
>
> But justice in this context refers to the dispensation of it by a tribunal charged with the duty of exercising judicial or quasi-judicial functions. The Board, however, is not such a tribunal... But this conclusion is no warrant for saying that in the field of human relations in modern industry, where sound management practices are essential to the preservation and development of harmony and co-operation between employer and employee and in which the country has a vital stake and interest, the principle

118 TD No. 27 of 2011 Oilfields Workers' Trade Union and Caribbean Packaging Industries. This decision was appealed and upheld by the Court of Appeal of Trinidad and Tobago.

> of giving an employee an opportunity to defend himself on a charge on which it is proposed to dismiss him has no application. Indeed we are convinced that it has and this conclusion has nothing to do with the justification or otherwise of converting the Board for present purposes into a judicial or quasi – judicial tribunal or investing it with such a status. Whether an employer should give his employee such an opportunity in any given case, however, will depend on the circumstances since each case is governed by its own facts."[119]

In **Bank and General Workers' Union and Home Mortgage Bank** the dicta of H H Khan are instructive on the principles of good industrial relations when dismissal is considered by an employer:-

> "The principles of good industrial relations practice dictate that no worker's employment may be terminated except for a valid reason connected with his capacity to perform the work for which he was employed or which is founded on the operational requirements of an employer's business. These principles are enshrined in writing in Convention No. 158 of the International Labour Organisation ("ILO Convention No. 158"). ILO Convention No. 158 has put in written form long standing principles of good industrial relations practice and it is of no consequence that the Convention has not been ratified by Trinidad and Tobago.
>
> At common law, an employer is not bound to give any reason for dismissing a worker. The principles of good industrial relations practice, on the other hand, require an employer, not only to inform a worker of the reason or reasons for a proposed dismissal but also to give a worker, save in exceptional circumstances, a fair opportunity to be heard before proceeding with a decision to dismiss for such reason or reasons. The two requirements are inseparable one from the other, since without being informed of the proposed

119 TD No. 2 of 1965 The Marketing Board and the Civil Service Association.

reason or reasons the worker will not have a fair opportunity to present to the employer material which may cause the employer to change his mind from his proposed course of action...in the event of a trade dispute concerning the dismissal of a worker, however, the Court is not restricted to the strict application of the terms of the individual contract or collective agreement. It is required to consider whether a worker has been dismissed by an employer in circumstances that are harsh and oppressive or contrary to the principles of good industrial relations practice." [120]

Summary Dismissal

Summary dismissal essentially, is the immediate termination of a worker by an employer, without notice, due to serious misconduct. The Courts have consistently stated that an employer can only summarily dismiss an employee in very exceptional circumstances such as, if the employee has committed an act of gross misconduct. The test is whether the employee has disregarded or breached a fundamental term of the contract.

"The idea still persists in some quarters that it is possible to terminate a worker's employment by merely giving him the required notice under the contract of employment. This was true under the common law but termination of workers by notice alone is insufficient under the Act... In addition, an employer must have an acceptable reason for terminating the worker's employment. Under the common law, the employer had the right to terminate without assigning a reason for the termination. This is not acceptable under the Act. An employer must have a valid reason for dismissal which must be connected with the worker's conduct or capacity to perform the work." [121]

120 TD No. 140 of 1997 Bank and General Workers' Union and Home Mortgage Bank.

121 TD No. 72 of 2000 Union of Commercial and Industrial Workers and El Dorado Consumers Co-operative Society Limited.

In **Bailey v BP Oil (Kent Refinery) Ltd**, Lord Lawson stated:-

> "In most unfair dismissal cases industrial tribunals are likely to be critical, and justly so, of an employer who has dismissed a man without giving him an opportunity of explaining why he did what he did; but cases can occur when instant dismissal, without any opportunity for explanation being given, would be fair, as for example when on the shop floor a worker was seen by the works manager and others to stab another man in the back with a knife. The dismissal in such a case would not be any the less fair because the employers did not follow a disciplinary procedure agreement with a number of trade unions containing the kind of provisions which are under consideration in this appeal."[122]

In **Communication Workers' Union and Varona Limited trading as Club de Vegas,** I delivered an ex parte judgment and reasoned that:-

> "The Industrial Court has pronounced in a plethora of judgments on the issue of summary dismissal in addition to the principles which govern such dismissals and the unreasonableness on the part of some employers in the exercise of their judgment to dismiss workers. We recognise and acknowledge that an employer's right to dismiss an employee is fundamental in the employer and employee relationship as we do the right of an employee to leave his employment. However summary dismissal ought to be used only in exceptional circumstances. In the instant Trade Dispute there is no evidence before the Court to justify the reasonableness in the dismissal of this worker. We therefore find that the Company's decision to dismiss the worker is devoid of the elements of natural justice and of the principles and practice of good industrial relations."[123]

122 [1980] ICR 642.

123 TD No. 252 of 2007 Communication Workers' Union and Varona Limited trading as Club de Vegas.

In **Communication Workers' Union and Busy Business Systems and Equipment Limited**, H H Khan discussed summary dismissal and the importance for workers to be given the opportunity to make good on their shortcomings in performance, a very important practice in Industrial Relations:-

> "It is well known in industrial relations practices that there are varying degrees of dissatisfaction with worker's services. For summary dismissal to result, there must be dissatisfaction of a very serious nature and the Company must have taken steps to bring the dissatisfaction to the worker's notice and allow a worker an opportunity to correct any deficiencies. There is also the matter of progressive disciplinary action. Summary dismissal is rarely justified where a worker has not been told beforehand of his shortcomings in performance and given an opportunity to improve his performance...In accordance with the principles of good industrial relations practices a system of progressive discipline is considered more appropriate and should normally be utilized to discipline poor performers." [124]

In **Oilfields Workers' Trade Union and Caribbean Packaging Industries**, I discussed the "audi alteram partem" principle and its importance in industrial relations and stated inter alia:-

> "The key issue in this trade dispute is whether a Supervisor who has a complaint against a Worker ought to be a part of an investigation team into the said complaint and at the same time give "evidence" to the said team. Moreover, whether that person (the complainant) can be the ultimate decision maker and in so doing determine the fate of that Worker.
>
> As stated in the Union's Evidence and Arguments the Union is the Recognised Majority Union for the

124 TD No. 101 of 1992 Communication Workers' Union and Busy Business Systems and Equipment Limited.

Company's hourly and weekly paid workers. The Court takes judicial notice of the fact that Trade Unions in this country acquire recognition to represent workers in this country in large and medium enterprises where there is structure in the management function, and where there is hierarchy in jobs positions. Unions are not known to seek recognition in the very small sole trading ventures or in very small businesses. Generally speaking, in enterprises where there is a Recognised Majority Union, due to the size and number of personnel in the business, it is expected that the Human Resources function, the Industrial Relations function and Decision Making function are separate and apart and do not reside with the person who is making an allegation against an employee.

The Industrial Court is not a court with an adversarial system; it is a Court of social justice to which Parliament has given inquisitorial powers. Section 17 of the IRA provides the Court with investigative powers and allows the Court to hear, inquire into and investigate every dispute which is before the Court. Moreover, section 9(1) and section 10 of the IRA provides that the Court may inform itself on any matter in such manner as it thinks fit and mandates that the Court acts in accordance with the principles of equity, good conscience and the substantial merits of the case before it, having regard to the principles and practices of good industrial relations.

By virtue of its investigative powers the Court was able to discern from the witnesses before the Court particularly from Mr. Kurt Allard, now a manager with the Company, that the machine was malfunctioning on the 21st April, 2009 and that Mr. Allard adjusted the machine by putting it on "skip feed". He explained to the Court that the adjustment did not fix the machine but it reduced the number of times the machine "jammed". He testified that he informed the Worker of this adjustment and stated that he told the Worker "that I put the machine on skip feed and to run the machine at a certain speed so he could get a consistent run". The evidence that Mr. Allard adjusted the machine before the incident occurred between the Worker and his Supervisor was not challenged by the Company.

The Company had a disciplinary hearing/meeting about the incident which occurred on the 21st April but Mr. Allard was not invited to attend this meeting to explain what role, if any, he played in this dispute. There is also no evidence that the person, who worked on shift which ended at 6:00a.m. on the morning of the incident, and who allegedly informed the Worker that the machine was malfunctioning, was called as a witness at the disciplinary hearing/meeting.

Good industrial relations requires employers to conduct enquiries and investigative hearings/meetings. This provides management with the opportunity to discover the relevant facts about incidents and allows management to make informed decisions. From the evidence, the Worker and the Company's witness, Mr. Cockburn, were the only witnesses who were invited to attend the disciplinary hearing/meeting. There is no evidence before this Court to suggest that the Company made any effort to get other witnesses to attend its disciplinary hearing/meeting and there is no evidence that an enquiry was conducted to assist the disciplinary panel in its deliberation. The disciplinary procedure which was adopted by the Company (which excluded potential witnesses) is flawed and is contrary to the principles of good industrial relations.

The right to a fair hearing is a fundamental right for all workers; decision makers therefore have a duty and obligation to be independent and unbiased when they hold disciplinary hearings into the conduct of workers.

Another issue is whether the Worker refused to carry out a "legitimate work instruction" and by his deliberate act cause the machine to malfunction, or; whether the machine was malfunctioning before the interaction between the Worker and his Supervisor. There is no evidence adduced by the Company to dispel the Union's contention that the machine was malfunctioning before the Worker began to work on that day. In fact, the evidence that another Worker tried to adjust the machine and to fix the problem before the incident occurred between the Worker and his Supervisor, is uncontroverted.

From the totality of all of the evidence presented to the Court, we find as a fact:-

a. that the Worker was not afforded a proper and fair hearing by the Company, this is contrary to the audi alteram partem rule and the principles of natural justice;

b. the Company caused a Supervisor (Shift Manager) who had a complaint against the Worker to be involved in the decision making process. Although the Company has a Human Resources Department, the Supervisor suspended the Worker and the Supervisor dismissed him. The Company by this very act deprived the Worker of his rights to a fair hearing;

c. the Company's investigative process did not include attempts to get other witnesses (apart from the Worker and Mr. Cockburn) to appear before the disciplinary hearing/meeting to provide information which may have been useful to determine what transpired with the machine, this flawed process violated the principle of fairness and good industrial relations;

d. that the Worker did carry out the instructions of the Shift Manager, his Supervisor on the 21st April, 2009;

e. that the machine was malfunctioning before the Worker assumed duties on 21st April, 2009 and that the instructions which the Supervisor issued to the Worker to increase the speed of the machine created further malfunctioning problems;

f. the instructions which were given to the Worker though lawful were reckless in the circumstance;

g. that the suspension and dismissal of the Worker were not for just cause;

h. that the Company is in breach of the rules of natural justice and of the principles and practices of good industrial relations;

i. that the Company dismissed the Worker in circumstances which were harsh, oppressive, unreasonable and unjust; and

j. that in the given circumstances reinstatement is the only equitable remedy.

The Court hereby orders that:-

1. the Worker be immediately reinstated to his position of Production Technician 1 without any loss of seniority and benefits;
2. any and all of the terms and conditions of employment which the Worker enjoyed prior to his dismissal remain intact; and
3. the Company computes the Worker's salary and pecuniary benefits from the date of his dismissal namely, 30th April, 2009 to 7th May, 2013, and pays to the Worker the sum of that computation on or before 31st July, 2013." [125]

125 TD No. 27 of 2011 Oilfields Workers' Trade Union and Caribbean Packaging Industries. This decision was appealed and upheld by the Court of Appeal.

In **Communication Workers' Union and Snooker World Recreation Club** the dicta of H H Aberdeen succinctly captured the practice of good industrial relations and the right to be heard:-

> "Every employer, no matter what the nature of the business he operates, whether it be Bank, Insurance Company, Manufacturing concern, commercial enterprise or indeed Recreational Club, is obligated in conducting his business and in employing workers, to act in accordance with the rules of national law and the principles and practices of good industrial relations. He cannot use ignorance as a shield against the consequences of a breach of any of these rules. It cannot be acceptable in Law or in Industrial Relations practice, for any employer to keep absolutely no record of the employment of workers or of the wages paid to them. It cannot be acceptable in Law or Industrial Relations practice, for any employer, to casually ignore the requirement to make statutory deductions and payments from the wages of his employees and keep appropriate records of such deductions and payment; and it certainly cannot be acceptable Industrial Relations practice, that any employer could dismiss a worker on the "flimsiest" of excuses or without giving that worker an opportunity to be heard."[126]

In **National Union of Government and Federated Workers and Battimamzelle Restaurant**, I examined the issue of summary dismissal and the need for a worker to be afforded an opportunity to be heard and to be informed of any shortcomings related to his/her performance at the workplace:-

> "Good industrial relations practices also require that an employee be given the opportunity to be heard when an allegation has been made against him or her of where there is some concern about the employee's performance.

126 TD No. 116 of 1998 Communication Workers' Union and Snooker World Recreation Club.

In John v Rees 1969 2 All ER 274 at page 309 Megarry J stated:-

> "It may be that there are some who would decry the importance which the courts attach to the observance of the rules of natural justice. "When something is obvious," they may say, "why force everybody to go through the tiresome waste of time involved in framing charges and giving an opportunity to be heard? The result is obvious from the start." Those who take this view do not, I think, do themselves justice. As everybody who has anything to do with the law well knows, that part of the law is strewn with examples of open and shut cases which, somehow, were not, of unanswerable charges which, in the event, were completely answered; of inexplicable conduct which was fully explained; of fixed and unalterable determination that, by discussion, suffer a change."

Thus, although an employer can dismiss an employee immediately for an infraction which has been committed such a dismissal is only justified when the worker's act or inadvertence is of a very serious nature. Summary dismissal is rarely justified where a worker was not afforded the opportunity to be heard and that worker has not been told what are the short-comings of his or her performance at the work place." [127]

In **National Union of Government and Federated Workers and Half Moon Belle and La Belle Creole Limited**, I emphasised that natural justice is a precursor to a decision of summary dismissal:-

> "The right for a worker to be heard before dismissal is one of the most important elements in the natural justice which is an inherent part of the dismissal of a worker. The Company has a duty to consider the nature of the allegations whether they have been proven and, if

127 TD No. 309 of 2004 National Union of Government and Federated Workers and Battimamzelle Restaurant.

> so, what should be the appropriate penalty. This process can only be properly achieved if the worker is afforded a proper hearing. Summary dismissal should only be used by employers in exceptional circumstances, in all other instances, an employer should afford an employee the proper opportunity to be heard." [128]

In **Banking, Insurance and General Workers Union and Hindu Credit Union Co-operative Society Limited**, H H Khan emphasised that:-

> "The employer should inform the worker of the substance of the allegations against him and listen to what he has to say about the allegations. This may be done in an informal manner. The two requirements are inseparable one from the other, since without being informed of the proposed reason or reasons the worker will not have a fair opportunity to present to the employer material which may cause the employer to change his mind from his proposed course of action. It is, therefore, necessary to read all workers' contract of employment subject to the requirements of the Act. What might constitute a good termination in accordance with the common law might not satisfy the requirements of the Act."

The dicta of HH Khan continued and he explained that:-

> "One of the best statements of this good industrial relations principle is contained in **ILO Convention No. 158 of 1982**, the salient parts of which are as follows:-
>
> 1. The employment of a worker shall not be terminated unless there is a valid reason for such termination connected with the capacity or conduct of the worker or based on the operational requirements of the undertaking, establishment or service.

128 TD No. 203 of 2004 National Union of Government and Federated Workers and Half Moon Belle and La Belle Creole Limited.

2. The following, inter alia, shall not constitute valid reasons for termination:-
   (a) union membership or participation in union activities outside working hours or, with the consent of the employer, within working hours;
   (b) seeking office as, or acting or having acted in the capacity of, a workers' representative;
   (c) the filing of a complaint or the participation in proceedings against an employer involving alleged violation of laws or regulations or recourse to competent administrative authorities;
   (d) race, colour, sex, marital status, family responsibilities, pregnancy, religion, political opinion, national extraction or social origin;
   (e) absence from work during maternity leave.
3. Temporary absence from work because of illness or injury shall not constitute a valid reason for termination.
4. **The employment of a worker shall not be terminated for reasons related to the worker's conduct or performance before he is provided an opportunity to defend himself against the allegations made, unless the employer cannot reasonably be expected to provide this opportunity.** (My emphasis)

It is essential that an employer should ensure that he makes a proper investigation of all the relevant circumstances, have a valid reason for terminating the worker's service, inform the worker of the exact reason for dismissal and give the worker an opportunity to answer the allegations made against him. Depending on the circumstances, an employer's failure or refusal to afford a worker an opportunity to be heard before dismissal may result in the Industrial Court finding that the worker's dismissal was

> not in accordance with the principles of good industrial relations practice.
>
> In determining whether or not he should proceed to dismiss a worker from his employment, an employer is not expected or required to apply the standard of a court of law in looking at the relevant facts and circumstances. He must, however, look at the facts and circumstances objectively and adopt a common sense approach in deciding whether or not dismissal is the appropriate penalty, having regard to all the circumstances of the particular case." [129]

It is evident from the judgments of the Courts, that the right to be heard and natural justice are fundamental principles which must be adhered to in the practice of good industrial relations. Moreover, it is also important to consider and explore other disciplinary measures before a decision is made to dismiss a worker.

However, there are many instances where Courts accept that the dismissal of a worker was fair and that he/she was given the opportunity to be heard. For example in **Oilfields Workers' Trade Union and Trinmar Ltd,** H H Tull discussed the principles of good industrial relations, the following dicta are from that judgment.

> "Except in the most exceptional cases, therefore, an employer we think, should always give a worker an opportunity to be heard before terminating his employment. This is one of the very important principles of good industrial relations practice. If such an opportunity is not given by the employer a Court may, depending on the circumstances, find the dismissal to be harsh and oppressive or not in accordance with the principles of good industrial relation practice.
>
> We fully agree with these dicta and also with the position of Brown-Wilkinson J, when he commented in Sillifant v

129 TD No. 2 of 2001 Banking, Insurance and General Workers Union and Hindu Credit Union Co-operative Society Limited.

Powell Duffryn Timber Ltd. (1983) IRLR 91 that:-

> "It will be a very rare case indeed when an employer can reasonably take the view that there could be no explanation or mitigation which would cause him to alter his decision to dismiss."

We do not think, however, that there should be any rigid or inflexible rules governing the grant of such an opportunity. It does not have to be a formal inquiry or investigation. It may be an entirely informal process provided always that the employee is given a fair opportunity to be heard.

A fair opportunity to be heard includes the provision of relevant information by the employer to the employee so that he may appreciate and understand the substance of the allegations made against him and an opportunity to reply to such allegations and to put forward any reasons in mitigation of any penalty or penalties which may be possible having regard to the nature of the allegations made against him. The underlying basis of the opportunity is the achievement of fairness and justice. In deciding whether there has been a violation of this principle of good industrial relations practice, each case must be considered on its own facts and circumstances.

We find in the present trade dispute that the Company gave the worker a full and fair opportunity to be heard and that it was possible for the worker to have made any representations on any potential penalty at that opportunity. In our view, it was unnecessary, on the facts of this dispute, for the employer to have consulted with the worker before dismissing him. It was a very serious act of negligence which fully merited dismissal." [130]

130 TD No. 12 of 1994 the Oilfields Workers' Trade Union and Trinmar Limited.

In **National Workers Union and Servisair Trinidad and Tobago Limited**, H H Jack held that the dismissal was not contrary to the principles and practice of good industrial relations:-

> "The questions therefore which had to be determined by the Court are:-
>
> I. Whether a reasonable management could find on the examination of the evidence before it, that the Worker is guilty of misconduct warranting dismissal.
>
> II. Whether the Worker in the circumstances was given a fair opportunity to be heard.
>
> We deal here with the first question. The evidence before us clearly supports the position taken by the Company that the Worker was indeed involved in the handling of private flight no. N28KA unknown to the Company although ostensibly acting on its behalf. Such conduct which the Company categorizes as dishonesty meets the criterion of gross misconduct and is undoubtedly a dismissible offence. The Company acted on the evidence emanating from its investigations as it satisfied the standard of proof that was required to determine the Worker's involvement.
>
> The requirements that an employer must satisfy before effecting dismissal have been enunciated by the Court in a plethora of previous judgments. These requirements conform to good industrial relations practice in accordance with the mandate by the provisions of the Industrial Relations Act. The investigative process must therefore be scrutinized to determine whether it was conducted fairly and in good faith and whether the Worker was given a fair opportunity to be heard in his defense.
>
> We accept the evidence that the Company's witnesses gave, of the manner in which the various interviews were conducted and of what was said to them. Meetings held between the Worker and the Security Manager in the first instance and the Human Resource Manager thereafter

seem to have taken a brief format that the Union contended was inadequate in satisfying the requirements aforementioned. However, was this information that was derived from this process sufficient to ascertain the Worker's culpability or was by an objective standard, a correct and justifiable conclusion? The Company carried out as much investigation into the matter that was reasonable in all the circumstances of the case. In British Home Stores Ltd v Burchell [131] the Employment Appeal Tribunal noted:-

> "In a case where an employee is dismissed because the employer suspects or believes that he or she has committed an act of misconduct, in determining whether that dismissal is unfair an Industrial Tribunal has to decide whether the employer who discharged the employee on the ground of the misconduct in question entertained a reasonable suspicion amounting to a belief in the guilt of the employee of that misconduct at that time. This involves three elements. First, there must be established by the employer the fact of that belief; that the employer did believe it. Second, it must be shown that the employer had in his mind reasonable grounds upon which to sustain that belief. And, third, the employer at the stage at which he formed that belief on those grounds, must have carried out as much investigation into the matter as was reasonable in all the circumstances of the case. An employer who discharges the onus of demonstrating these three matters must not be examined further."

In the instant case the Company gave the Worker an opportunity to first respond to the allegation during the course of a meeting and to provide a written statement. All of the Worker's responses were taken into consideration in arriving at a decision. In addition to which the Company

131 [1978] IRLR 379.

carefully examined the Worker's declaration, firstly that it was S. Colai that handled the private flight then saying it was his other brother P. Colai. Maraj from Katerserv indicated that it was the worker who requested catering services and the Worker admitted that he made that request albeit on behalf of his brother. The matter was certainly investigated during which period the Worker was given an opportunity to be heard.

The Court stated in a judgment in Trade Dispute No. 24 of 2005 between Oilfields Workers' Trade Union and Trinidad and Tobago Electricity Commission that:-

> "Before taking disciplinary action against any employee, an employer is required to observe certain basic principles. The employee must be informed as to any alleged default on his part with reasonable particulars and be afforded a reasonable opportunity to respond to the allegations. There is no formula for this and no requirement that all the formalities of a Court of Law are to be followed. The employer must act fairly and this includes assessing all the facts and coming to a conclusion which is not perverse or imposing a sanction which bears no proportion to the default."

We have listened to the oral testimony and read the evidence and the submissions of both sides and have concluded that the Company's case is substantiated. We are satisfied that while not perfect those criteria pertaining to good industrial relations practice have been met during the Company's conduct of the matter. The Company displayed good faith during the course of its investigation by pursuing every response made by the Worker in his defense. On the totality of the evidence we find that the Worker's dismissal was not contrary to the principles of good industrial relations practice. We are therefore unable to support the Union's claim that the Company failed to adhere to the principles of good industrial relations

> practice and that the dismissal of the Worker was harsh and oppressive. Consequently, the relief prayed by the Union is not supported. The Court hereby orders that the matter be dismissed." [132]

In **Contractors and General Workers Trade Union and National Quarries Company Limited**, I accepted the Company's case of loss of confidence in the worker:-

> "The parties agree that apart from its regular workers the company hires contractors to perform certain tasks at its quarry operation. One such contractor is Mr. Neville Rajnauth whose equipment is also stored on the Company's compound. Some of Mr. Rajnauth's workers operate from the Company's compound and at times they work alongside the Company's employees. Mr. Simon Bowen is a past employee of Mr. Rajnauth who had worked prior to the issues giving rise to this trade dispute with Mr. Rajnauth for seven years at the Company's quarry. The worker and Mr. Bowen were very familiar with each other since they grew up in the same area and at some point they both worked on the Company premises...the Union case is riddled with inconsistencies from the most minor detail to the most important. Here are a few of the inconsistencies: The worker testified that he had known Mr. Bowen for a very long time and that he, Mr. Bowen, resided in Guaico with his grandmother. Mr. Bowen appeared confused at the suggestion that his grandmother resided with him and he informed the Court that he lived at Guaico with his mother. The worker testified that Mr. Bowen asked of him to request from Mr. Lee King four thousand ($4,000.00) dollars for the repairs done to the parts. Mr. Bowen stated in evidence that he told the worker to collect One thousand five hundred ($1,500.00) dollars from Mr. Lee King for the repairs, he denied ever requesting that the

132 TD No. 377 of 2010 National Workers Union and Servisair of Trinidad and Tobago.

worker collect four thousand ($4,000.00) dollars from Mr. Lee King.

Mr. Bowen stated that his meeting with the worker occurred on a Friday. The worker stated that it occurred on a Saturday. Although Mr. Bowen was seated in the back of the car at all material times the Union insisted that when Mr. Lee King put his head in the front passenger window to view the parts on the "floor" between the back and front seats of the car, he may not have seen Mr. Bowen. The worker in our view has not properly explained why he chose to give the parts to and conduct the transaction with Mr. Lee King when Mr. Bowen was present in the car to do so himself. The general explanation of his role in the said transaction is very questionable.

The central issue in this trade dispute is whether the Company's decision to dismiss the worker for loss of confidence was reasonable in all the given circumstances. The Company for good reason conducted an investigation into the matter to ascertain the extent and nature of the Worker's involvement in the incident. The worker who at the time was the Vice President of that branch of the Union was given adequate notice of the date of this enquiry and the reason why the enquiry was held. The Worker appeared at the said enquiry with his representatives and there he gave his account of the incident. He had the opportunity to ask questions of all the witnesses at the enquiry and he also had ample opportunity to call witnesses to testify on his behalf but he did not call Mr. Bowen to appear as a witness at the enquiry. The notes of the enquiry were tendered into evidence, from these notes and from all of the evidence there is nothing to suggest that the worker was denied the opportunity to be heard or that a proper enquiry was not conducted.

The worker and Mr. Slater have agreed that they had some experience in industrial relations by virtue of their positions and responsibility in the Union and there is no evidence to suggest that they had a concern or voiced a concern about the manner in which the enquiry was conducted. It is a stated principle in industrial relations that where a company chooses to dismiss a worker for reason of loss of confidence that the Company must provide a proper explanation and a good reason to the worker in support of its decision and those reasons should be clear and cogent. In the instant case, the worker was informed in writing by the Company as to the reason why it was conducting an enquiry. After the enquiry was conducted he was also given the precise reasons why the Company lacked confidence in him as a worker. It is our view from the totality of the evidence that the worker was given sufficient and legitimate reasons why he was dismissed by the Company for reason of loss of confidence. Thus, after careful consideration of all of the evidence of this trade dispute, we find that the Company's decision to dismiss the worker was reasonable. We therefore uphold that decision and dismiss this trade dispute." [133]

In **Eural Baptiste and Bank of Nova Scotia**, the Industrial Court of Antigua and Barbuda examined the issue of unfair dismissal and reasoned that:-

"The Employee claims to be unfairly dismissed. The Employee's Memorandum was filed on January 12, 2006. In that Memorandum Mr. Baptiste claims loss of employment security, loss of immediate earnings, loss of future earnings, loss of employment benefits, and loss of employment opportunities...By a letter dated June 22, 2004 the Bank dismissed Mr. Baptiste. The Bank submitted two reasons why it dismissed Mr. Baptiste.

133 TD No. 315 of 2002 Contractors and General Workers Trade Union and National Quarries Company Limited.

They are as follows:-

i. That Mr. Baptiste "recorded an excessive number of uncertified absences ... resulting in continuous disruption of the Bank's operations".

ii. That the Employee never worked for a monthly sum of $3,200.00 and that as at the date of his dismissal he was not employed by Sinsational Intertainment. The Employer's Memorandum was filed on July 30, 2007. The Bank contends that Mr. Baptiste was terminated for just cause. He is therefore not entitled to any relief.

In Cable & Wireless (WI) Ltd v Hill and Others (1982) 30 W.I.R. Berridge JA in delivering the Judgment of the Court of Appeal stated inter alia:-

> "The burden of proof was on the company to show 'just cause' for dismissing the employees and that since summary dismissal constituted a "strong measure" the standard of proof should be strict, persuasive and convincing. Further, understanding the fact that this is a matter of civil nature requiring proof on the balance of probabilities, since the matters to be proved were of a grave and weighty nature, it would expect the evidence to be corresponding cogent and weighty in nature and content."

The Employee must bear his proportion of responsibility for the circumstances which led to his dismissal. This is a well-established practice in this Court. In the circumstances of this case I assess his degree of responsibility to be 50%. If any authority is required, see Alexander Hughes v Antigua Brewery Limited Ref. No. 35 of 2002...The Employer shall pay to the Employee the sum of $51,700.75 (being $103,401.50 less 50%) on or before December 31, 2008. There shall be no order as to costs." [134]

134 Reference No. 25 of 2005 Eural Baptiste and Bank of Nova Scotia.

In **National Union of Domestic Employees and Superstore Limited,** H H Daniel in his judgment upheld the Company's decision to dismiss a worker and stated as follows:-

> "The Union contends that the Worker was dismissed in circumstances which were harsh, oppressive and contrary to the principles of good industrial relations practices. The Worker commenced employment with the Employer on the 5th March, 2012. She held the position of Cashier. On the 18th March, 2014, in the course of her employment the Worker sold to a customer a brownie and a classic select wherein he gave her a hundred dollar note ($100.00) and the Worker gave him in return two dollars ($2.00) change. The cost of the items amounted to $8.99. The Worker it seemed had believed the customer gave her a ten dollar note ($10.00). The customer queried the correctness of the change and the Worker maintained that the Customer had given her only ten dollars ($10.00). An internal inquiry commenced wherein the owner/director showed the Worker video footage which showed the Worker had indeed received a hundred dollar ($100.00) note. The Worker stated she had made a mistake. The Worker further maintained under cross-examination by the Company's representative that she was not aware of any Company's policy regarding dishonesty. In answer to the Court, the Worker admitted having seen the video footage which showed that she did in fact collected a hundred dollar note.
>
> Issue 1
>
> The Union's contention predicated upon the evidence of the Worker that a mistake took place wherein a hundred dollar note was mistaken for a ten dollar note. The Employer submitted that it was a theft and not a mistake. In arriving at a finding of fact herein the Court considered the following:-

a) If indeed there was a mistake by the Worker in believing it was a ten dollars, then the cash register ought to reflect an excess or overage? Notwithstanding the register was checked by three (3) different persons contemporaneous with the incident none was found. This evidence was not challenged by the Union, as such the Court accept it as being true. The Court found as a fact there was no excess or overage...

e) ...When asked to explain the absence of any excess monies in the cash register the Worker did not advance any reasonable explanation.

For these reasons the Court found as a fact that the conduct of the Worker is not consistent with that of a mistake being made, and we so hold.

Issue 2

It is the contention of the Company that the Worker stole the money. Moreover given their policy is one of zero tolerance to dishonesty and theft, they submitted that they were justified in their decision to dismiss the Worker.

In the instant case there was video footage contemporaneous with the act. In the face of such video evidence the Worker could not and did not proffer any reasonable explanation. This Court is not unmindful of the indispensable need for an employer to repose trust and confidence in their employees. The breach of such trust and confidence is tantamount to the removal of the glue that bonds and keeps an effective and productive working relationship. It is the respectful view of the Court that no Employer should be carrying the burden of an untrustworthy employee; as such the Employer was justifiable in the circumstances to dismiss the Worker.

It's the Court's view that the cash transaction and the video footage were all contemporaneous, as such, it was quite reasonable for the Employer to request an explanation instantaneously. The event would have been quite fresh in the mind of the Worker and the customer who made the allegation and who was still present on the scene. The need to give notice to the Worker was not necessary in the instant factual matrix. The Court found as a fact there was not any breach of rules by the Company in its investigatory process.

Decision

Based on the totality of the evidence herein, the Court is satisfied that there is evidence to justify the reasonableness in the dismissal of the Worker.

We therefore find the case for the Company to be credible and in accordance with Section 10(5) of the Act, we hold that the termination of the Worker's services were effected in circumstances that were fair and justifiable and consistent with the principles of good industrial relations practice and procedure." [135]

Harsh and Oppressive Dismissals

As previously stated, by virtue of the provisions of sections 10(5) and (6) of the IRA, the Industrial Court can determine on the facts of a case whether a dismissal is *harsh and oppressive or not in accordance with the principles of good industrial relations practice*. Many of the Court's judgments contain rulings on whether a dismissal is *harsh and oppressive and contrary to principles and practices of good industrial relations.*

In **Banking, Insurance and General Workers Union and North-West Regional Health Authority**, H H Achong, Chairman ESD examined a decision to terminate a worker after two weeks of assumption of his duties:-

135 TD No. 365 of 2014 National Union of Domestic Employees and Superstore Limited.

> "The Worker assumed duties on June 14th, 2010 as per the letter to the Permanent Secretary, Ministry of Health dated June 18, 2010 the Chief Executive Officer (Ag.) of the Authority. His services were terminated on June 28, 2010 exactly two weeks after his assumption of duties. Therefore the termination occurred before the expiration of one (1) month whereas clause 13 is quite explicit i.e. the Employee's service with the Authority may be terminated at any time after the expiration of one (1) month...If ever there was a case of gross mismanagement and incompetence on the part of an organization and its executive, it is this one. The Court finds that the Worker was dismissed in circumstances that were harsh and oppressive and contrary to principles and practices of good industrial relations pursuant to section 10(6) of the Industrial Relations Act." [136]

In **Transport and Industrial Workers' Union and Public Transport Service Corporation,** I ruled that a decision to terminate a worker without a proper enquiry was harsh and oppressive. The facts are as follows:-

> "The worker was employed with the Corporation in 1976...He worked as a driver/conductor until 1994, when he accepted a voluntary separation package from the Corporation in December of that year. Some two weeks after the said voluntary separation, the worker was reemployed by the Corporation...For a period of time he worked "one fortnight on and one fortnight off' each month. However, from April 2000 he began working continuously from Monday to Friday each week, and he was assigned as the driver/conductor to transport school children along the Mayaro to Sangre Grande route. On 2nd January, 2001 the worker was driving bus Registration No. HAX 9836, from Mayaro to Sangre Grande. At the

136 ESD TD No. 52 of 2013 Banking, Insurance and General Workers Union and North-West Regional Health Authority.

time thirty (30) school children and a school teacher were passengers in the said bus when in the vicinity of the 62 km mark the bus "ran off' the road. The teacher, the driver and school children were injured and they all received treatment at the Sangre Grande Hospital. As a consequence, the worker was fired by the Corporation.

The Union's case is that on 2nd January, 2001 the worker was driving within the speed limit from Mayaro to Sangre Grande. While he was negotiating a double bend along the Manzanilla Road the bus he was driving experienced mechanical problems which caused him to lose control and this resulted in the accident...The Union has contended that the right front man leaf of the bus broke and this was the primary cause of the accident. A memo dated 2nd January, 2001 from the Corporation's Corporate Manager of Operations was tendered to the Court in support of this contention.

The Union has contended that the worker was not given the opportunity to be heard by the Corporation before he was dismissed and also that...there was no written report and/or finding that the Corporation produced to the worker which revealed that the worker was grossly negligent and/or careless in operating bus fleet #E066 registered number HAX 9836, on January 2nd 2001 prior to, and/or even thereafter, his dismissal by memo dated January 11, 2001 from the Corporation.

The Corporation has contended that on the day of the accident the bus had no mechanical problems, however, the computer in which the respective supporting data was stored "crashed and all of the data was lost. Mr. Subiah said that it was his opinion that the bus was in good working condition. His opinion was based on "first line check documents" which he perused.

We find as a fact that although there was a meeting with the Corporation, the worker was not called lo an inquiry

> to give his account of what transpired on January 2nd 2001...It was important for the Corporation to conduct a thorough and balanced inquiry into the events which led to the bus leaving the road and colliding with a tree or trees. Such inquiry is critical to the investigation into allegations of recklessness and/or negligence on the part of the worker on the day in question. There is no evidence forthcoming from the Corporation to indicate that the worker was given the opportunity to properly explain the circumstances which led to the accident at an inquiry. There is no evidence that he was afforded the opportunity to respond to allegations of negligence and speeding.
>
> The Court finds, that the Corporation has not conducted a proper and fair inquiry and/or investigation of this accident, the dismissal of the worker was harsh and oppressive and not in accordance with the principles of natural justice and good industrial relations practices and that reinstatement is not an appropriate relief in the circumstances. We hereby order that the Corporation do pay to the worker compensation and damages."[137]

In **Toucan Inn & Bonkers Restaurant and Bar and Oilfields Workers' Trade Union,** the workers refused to work and disrupted the operations of the business. I did not accept that the dismissal was harsh and oppressive:-

> "The Company, following an incident which arose on the workplace on the 19th of December, 2003 terminated the services of Sandra Joseph, Kitchen Assistant, Marvin Mckenzie, Chef, and Junior Melville, Assistant Cook...On the evening of December 19, 2003 the restaurant was the venue for a local church Christmas dinner and forty (40) persons from the said church were expected to attend the function and to participate in a buffet dinner, while

137 TD No. 187 of 2002 Transport and Industrial Workers' Union and Public Transport Service Corporation.

the other guests and/or patrons of the restaurant were expected to order a la carte from the menu.

Mr. Troy Murray (Manager) stated that when he spoke to the workers, who at the time were standing in the carpark, they voiced their dissatisfaction with the recent Christmas bonus they had received. He pleaded with them to return to the kitchen and to continue to perform their duties but they refused.

We do not believe that the workers completed the preparation of the meals on the evening in question and that their actions were not disruptive. We believe that the workers did voice their concern about their remuneration albeit bonus or salary on the evening of December 19, 2003 at a time when they were aware that the Company's restaurant was the venue of a function and that their services were critical for the smooth operation of the business.

It is clear that the Company was put in the unfortunate position where it was forced to entertain the demands of its workers and make an immediate decision on the issue of increased remuneration for staff. The Management instead made the decision to close the restaurant...While a Court can understand and empathise with workers in their relentless quest for improved conditions and benefits at the workplace, this Court will not endorse actions by workers which in effect cripples the operations of any Company for no good and/or proper reason. There is absolutely no evidence before us to suggest that the workers had been attempting to hold discussions with the Company before the day in question and that they were frustrated by the Company in their attempts. There is also no evidence forthcoming from the Union to suggest that up to that point in time the management style of the Company was oppressive.

> Thus, for the workers to decide for no good reason to literally impede and abruptly halt the operations of the Company on the evening of a very important event in order to have discussions on a matter which from the evidence did not appear before that evening to be of great importance and urgency is totally unacceptable.
>
> After carefully examining all of the evidence we rule that:-
>
> (1) the workers knew or ought to have known that if the meals were not prepared and served to the guests in a timely manner the Company will not only be embarrassed but also it will not be able to operate its business effectively.
>
> (2) the workers did bring the Company's operations to a halt on the evening in question.
>
> (3) the Union's account of what had transpired on that evening in question to be less than credible.
>
> Accordingly, this trade dispute is therefore dismissed." [138]

In **Oilfields Workers' Trade Union and Nestle Trinidad and Tobago Limited**, H H George-Marcelle held that the Company's action was harsh and oppressive:-

> "The Court must now ask itself whether when Mr. Llanos (The Company's Customer Service Manager) said, "I want you to get off this compound," and he called the security to escort Mr. Walters (the worker), was Mr. Walters summarily dismissed by the aforementioned words. The Court's analysis and conclusion is yes...The authority for this conclusion can be found in Kendrick v Aerduct Productions (supra) which states that traditionally the words used by an employer to denote a dismissal can be clear and explicit. It is also important to note that it is not only the actual words used which are important but also

138 TD No. 262 of 2004 Toucan Inn & Bonkers Restaurant and Bar and Oilfields Workers' Trade Union.

the intention behind the words used which can be gleaned from the surrounding circumstances such as the security escort of the worker.

Indeed it must be stated in this case that the words used by Mr. Llanos were clear and unambiguous. Most definitely by putting the worker off the compound he summarily dismissed him. Actually, if it is that his words were not clear enough then the fact that he called security to ensure, that the worker left clearly showed his intention. Clearly, he had intended by his words to summarily dismiss the worker and the use of security was to ensure that his intentions were carried out.

Did the worker deserve to be treated that way? That is to say, did the worker deserve to be summarily dismissed? This question brings the court to consider the third issue. The third issue being whether or not the Company had acted reasonably under the circumstances of alleged threatening and intimidating behaviour...In this Lever Brothers case the Court held that in cases involving dismissal on grounds of alleged or proven criminal acts the test is whether the employer acted reasonably in light of the circumstances known to him. The fundamental principle concerning this issue of reasonableness is whether or not the employer had conducted the necessary inquiries to allow them to function in the manner in which they did. The Court stated that it is not the function of the employer to adopt the role of a Court of law and attempt to establish innocence or guilt of the person concerned...clearly, by summarily dismissing the worker he left no room for inquiries to establish the worker's guilt or innocence.

Any subsequent attempt of an enquiry was otiose...indeed, the charge of threatening and intimidating behaviour is criminal in nature and the use of the security gave effect to the criminal charge. The criminal element therefore legitimately introduces the concept of reasonableness,

> where in Industrial relations, the burden of proof is on the balance of probabilities. Instead of conducting a reasonable investigation a security officer was called and the worker was dismissed in a harsh and oppressive manner. Additionally, the Company was bold enough to attempt to suspend him the next day after being already dismissed by the words and action of Mr Llanos. Then the disciplinary procedure was instituted and the worker was again dismissed. This disciplinary procedure and subsequent dismissal was a sham to mask the Company's harsh and oppressive conduct." [139]

In **All Trinidad Sugar and General Workers' Trade Union and Fen Mohammed Stores Limited**, I discussed the misconduct of a worker and whether such misconduct warranted dismissal:-

> "This Court accepts that there are a number of well recognized grounds on which an employer may dismiss an employee summarily such as gross misconduct, dishonesty, and so forth, but the pertinent question is whether the conduct of this worker is serious enough to warrant summary dismissal.
>
> In Trade Dispute No. 2 of 1992 the Industrial Court stated that the worker in question committed mistakes. However, as soon as the mistakes were discovered, he took all reasonable steps to rectify his errors. He went to his supervisor to made (sic) a report, his supervisor was not available, so he went to another supervisor, who had responsibility and made the report.
>
> Similarly in the instant case the worker made an error at the workplace and as soon as she discovered it she too, informed her supervisor who directed her to inform another worker and she was given the assurance that the matter would be resolved. While we are not condoning the mistake which the worker has made, we accept her

139 ESD No. 371 of 2011 Oilfields Workers' Trade Union and Nestlé Trinidad and Tobago Limited.

evidence that the spoons were returned and replaced. We also accept the worker's evidence that the customer was Tital Methanol, a company, and not a person as was advanced by the Company. In the absence of such conduct it was incumbent on the Company to conduct a proper investigation into the matter and to examine all of the possible options which were available, so as to determine which penalty best serves the objective of discipline in the given circumstances. We find that the worker's dismissal was indeed harsh and oppressive and not in accordance with the principles of good industrial relations practice."[140]

In **Jennifer Geran and Dream Company Ltd (K-Club Barbuda)** the Hon. Edward T. Henry OBE, Chairman of the Industrial Court of Antigua and Barbuda, ruled that the dismissal was unfair. He asked the following questions:-

(a) "Did the Employer institute any investigation of the two "heavy complaints" which it made against the Employee before dismissal?

(b) Was the summary dismissal fair?

(c) Did the Employee mitigate her loss?

(d) What compensation is payable to the Employee if the dismissal is found to be unfair?

An employee, who is dismissed is under a duty to mitigate his loss by seeking similar or alternative employment. In an appropriate case he is required to resort to self-employment and to set up his own business. Failure to do any of the foregoing will result in a reduction of the award. Notwithstanding, it must be borne in mind that the employee was hired under a fixed-term contract, and in circumstances of unfair dismissal and breach of contract, she is entitled to the outstanding salary and perquisites that she would normally have enjoyed if her dismissal is held to be unfair...It is a requirement of natural justice

140 TD No. 90 of 2004 All Trinidad Sugar and General Workers' Trade Union and Fen Mohammed Stores Limited.

that if any allegations against an employee are alleged by an employer to have been committed by an employee, then it is incumbent upon the employer to allow the employee to be aware of them so that that employee may have the opportunity to rebut them if there is evidence upon which he has in his possession.

Maundy, P. in Carlene Vigo and David Jarvis V Swiss American National Bank References Numbers 27 and 40 of 1996 stated the following proportion at paragraph 18 inter alia as follows:-

> "This Court has always maintained that in cases of Industrial Relations, except perhaps in instances where an employee is caught in flagrante delicto, he should be given an opportunity to be heard in keeping with the rule of Natural Justice, Audi alteram partem...Not only must both sides to a dispute be heard but no undue pressure or coercion must be put on an employee to e.g. admit a wrong. By extension, all the parties to a dispute must be heard prior to a finding."

In arriving at a decision, the Court has taken into consideration all of the evidence led on behalf of the employee, has observed her demeanour, has listened to her counsel's submissions, the submissions made on the Employer's behalf, has read the Employer's Memorandum has considered the authorities cited, and the provisions of the Labour Code, the Industrial Court Act, Cap.214, and the relevant case law. The decision of this Court is that in all the circumstances of this case, the Employee was unfairly dismissed by the Employer.

The Labour Code makes it clear that an employee is entitled to more than his contractual rights. He has an equity in his job which requires protection and he has a right not to be unfairly dismissed. This is affirmed by section 10 (3) of the Industrial Court Act.

In this case the Employee was employed under the terms of a contract. Since the dismissal is deemed to have been unfair and the contract breached, it follows that she is entitled to the amount of salary she would have earned from the time of her dismissal up to the closing date of the contract. In addition she is entitled to paid leave, any other perquisites provided by the contract together with her equity." [141]

In **Bank and General Workers' Union and Public Service Association of Trinidad and Tobago,** H H Aberdeen examined several cases and legal principles with respect to the concepts of harsh and oppressive and natural justice. He stated that:-

"The Union "alleges that the worker's dismissal was unfair, unjustified and contrary to good industrial relations, practice. The Union is seeking compensation "to meet the justice of the case." For its part, the Association contends that on the 13th, 14th and 16th April 1999, the worker committed breaches of duty which separately and cumulatively were considered sufficiently serious to warrant his dismissal...In summary the Union's case according to its written and oral submission is as follows:-

- That the worker's explanation for the incident of the 13th April, 1999 is reasonable since his action was in the interest of the Association and that he was.... under the impression that the Secretary/Treasurer accepted his explanation since he was not told that he would be charged for an offence.
- That with respect to the incidents of 14th and 16th April 1999, the worker was only made aware of the allegations against him in connection with those dates when he received the letter of dismissal.

141 Reference No. 4 of 2004 Jennifer Geran and Dream Company Ltd (K-Club Barbuda).

- That the worker was not given any opportunity to be heard by the Association in answer to any charge or allegation in connection with his conduct on the 13th, 14th and 16th April, 1999, and that such a denial is a fundamental breach of the rules of natural justice and therefore a breach of good industrial relations practice.
- That the worker's past record does not cause a forfeiture of his right to be heard and that he was still entitled to be treated fairly by being allowed an opportunity to defend any charge against him.
- That the Association in dismissing the worker acted in contravention of its own constitution by not informing him in writing about allegations made against him and affording him reasonable opportunity to defend himself before taking disciplinary action against him.
- That there was no just cause for the dismissal of the worker, that his dismissal was contrary to good industrial relations practice and that he should, as a consequence be compensated.

In support of its submission the Union cited the Court's judgment in Trade Dispute No. 20 of 1990 between UCIW and American Stores Ltd. The Association's case is succinctly summarized in its written submission to the Court as follows: Mr. Dale Boxill was employed by the Association as a Security Officer and during the course of such employment displayed characteristics which were totally incompatible with the duties attached to his office. Repeated warnings in writing to him proved to be of no effect. On the 13th 14th and 14th (sic) April, the worker again committed breaches of duty which separately and cumulatively the Association considered to be sufficiently serious to warrant his dismissal. On the 19th April 1999 he was dismissed.

The Association contends that the worker's conduct on the relevant occasions referred to, at paragraph 3 above together with his past conduct justifies his dismissal.

The question this Court has to determine is whether the dismissal of the worker occurred in circumstances that were harsh and/or oppressive and/or contrary to good industrial relations practice. We have been greatly assisted in this task by the input of the very learned and experienced representatives of the Union and Association for which we are grateful. In TD 98 of 1997 between Barclays Bank and Barclays Employees Union, cited by representative for the Association, the Court held that the dismissal of Wayne Corbie, a worker who had been dismissed for writing an abusive and insulting letter to his Manager, was not in accordance with the principles of good industrial relation practices. The court found that **"The management section dealing with discipline never interviewed him. The Managing Director who alone could dismiss an employee, did not interview him and so he had no opportunity to put his case or to apologize before dismissal..."**

In coming to its conclusions, the Court reviewed certain cases cited as the case of Bryden & Co. v C. Thomas reported in IRLA Vol.5 No.6 pg. 174 and Charles Lett & Co. Ltd v A.E.C.T Howard I.R.L.R Vol.5 pg. 246. The Court also reviewed Recommendation of the ILO No.119, and concluded that:-

> "A fundamental principle of natural justice developed under the common law is that a person has the right to be heard in defense of his person or property and the ILO recommendation only restate this principle." The Court declared that "...the cases cited emphasize the right to be heard in one's defense which is embodied in our system and with respect we adopt the conclusions therein. "They are in essence that: "Whatever the circumstances, whatever an employee

> is alleged to have done and however serious it might be, it is always necessary that an employee be afforded some opportunity of explaining himself to the person in management who will in the first instance take the decision whether or not he is to be dismissed... When this procedure has not been followed in order to sustain a dismissal, management must prove that the result would have been the same if it had been followed."

In TD 15A of 1982 and TD 15B of 1982 between the OWTU and Trinidad & Tobago Electricity Commission, the Court after hearing the two disputes separately, ordered the reinstatement of the two workers who had in each case been dismissed by the Commission for alleged acts of gross misconduct. In each case the Court found that the involved worker had been dismissed without first being given an opportunity to be heard in his defense. In TD 15A of 1982 the Court found that:-

> "There was a breach of fundamental principles in law and industrial relations in the Commission's denying of the worker the right to be heard on the issue."

The Court went on to hold that: "The dismissal of the worker Mr. Kurt Murray was harsh and oppressive and contrary to the principles and practice of good industrial relations."

In TD 15B of 1982 the Court declared that:-

> "It should be noted that the right to be heard is not only a rule of natural justice but a fundamental principle of industrial relations. (See I.L.O recommendations 119). 'Dismissal for serious misconduct should take place only in cases where the employer cannot in good faith be expected to take any other course'. 'Before a decision to dismiss a worker for serious misconduct becomes effective, the worker shall be given an opportunity to state his case promptly'..."

In TD 140 of 97 between Banking General Workers Union and Home Mortgage Bank Ltd at page 9 H H Khan then Vice President of the Court, stated:-

> "The principles of good industrial relations practice dictate that no worker's employment may be terminated except for a valid reason connected with his capacity to perform the work for which he was employed or which is founded on the operational requirements of the employer's business...these principles have been enshrined in Convention 158 of I.L.O...it...affords evidence of good industrial relation practices which have been accepted at an international level...**The principles of good industrial relations practice require an employer not only to inform a worker of the reason/reasons for a proposed dismissal but also give a worker, save in exceptional circumstances a fair opportunity to be heard before proceeding to dismiss him for such reason/reasons the worker will not have a fair opportunity to present to the employer material which may cause the employer to change his mind from his proposed course of action..."**

The effect of these and the numerous other judgments of this Court including that cited by the able representative of the Union in TD 20 of 1999 between UCIW and American Stores, as well as ILO Convention 158 cited by the learned representative of the Association, is to establish, that in our system of industrial relations, every worker has the right to a fair opportunity to defend himself against any charge or allegation made against him, as well as to be heard in mitigation of any possible penalty (especially dismissal) by the person/s in management responsible for taking such decisions, before they are effected.

This is not a trifling matter to be taken lightly or viewed as a mere technicality. It is a fundamental principle of good industrial relations. It is to industrial relations practice what natural justice is to the common law. Its omission from common law practice, would make a fair trial impossible to achieve and would nullify any finding of guilt by common law courts. Its omission by an employer from any disciplinary process, would amount to a fundamental breach of the principles of good industrial relations practice and render any disciplinary action by an employer (especially dismissal) harsh and oppressive and unsustainable, except in the most exceptional circumstances.

An employer seeking to sustain and justify the dismissal of a worker in such circumstances, places on his own shoulders, the very difficult task and perhaps unbearable burden of proving on the one hand, that he could not reasonably have been expected to provide the worker with the opportunity to be heard; and on the other hand, that even if he had done so, it would have made no difference to the outcome.

In this instant case, the worker has stated and the Association has admitted, that he did not know of any of the allegations against him prior to being dismissed. He was never charged with anything; there was no investigation or disciplinary inquiry in which he was involved; he never had any opportunity to be heard in his own defense. He never had an opportunity to be interviewed by or to give any explanations to or make any plea in mitigation, to the President of the Association, who in the final analysis issued the letter of dismissal. His dismissal was executed by the President of the Association, who did not have the benefit of the worker's explanations in response to the allegations contained in the letter of dismissal. There was no process undertaken beforehand, to determine his guilt in relation to "reports" which we assume, must have been made by the Association's Secretary Treasurer, 2nd Vice President, and Assistant Secretary.

There was also no opportunity provided to the worker, to be heard in mitigation of the possible-penalty of dismissal. His guilt and punishment were decided without charge or trial or chance to speak in his own defense. The Representative of the Association has argued, that the worker had a bad disciplinary record and that he was given a final warning by letter dated 19/3/99, to the effect that should he engage in any further infractions, his services would be terminated. This, he explained meant, that if the worker was found guilty of any further infractions he would be dismissed. He further posited, that the worker's admission that he disobeyed the Association's instructions and turned off the lights, left no doubt as to his guilt and as such the Union's case was without foundation. The Association, he submitted, in frustration as a result of the numerous infractions by the worker, acted summarily in terminating his employment and as such should be excused by the Court for so doing.

We find in this present dispute that the Association has not shown evidence of any circumstance that could be said to have reasonably prevented it, from undertaking its obligation to inform the worker of the charges or allegations against him and provide a fair opportunity to him to be heard in his defense. The Association has not proven that, had the worker been heard, it would have made no difference to the penalty of dismissal that it imposed on him. Indeed the reasons for the worker's dismissal are in our view, not such as could in themselves, justify the action of summary dismissal.

The worker certainly had an unenviable record of employment, with numerous letters recording his persistent breaches and infractions. It is clear that the Association became frustrated by this and had reached the point where it considered the worker to be more of a liability than an asset. This appears to be what the Association was most influenced by, when it dismissed the worker in the way that it did. But bad though it maybe, a worker's past disciplinary record, is relevant only after he has already been heard and found guilty of any alleged misconduct or breaches. His past record goes not to a finding of guilt or innocence, but to determining the nature of the consequence or penalty an employer may reasonably impose, after guilt has already been established; it should not be allowed to predetermine a worker's guilt or prejudice the employer's mind in relation to present allegations. Indeed, it is by no means an excuse for denying a worker a fair opportunity to seek to establish his innocence, or to be heard in mitigation of any possible penalty, by the person with whom the authority to take disciplinary action resides.

Having heard and evaluated all the evidence and in particular the oral evidence of the worker; and having heard the oral submissions of the learned and experienced representatives of the Union and the Association, for which we are grateful, it is our opinion and we so hold, that the worker Dale Boxhill, was dismissed in circumstances that were harsh and oppressive and not in accordance with the principles of good industrial relations practice.

By section 10(4) of the Act (IRA) the Court is empowered to order the reemployment or reinstatement of any worker or the payment of compensation or damages whether or not in lieu of such re-employment or reinstatement, or the payment of exemplary damages in lieu of such re-employment or reinstatement. And by section 10(5) of the Act, the Court in making an order for compensation or damages is, not bound to follow any rule of law for such and may make an assessment that is in its opinion, fair and appropriate. The union's prayer in this matter is for "...compensation to meet the justice of the case." We have considered the Union's view in this regard as well as the views of the Association. We have considered also the evidence of the worker regarding his earnings and employment since his dismissal. We are of the view that this is an appropriate case for an award of damages." [142]

142 TD No. 15 of 2000 Bank and General Workers' Union and Public Service Association of Trinidad and Tobago.

Abandonment

Abandonment, in the industrial relations context, essentially is the deliberate and unjustified refusal of a worker to report to work and perform his/her duties. There are elements to be satisfied to prove that a worker has abandoned his/her job, namely:-

1. Failure to report to work or absence without a valid or justified reason
2. A clear intention to sever the employment relationship

Banking, Insurance and General Workers Union and Cariflex Limited is one of the cases of summary dismissal and abandonment upon which I presided where the employer demonstrated a disturbing disregard for the rule of law and for the principles and practice of good industrial relations. The following is an abridged version of the judgment:-

> "The main issue which the Court is asked to determine is whether Company through its Managing Director dismissed the worker on 30th October, 2001 when he allegedly told him "go from here, go from here, go home and don't come back or whether the worker left his job on the 30th October, 2001 and did not return to work thereby abandoning his job. The Company also stated that the worker failed to attend a meeting on 5th October 2001 to discuss his status with the Company. Mr. Sooknarine stated in evidence that on the 30th October, 2001 he invited the worker to attend a meeting at the Litho Department where he and the worker joined four other persons. He stated that the worker left the meeting after ten minutes. Mr. Sooknarine said quite clearly that the worker then left the meeting without a single exchange of words between the worker and the Company, he subsequently discovered that the worker had left the compound and did not return. He denied ever referring to the worker as a "jackass" and he testified that at no time did he tell the worker to "go from here, go from here, go home and don't come back...

Now although Mr. Sooknarine categorically denied that there was conversation with the worker at the meeting, correspondence dated 31 October, 2001 which forms part of the Company Evidence and Arguments states as follows:-

> "Please be advised that the meeting with Mr. Hernandez ended abruptly yesterday when he took his bag and left. The meeting was being held with other production supervisors at the Offset department when Mr. Hernandez was told clearly that the company would continue to hold him liable for the damaged gearbox on the Scriber."

The letter supports the worker's evidence that the issue with the gear box was discussed at the meeting. The worker said that he left the Compound only after he was told "go from here, go from here, go home and don't come back" by Mr. Sooknarine, to use the worker's own words, "he (Mr. Sooknarine) run me like a dog..." Mr. Sooknarine's correspondence aforesaid to Miss Sankar corroborates that bit of the worker's account of what happened at that meeting and it raises questions about the veracity of Mr. Sooknarine's evidence. Indeed we accept the worker's evidence as a credible account of what transpired at that meeting on 30th October, 2001. We find as a fact that the worker was ordered to leave the Company premises by Mr. Sooknarine and he was also told that he should not return. This in our view amounted to the dismissal of the worker by the Company. Thus there was no duty on the part of the worker after he was dismissed to return to the Company to attend any meeting whatsoever.

This worker was employed with the Company for eight and a half years with an unblemished work record, that he was the only person working as printer in that section before the incidents which are stated aforesaid has not been challenged. After a careful and critical examination of all of the evidence, we find that the worker is a very credible witness and we accept his account of what transpired between the parties at the material time.

We find that the worker did not abandon his job on 30th October, 2001 but that he was summarily dismissed by the Company. It is a well-established principle in industrial relations and the laws of natural justice that in only exceptional circumstances should an employer dismiss an employee without giving that employee an opportunity to be heard.

This principle is enunciated by the Privy Council in Jupiter General Insurance Co. Ltd. v Ardeships Bomarji 1937 3 All ER 67. In John v Rees 1969 2 All ER 274 at page 309 Megarry J stated,

> "It may be that there are some who would decry the importance which the courts attach to the observance of the rules of natural justice. "When something is obvious," they may say, "why force everybody to go through the tiresome waste of time involved in framing charges and giving an opportunity to be heard? The result is obvious from the start." Those who take this view do not, I think, do themselves justice. As everybody who has anything to do with the law well knows, that part of the law is strewn with examples of open and shut cases which, somehow, were not, of unanswerable charges which, in the event, were completely answered; of inexplicable conduct which was fully explained; of fixed and unalterable determination that, by discussion, suffer a change."

In Western Excavating (ECC) Limited v Sharp 1978 QB 761, Lord Denning had this to say,

> "If the employer is guilty of conduct which is a significant breach going to the root of the contract of employment or which shows that the employer no longer intends to be bound by one or more of the essential terms then the employee is entitled to treat himself as discharged from any further

> performance. If he does so, then he terminates the contract by reason of the employer's conduct. He is constructively dismissed. The employee is entitled in those circumstances to leave at the instant without giving any notice at all..."

It is clear that when the Company discussed the transfer of the worker to another section at a lower rate of pay without any form of consultation and or agreement, the Company was indeed considering the dismissal of the worker. On a critical examination of the evidence of what transpired on 30th October, 2001 we find as a fact that the worker was not given the opportunity to be heard.

We find also that he was called to a meeting without any knowledge of the purpose of the meeting beforehand and then he was summarily dismissed.

There is a plethora of decisions which have emerged from the Industrial Court of Trinidad and Tobago which adequately explain the law on summary dismissal of a worker. Among them are Trade Dispute No. 352/1997; Trade Dispute No. 40/1997; Trade Dispute No. 308/2002; Trade Dispute No. 90/2004. These decisions speak to gross misconduct, dishonesty, gross negligence etc. which are regarded as exceptional circumstances to justify summary dismissal. In this Trade Dispute, there is no evidence before this Court to suggest that there are exceptional circumstances to justify the Company's decision to dismiss the worker summarily.

It is our view that an award of exemplary damages to the worker is a just, fair and appropriate award in all of the given circumstances. The Court wishes to signal its abhorrence to the manner in which the worker was treated by the Company especially the humiliation which the worker was made to suffer especially at the meeting on the 30th October, 2001." [143]

143 TD No. 303 of 2002 Banking, Insurance and General Workers Union and Cariflex Limited.

In **Westend Sawmill and Lumber Yard and National Union of Government and Federated Workers,** I examined the Company's allegation that the worker had abandoned his job:-

> "The worker in this case is extremely incapacitated and appeared almost to be a paraplegic. These symptoms we are told were as a result of a stroke which the worker suffered in November 2003. As we stated in open court and we wish to reiterate in this Judgment, the Industrial Court was never intended by the powers that be, to be a court which is adversarial in nature. The main purpose of the Court is to facilitate the amicable resolution of disputes in a civil manner, indeed, the Industrial Court has been described in some quarters as a court of Social Justice.
>
> The Union's case is that the worker was employed with the Company as a watchman since 1980. He left the Company for a two year period sometime after 1980 and he returned to work with the Company thereafter and remained there as the watchman until he suffered a stroke in 2003 and was unable to work...Miss Lutchmansingh, the worker's common law wife testified that after the worker became ill she went to the Company to collect his wages and she also submitted a sick leave certificate on behalf of the worker for a further period of thirty days commencing 1st January, 2004. However she did not receive any wages for the worker from the Company.
>
> The Union contends that the action taken by the Employer to terminate the worker's services was harsh, inhumane, and contrary to the custom and practices of good Industrial Relations, in that after having worked for so many years with the Employer (twenty three (23) the worker fell ill at age sixty six (66), and the Employer is refusing to accept Sick Leave submitted by the worker. Upon being approached by the worker representative, who requested that the worker be paid an Exgratia payment in

lieu of his services, the Employer refused to reply...There was very little evidence forthcoming from the Company to assist the Court in its deliberations. The Company argued that the worker had abandoned his job since he has not reported for duty since November 2003. Counsel for the Company Mr. Manwah in his submissions to the Court stated:-

> "What is before us is the termination of service. They are claiming that we terminated his service. We never terminated his service. This man just did not show up for work. He came in November and that is the last time we saw him; he never came back."

It is noteworthy that the Company was informed of the worker's health in November 2003 by a medical certificate which was submitted for and on behalf of the worker, yet the Company chose to ignore this information and it also refused to accept a further medical certificate related to the worker's medical condition.

It is stated in Patterson vs Messrs. Bracketts (1977) IRLR 137 that when the health of a worker is considered by the employer the following is a useful approach:-

> "What is required in a particular case as for the employer informing himself about the ...employee's health is concerned will depend on the circumstances of the case. But the principle is twofold; first there should be consultation or discussion with the employee: and secondly such other steps as are necessary should be taken to enable the employer to form a balanced view about the employee's health."

It is clear therefore that when it was informed of the worker's health, there was a basic obligation on the Company to inquire into the nature of the worker's illness, this certainly was not done. It is clear that in cases of long term ill health, a company cannot reasonably be expected to keep a worker in its employ, the nature of the illness and the likely length of a worker's continued absence from work are certainly some of the circumstances that a Company must take into account to determine whether or not to continue the contract of service.

If we were to accept the Company's assertion that the worker did not return to work in November 2003 and he therefore abandoned his job, then we need to critically examine the evidence to see whether the Company made any efforts to contact the worker after the last day when he reported to work. There is no evidence before the Court which suggests that the Company made any effort in this regard.

We find also, that the Company had a duty to inquire about the worker's whereabouts and the state of his health when he failed to report to work in November 2003 before it could conclude that he had abandoned his job.

On the totality of all of the evidence we find as a fact that the worker did not abandon his job as a watchman but that the Company abruptly ended its contract of service with the worker without first ascertaining the true status of the Worker's health.

It is the ruling of this Court that the Company by its very act had dismissed the worker in circumstances which were harsh, oppressive and contrary to the principles of good industrial relations practices." [144]

In **Sissons Paints (W.I.) Limited and Transport and Industrial Workers' Union**, H H Sealy also examined the issue of abandonment:-

"Errol Mahabir a Process Operator, was dismissed on October 12th 1977. Mahabir had been employed by the Company from February, 1976 and at the time of his dismissal was in receipt of a wage of two dollars and eighty-one cents per hour. Mahabir received chemical burns at work on his left wrist on Wednesday October 5, 1977.

144 TD No. 204 of 2004 Westend Sawmill and Lumber Yard and National Union of Government and Federated Workers.

He was attended to at the Factory and continued to work up to Friday, October 7, 1977. He did not report for work from Monday October 10 to Friday October 17, he was informed that he was dismissed with effect from October 12, on the ground that he abandoned his job.

During the weekend following his injury, the condition of his wrist had become worse. He went to the doctor on October 10 and obtained a medical certificate recommending five (5) days leave from that date. His wife went to the doctor with him and he asked her to take the certificate to the Company. She did not do this. According to Mahabir, she had forgotten to deliver the certificate and did not tell him until Wednesday October 12. The next day he gave the certificate to a co-worker and the Company received it on the 13th.

There is no doubt from at least two (2) of these documents that Mahabir had built up an unenviable record of absences and the Company had given thought to what would be the future of his relationship with them in light of this record. Against this background when Mahabir failed to turn up for work during the week October 10-14, that the Company terminated his services, reason given however, by the Company for termination is the fact that he abandoned his job.

The Company was aware that Mahabir had received injury on the job on October 5th and had no reasonable ground for drawing the conclusion that he abandoned his job...We accept that Mahabir gave his wife the certificate to deliver to the Company...it was argued by the Company that Mahabir displayed irresponsibility in ascertaining from his wife whether the certificate had in fact been submitted. We do not find him as being irresponsible or negligent. Nevertheless, the Company became aware of a reason for Mahabir's absence when they received the certificate and in our view, this was an occasion for a

> reasonable employer to reconsider a decision taken the day before to dismiss a worker on abandonment of his job.
>
> While we understand the anxiety to be rid of a Worker with a record such as Mahabir, we think the employer should have exercised a little more caution than they did in dealing with the circumstances of the case on October 13, 1977.
>
> We consider that the employer acted unreasonably in that there was on the basis of the medical certificate reasonable ground for re-consideration of its decision and secondly, the employer having indicated on 14th September, the manner in which he proposed to register his disapproval of Mahabir's absence; that is suspending him should have issued a warning to the worker if he intended to visit upon his sterner form of discipline, namely dismissal."[145]

In **Prison Officers Association of Trinidad and Tobago and Ship Builders, Ship Repairers & Allied Workers Trade Union** H H Bramble rejected the contention that the worker had abandoned her job and he held that the dismissal was harsh and oppressive:-

> "In this trade dispute, the Union contested the dismissal of a Barmaid employed by the Prison Officer's Association of Trinidad and Tobago...It was agreed that the worker was on two (2) weeks' sick leave from the 16th March 1979. It is common ground that the worker did not report for duty on Saturday, March 31 but did turn out to work on the next working day, the 2nd April.
>
> The Association contended that the worker abandoned her job as barmaid...It sought to substantiate its case by the evidence of its General Secretary Rafael Sequea, who said the worker came to the Club on the afternoon of Friday March 30 and in a boisterous manner said that she was not coming to work the following day and that the

145 TD No. 50 of 1978 Sissons Paints (W.I.) Limited and Transport and Industrial Workers' Union.

Association could do as it pleased about that. On Monday, April 2, she did report and when asked by him why she was not out to work on Saturday, March, 31, indicated that she had done exactly what she had intimated on Friday. The Secretary thought the worker's behaviour extremely arrogant and proceeded to suspend her verbally and told her to report for further instructions on Friday, 6th April. She did not come back at that time. Subsequently he reported to his executive committee and it was decided to treat the worker as having abandoned her employment with the Association.

It would seem that the Association as an employer would know it is normal industrial relations practice in this country for a worker to be granted at least a two (2) or three (3) days grace period either for the presentation of a medical certificate or before being deemed to have abandoned the job. The Association's own admission that the worker had indicated that she would be absent on the 31st, and its knowledge of recent surgery undergone by her should have inhibited any drastic action.

The Worker, however, claimed that she was not suspended on the 2nd April but was told that her services were no longer required. This emphasizes the necessity of an employer's putting in writing any disciplinary action taken and the reason for it.

In the general setting we accept the worker's version of what occurred. In the result we find that the dismissal was harsh and oppressive and award compensation in the sum of four hundred and eighty dollars ($480.00) to be paid on or before the 1st May, 1980." [146]

146 TD No. 125 of 1979 Prison Officers Association of Trinidad and Tobago and Ship Builders, Ship Repairers & Allied Workers Trade Union.

The Use of Narcotics in the Workplace

From time to time the Court has to deliberate upon disputes related to drug policies and the use of illegal drugs in the workplace.

In **Transport and Industrial Workers' Union and Public Transport Service Corporation**, I upheld the Company's decision to dismiss a worker for the use of marijuana at the workplace. The Union's case essentially was that:-

> "On June 10th, 2003 the worker and a trainee by the name of Kenwyn Seales were assigned to work on Bus R.T.S. 28. That bus was in need of a rear bumper bracket. The worker went to the Corporation's store to obtain a bracket for use on the said bus but there was no rear bumper bracket available at the store. He then went to the scrap yard to see if he could locate the said bracket from any of the derelict buses. He eventually located a rear bumper with a bracket in bus R.T.S. 006.
>
> The Company's case is that around 9:35 a.m. on June 10th, 2003 Mr. Drolly Francis and Mr. Lakhan Mahabir were alerted by a strange scent which appeared to emanate from the area of the scrap yard. They went in the area and they saw the worker and Seales sitting in one of the derelict buses. This area was not a designated work area. Mr. Francis told the Court that he saw the worker "with a joint in his hand. So when we went in the bus, he dropped it".
>
> At about 3:30 pm the worker was served with a notice of suspension from the corporation dated the 11th June, 2003.
>
>> "....We wish to advise that you are suspended from duties with immediate effect as the undermentioned charges are preferred against you...On Tuesday 10th June 2003, you were caught engaging in the use of illicit drug, namely marijuana, in E060, which is a derelict Unit. At approximately 9:35 am, on Tuesday 10th June, 2003 you abandoned your work assignment

and was seen malingering in EO60, which is a derelict Unit."

An inquiry which lasted for approximately four (4) to five (5) days was held into the matter. The worker, two shop stewards from the Union and a representative from the Company were present at the inquiry on ail days. Sometime after the end of the inquiry the Corporation informed the worker by letter dated 23" July, 2003 that he was dismissed. The Union has argued that:-

a) That there is no proof beyond a reasonable doubt "as to whether the substance allegedly found by Mr. Francis was the said substance that Mr. Juanette handed over to the forensic sciences center (sic)."

b) That there is no proof that the integrity of the exhibit was intact when it was under the control of the Corporation

c) Additionally that there is no exhibit before the Court to support the Corporation's contention that the worker was allegedly found with a narcotic.

Beyond a reasonable doubt is the criminal standard of proof. The burden of proof in civil cases and in trade disputes before the Industrial Court is the civil standard of proof which is the balance of probabilities. Thus this Court is required to use the lower level of proof as opposed to the higher level (beyond reasonable doubt) to determine if the allegations which were made against the worker were "more probable than not" to coin the phrase made popular by Lord Denning in Miller vs Minister of Pension. The Corporation therefore does not have to establish its case beyond reasonable doubt in this dispute.

In civil matters and trade disputes one cannot reasonably expect that companies and/or organizations have special rooms to store a narcotic when it is found on their compound. Indeed there is no provision in law for a narcotic, when found by employers to be sent to the Police property keeper for safe keeping. Therefore it is reasonable to expect that an employer would make some sort of arrangement to keep this narcotic safe.

We believe the evidence of Mr. Juanette when he testified that the plant material in the plastic bag was handed over to him and he placed it in an envelope which he locked in his drawer. He subsequently handed the envelope at the Forensic Science Centre, to Mr. Maharaj, a forensic analyst at the Centre who in the presence of Mr. Juanette, placed the markings 10306/03 on the envelope. The said items in the envelope were then sent to the lab for testing and analysis.

There is nothing in the Corporation's evidence to suggest that the integrity of the exhibit was compromised and that the plant material which was referred to on the Certificate of Analysis is different from what Mr. Francis has alleged that he found...In this dispute a Certificate of Analysis was given to the Court and it has identified the plant material which was analyzed as marijuana. It seems reasonable to expect that after a narcotic is produced and shown to the relevant parties in a trade dispute together with a Certificate of Analysis which has been accepted by both sides that lawful arrangements be made for the disposal of the said narcotic. In this case the Corporation sent the narcotic to the Police for disposal. There is no evidence before the Court to suggest that at any time during the inquiry that the Union objected to the plant substance which was allegedly found by the Company. There is also no evidence that the findings of the forensic analyst which were contained on the Certificate of Analysis were ever challenged by the Union at the inquiry.

We further find that the worker was engaged in the illicit use of a narcotic, namely marijuana, on the Corporation's premises and that a proper and thorough inquiry was

> held into the matter. Thus, we find that the Corporation's decision to dismiss the worker to be a reasonable one. This trade dispute is therefore dismissed." [147]

In **All Trinidad Sugar and General Workers' Trade Union and Seereeram Brothers Limited,** H H Khan, Acting President (as he then was) held:-

> "The facts are within a short compass and not in dispute. They show that the Company dismissed the Worker from its employment on March 17, 1995. At the time of his dismissal, the Company employed the worker as a specialist truck driver. The Company dismissed the worker after it received an Analyst's Report that the worker had an excessive amount of marijuana in his urine.
>
> The All Trinidad Sugar and General Workers' Trade Union ("the Union") did not contest the Analyst's Certificate or the facts relating to the dismissal. Mr. Cowie, who appeared for the Union, submitted, however, that the Company had an obligation to offer the worker an opportunity' to undergo rehabilitative treatment as an alternative to his dismissal. Mr. Cowie was unable to point to any duty or obligation either in law or in the registered collective agreement or the principles of good industrial relations practice to show that there was any such duty or obligation placed on the Company. To show such an obligation, it is necessary that there must be some statutory requirement or an undertaking by the employer, either in a contract of employment or in a registered collective agreement. On the facts of this trade dispute, I find that there was no obligation imposed on the employer to rehabilitate the worker instead of dismissing him.
>
> A motor vehicle driver, such as the worker, who consumes illegal drugs, is not only a danger to himself but also to

147 TD No. 131 of 2005 Transport and Industrial Workers' Union and Public Transport Service Corporation.

> his fellow workers, the property of his employer and its customers, and the public at large. He should not be permitted or placed in a position to cause death, damage or injury to other persons or to property. I accordingly found that the Company did not dismiss the worker in circumstances that were harsh and oppressive or not in accordance with the principles of good industrial relations practice and I dismissed the trade dispute." [148]

In **Oilfields Workers' Trade Union and Schlumberger Trinidad Incorporated**, H H Soverall considered the issue of the use of illegal drugs by employees when there was a written workplace policy:-

> "The Trade Dispute concerns the termination of the services of Dave Gumbs (the worker) on 30th August 2001 as certified by the Minister with responsibility for Labour. The worker was employed as an Operator...At times, he drove the Employer's vehicles in the discharge of his duties. The worker was selected to attend and did attend a two week course on Heavy Vehicle Training at Kellyville Training Centre, U.S.A from 20th August to 31st August, 2001. During his attendance at the training session, a random drug test was conducted on the worker and he was found to have traces of an illicit drug, namely marijuana, in his system.
>
> The Employer had in force a strict Drug and Alcohol Policy, which prohibited the use of illicit drugs by its employees. The worker knew of the policy. As a result of that finding, the worker was asked to return and did return to Trinidad. By letter dated 29th August, 2001, the Employer terminated the worker's services on the ground that he has used marijuana in violation of the Employer's policy.

148 TD No. 90 of 1995 All Trinidad Sugar and General Workers' Trade Union and Seereeram Brothers Limited.

> The Judgment in Trade Dispute No. 90 of 1995 between All Trinidad Sugar and General Workers' Union and Seereeram Brothers Limited which was almost of the same kind of facts, supported the dismissal of the worker. Unlike the Employer in that dispute, this Employer dealt with petrochemicals, gases, radioactive substances et. al. The Employer did not and could not give any undertaking to the worker as to his rehabilitation since there was no existing rehabilitation programme, a fact which the worker admitted.
>
> We conclude that there is no existing collective agreement between the parties on that policy and the union had failed to provide evidence of such a policy or that such a policy was in accordance with the principles of good industrial relations practice. As a result, we are unable to fault the Employer's action in the matter, to wit, to terminate the worker's services." [149]

The Importance of Union Representation

The International Labour Standards are legal instruments which set out the basic principles and rights at work. These labour standards have been drawn up by the ILO 187 Member States (governments, employers and workers) and take the form of Conventions and Recommendations. There are eight (8) "fundamental" Conventions which are considered to be fundamental principles and rights of work, namely:-

1. Freedom of Association and Protection of the Right to Organise Convention, 1948 (No. 87)
2. Right to Organise and Collective Bargaining Convention, 1949 (No. 98)

149 TD No. 110 of 2003 Oilfields Workers' Trade Union and Schlumberger Trinidad Incorporated.

3. Forced Labour Convention, 1930 (No. 29) (and its 2014 Protocol)
4. Abolition of Forced Labour Convention, 1957 (No. 105)
5. Minimum Age Convention, 1973 (No. 138)
6. Worst Forms of Child Labour Convention, 1999 (No. 182)
7. Equal Remuneration Convention, 1951 (No. 100)
8. Discrimination (Employment and Occupation) Convention, 1958 (No. 111) [150]

Trinidad and Tobago has ratified the eight (8) Fundamental Conventions (along with three (3) Governance Conventions and eleven (11) Technical Conventions). Several other countries in the Commonwealth Caribbean have also ratified these Fundamental Conventions:-

- **Antigua and Barbuda** has ratified eight (8) Fundamental Conventions, three (3) Governance Conventions and eighteen (18) Technical Conventions.
- **Bahamas** has ratified eight (8) Fundamental Conventions, two (2) Governance Conventions and twenty-five (25) Technical Conventions.
- **Barbados** has ratified eight (8) Fundamental Conventions, three (3) Governance Conventions and twenty-nine (29) Technical Conventions.
- **Dominica** has ratified eight (8) Fundamental Conventions, two (2) Governance Conventions and sixteen (16) Technical Conventions.
- **Grenada** has ratified eight (8) Fundamental Conventions, two (2) Governance Conventions and twenty-four (24) Technical Conventions.

150 www.ilo.org, last visited on 7th December, 2020.

- **Guyana** has ratified eight (8) Fundamental Conventions, three (3) Governance Conventions and thirty-six (36) Technical Conventions.
- **Saint Kitts and Nevis** has ratified eight (8) Fundamental Conventions, one (1) Governance Convention and one (1) Technical Convention.
- **Saint Vincent and the Grenadines** has ratified eight (8) Fundamental Conventions, four (4) Governance Conventions and fifteen (15) Technical Conventions.

The Freedom of Association and Protection of the Right to Organise Convention and the Right to Organise and Collective Bargaining Convention are at the top of the list of the Fundamental Conventions and they are regarded as primary safeguards of peace and social justice. They are also the oldest fundamental Conventions, having been entered into force just after the end of World War II.

The ILO constituents are committed to the effective global implementation of the principles of Freedom of Association, the Protection of the Right to Organise and the Right to Collective Bargaining. These principles promote, among other things, the right of workers to become members of Trade Unions.

It is therefore critical in any workplace environment where there is a Trade Union present, for the employer to have consultation with that Trade Union. Moreover, it is equally important for the workers to be afforded with the opportunity to have Trade Union representation on work related issues, especially if the workers are accused of or charged for an infraction.

In **Transport and Industrial Workers' Union and Penta Paints Caribbean Limited,** I examined the importance of representation of a worker by a Union when he/she appears before an internal workplace tribunal. In this dispute the Union's shop steward changed roles and became a witness for the Company:-

> "The facts are that on the 26 April 2008, after working hours, there was an altercation between the worker and Collin Ottley, another worker. The Company, in

its Evidence and Arguments, stated that the incident occurred when the worker was "in the Company's uniform in an area with direct access and view of the public road". The Union stated that the incident occurred "outside the Company's compound". The two workers appear to have a non-work related issue about a transaction for the sale of honey and there are different versions to the Court about who was the aggressor on that day. The following day, a verbal report of the altercation was first brought to the attention of Ms. Cintra Singh, the Company's Human Resource Manager by the Union's shop steward, Mr. Fidel Plaza. As a result of Mr. Plaza's report Ms. Singh testified that she conducted an "investigation". She also verbally informed the worker on the said day that he was charged with gross misconduct and that he was required to attend a disciplinary hearing the following day.

At the disciplinary hearing Mr. Plaza, the Union's shop steward who was a part of the Company's "investigative panel" was asked to give an account of his version of the incident which transpired on 25 August 2008 and he did so. At no time in the hearing was the worker afforded the opportunity to face his accusers. At the end of the hearing a decision was taken to dismiss the worker with "immediate effect".

The worker was informed of the decision to dismiss him by a letter dated 27 August 2008. Curiously, although the letter of the 27 August 2008 informed the worker that his services were terminated with immediate effect and that he should return all company property, he was also asked in the same correspondence to "indicate to the Company within forty-eight (48) hours in receipt of this letter if there is any reason why your services should not be terminated."

The Company's Human Resource Manager, Mr. Singh had this to say about the process which was adopted:-

"At this grievance meeting the Union raised the following concerns:-

- Mr. Cassar was not given proper opportunity to be heard – as the witnesses did not give their verbal testimony in front of him.
- That the alleged assault did not occur on the Company's premises.
- There was no report presented from security although the booth was in close proximity.
- The company acknowledged that there was some merit in the concerns raised by the Union but after a detailed review concluded that none of the issues raised were compelling enough to warrant a change in its decision."

One of the main issues is whether or not the altercation occurred on the company's premises. The Company as part of its written policy has a list of disciplinary offences for which various penalties can be imposed. One such policy is a policy related to fighting. This policy states that acts of fighting or acts of assault or provocation on Company's premises will be punished with dismissal. The Company's policy is clear and unambiguous and ought to be distinguished from those cases where there is no clear or written policy. All of the witnesses have testified that the incident occurred at a place before the entrance to the company's security booth and outside of the fence of the Company's compound.

The Company has argued however, that the area outside of the fence is regarded as part of its compound. The key ingredients of this offence of misconduct, so to speak, are (1) whether there was a fight and (2) if there was indeed a fight, whether this fight was on the Company's compound...The Parties agree that the Company's guard booth was a short distance away from where the altercation occurred and that the area where the altercation occurred is a public thoroughfare. The Company did not obtain a report from the security guards who were on duty at the time of the incident. We have heard several different versions of the actual disciplinary process which was adopted in this Trade Dispute from various witnesses. Moreover, there are several inconsistencies in the Evidence and Arguments which were prepared and filed by the Company and the overall oral evidence of the Company's witnesses. However, what has not been refuted by the Company is that the Worker's Union representative Mr. Fidel Plaza reported the incident to management and the said Mr. Plaza was part of the Company's team which investigated the worker's conduct. A rather curious state of affairs indeed.

The worker was called to a disciplinary hearing where he faced a team which was put together by the Company, included in this team was the Union's shop steward. This rather curious course of events caused the worker to appear at the inquiry without any representation and the person whom he ought to rely upon to represent his interest was on the other side of the table. This type of situation does not augur well for Industrial Relations.

The role of a Union in representing workers is critical to the grievance process and central to good industrial relations. From the facts there appears to be a grave breach of duty by the Union to represent this worker and a flagrant departure of the role and purpose of the Union to provide representation for its members. The duty and responsibility of a Union is recognised and accepted by the Industrial Relations Act Chapter 88:01 and also by the ILO Convention to which this country is signatory.

The main purposes of a disciplinary hearing are two fold, firstly, to give the worker the opportunity to have his input on the facts which are presented by the employer and secondly to allow the worker the opportunity to be represented by his Union official. A worker has the right to a proper hearing, which includes his right to representation so that he can have an opportunity to respond to any allegation which has been made.

Although there is no question that this worker was involved in an altercation with another worker, the procedure which was adopted by the Company meant that he did not have any representation at the hearing and that he did not have sufficient or any detail of what was being said against him before the meeting. Natural justice, in a case such as the present one, requires not merely that the worker has a chance to state his case, he must be afforded proper representation and he must know sufficiently what are the allegations against him so that he can properly put forward his own case. There is no evidence that the worker was informed before the meeting or at the start of the said meeting of what was said against him. In addition the worker was not given the opportunity to face his accusers and he was not represented by his shop steward Mr. Fidel Plaza who changed roles and opted to become "a company witness".

From the totality of the evidence presented to the Court, we also find as a fact:-

a. that the worker was not represented at the meeting and that he was not afforded a proper and fair hearing;

b. that the altercation occurred outside the Company's compound in an area where the public has access. We therefore find that the worker was not in breach of the Company's written policy;

c. that the Company by its very action has deprived the worker a fair hearing;

d. that the Company is in breach with the rules of natural justice;

e. that the dismissal of this worker was harsh, oppressive and in breach of the principles and practices of good industrial relations.

The Court hereby orders that:-

a) the worker be immediately reinstated to his position of Warehouse Attendant without any loss of seniority and benefits;

b) any and all of the terms and conditions of employment which the worker enjoyed prior to his dismissal remain intact; and

c) the Company computes the worker's salary and pecuniary benefits from the date of his dismissal namely, 27th August, 2008 to 24th April, 2013, and pays to the worker the sum of that computation on or before 1st July, 2013." [151]

In **Trinidad and Tobago National Petroleum Marketing Company Limited and Oilfields Workers' Trade Union,** I examined the denial of a request which was made by two workers to have their Union representatives present at a meeting and held:-

> "It is highly unacceptable where there is a Recognised Majority Union in a Company that a worker has to use the guise of going to the washroom to seek representation from that Union. The right to representation, which is a right guaranteed under the Constitution, is a pillar of the IRA and fundamental to the practice of good industrial relations in this country. The denial of the workers of their rights to representation when there is a dispute over the duties and job functions can only be described as self-serving and misplaced arrogance." [152]

151 TD No. 275 of 2009 Transport & Industrial Workers' Union and Penta Paints Caribbean Limited.

152 TD No. 717 of 2013 and IRO 23 of 2013 (consolidated) Trinidad and Tobago National Petroleum Marketing Company Limited and Oilfields Workers' Trade Union.

Indefinite Suspension

It is an important principle in industrial relations that a suspension must have a commencement date and an end date. An indefinite suspension is therefore regarded as a dismissal which is harsh, oppressive and contrary to the principles and practice of good industrial relations.

H H Mahabir in her dicta in **The Amalgamated Workers Union and the Chief Personnel Officer** held that:-

> "Suspensions are temporary by definition. Accordingly, an indefinite suspension is unlawful and may also give rise to a personal grievance for an unjustifiable dismissal. Moreover, it is impossible as a matter of good industrial relations practice for an employer to indefinitely suspend an employee merely because the employer seeks to investigate the claim against the employee." [153]

In **Transport and Industrial Workers' Union and National Maintenance Training and Security Limited**, H H Rousseau reasoned, inter alia:-

> "The worker was suspended on the 10th January 2000 while the Union reported the dismissal of the worker on 21st June 2002, these are two fundamentally different issues. On the basis of the evidence before the Court, I have found that contrary to the commitment given in its letter of 10th January 2000, the Company failed to determine this matter by not issuing correspondence affirming as they alleged that the worker abandoned her job or by a letter of dismissal.
>
> A suspension cannot be for an indefinite period of time, it must be the responsibility of an employer to determine and to communicate its findings to a worker who has been suspended without pay pending further investigations.

153 TD No. 25 of 2008 The Amalgamated Workers Union and the Chief Personnel Officer.

> This must be done as quickly and as efficiently as is reasonably possible." [154]

In **Banking, Insurance and General Workers Union and Fibis Wireless Limited, trading as Wireless and Mobility Solutions (WAMS)**, I highlighted in this judgment the issue of indefinite suspension and its implications:-

> "The Company is involved in the trade of electronic equipment and gadgets. At all material time a Ms. Susan Holder, Manager, was the worker's supervisor. The Union contends that the worker was employed with the Company on December 9, 2005 as a Customer Service Representative. As a Customer Service Representative, his duties included among other things the sale of items to the public. Sometime in December 2005 within weeks after he assumed official duties at the Company, the worker was informed by his supervisor (Ms. Holder) that several items were missing from the stock at the store.
>
> As a result, a decision was taken by the Company to deduct the cost of the missing items from the wages of all workers (including the worker) to compensate for the loss. In this regard, a sum of money was deducted from the worker's wages for a period of time. The Union's case is that on 17th February, 2006, Ms. Holder had a conversation with the worker during which she disclosed that several items of stock were again missing, she also informed him that he was suspended from his job at the Company until an Investigation was conducted to determine what happened to the said items. The worker was officially suspended without pay on that day. The Union has alleged that since that date, the Company has made no further contact with the worker and he has not been given the opportunity to be heard. The Company in cross examination has challenged the worker's account of his suspension and has

154 TD No. 148 of 2003 Transport and Industrial Workers' Union and National Maintenance Training and Security Limited.

stated instead that it made several unsuccessful attempts to contact the worker.

There is no tangible evidence forthcoming from the Company to contradict and/or militate against the Union's claims. The Court accepts the evidence which was given by the Union in its entirety as evidence of fact in this Trade dispute. It is the duty of an Employer to conduct proper investigations into allegations of wrong doing against a worker. It is also the duty of the Employer in such circumstances, to ensure that the worker be given the opportunity to be heard and to defend himself against any such allegation of wrong doing during the course of such an investigation. In the instant Trade Dispute this was not done...From the evidence before the Court the worker was not informed by the Company that there was indeed an inquiry nor was he invited to attend one. We wish to emphasize that it was the duty of the Company to hold an inquiry into the allegations which were made against the worker, such an inquiry is indeed an integral part of any reasonable procedural approach to be adopted in the circumstances.

It is trite law that an Employer cannot suspend a worker indefinitely. Such a suspension clearly is in breach of law and good industrial relations practices and it is tantamount to a dismissal. There is a plethora of rulings and judgments from the Industrial Court on this subject. The excessive delay between the date of the alleged act of misconduct and the date of hearing can be legitimately regarded as the basis for finding that the employer is in breach of the principles and practice of good industrial relations. On the totality of evidence we find that the worker was summarily dismissed by the Company. Further, we find that the dismissal was harsh and oppressive and not in accordance with good industrial relations practice." [155]

155 TD No. 21 of 2008 Banking, Insurance and General Workers Union and Fibis Wireless Limited trading as Wireless and Mobility Solutions (WAMS).

Considerations before a Dismissal is Effected

In a landmark decision in what has become known as the **"Chubby Bottle Case"**, the Industrial Court provided guidelines which should be considered when a dismissal is contemplated by an employer. In this case the Court provided a list of considerations that an employer should take into account before he/she makes a decision to dismiss a worker. The Court ruled that the dismissal was harsh and oppressive and ordered the reinstatement of the worker. This Order for reinstatement was appealed to the Court of Appeal and the dicta of Sharma CJ on the salient points are of great importance.

I therefore think that it is very useful to present the judgment of the Industrial Court which was delivered by H H Ramsubeik and the main points of law which were addressed at the Court of Appeal of Trinidad and Tobago:-

> "In this case the Union contends that the action of the employer to dismiss the worker was wrong, inconsiderate, harsh, inhumane and not in keeping with good industrial relations practices...The Company contends that the dismissal was justifiable because of the action he took by requesting his subordinate to put some paint belonging to the Company in his car. Balloon asked his subordinate to put a bottle with paint, in Balloon's car in a clandestine manner. The paint belonged to the Company. His dismissal was therefore justified. The worker testified that at the time of his dismissal he had completed twenty years of service with the employer. He commenced working with Caribbean Development Company as a labourer, on the 31st October, 1977. His duties included cleaning the lawn sweeping the road and cutlassing the grass on the compound of the Company. He also cleaned inside and outside of the Presidential buildings and the surroundings on a monthly basis...When he was dismissed he was an Estate Supervisor receiving a salary of Five thousand three hundred and forty-five dollars and seventy-five cents [$5,345.75] per month. The gangs would collect

the refuse from all over the compound and dump it in a large bin, for disposal. Balloon also said the duties of the workers included painting the outside and inside of the compound, including the car park.

Balloon, further testified that on the 24th March, 1998, he reported to work between 5.00 a.m. to 6.00 a.m. When he entered the "carpenter shop" it was in a "mess", with debris strewn everywhere. There were pieces of boxes, paint pans and sawdust. He instructed Mr. Maharaj, a worker to clean up the place while he dispatched the other workers to do their normal duties.

The worker further testified that Maharaj informed him of some "old paint" which was hard on top but soft below. He said he told Maharaj to put aside the pan with the hard paint for him. He then got a small [chubby] "sweet drink" bottle in which he poured out the entire amount of soft paint. He left the paint on his desk for a while as he intended to inform Kenneth Joseph, his Supervisor about it. Kenneth Joseph came and left before he could have spoken to him. At about 10.20 a.m. a female employee from the Advertising Department of the Company called and told him to remove some rubbish that was near a sign in the car park. He sent Kumar and Maharaj to pick up the sign and the rubbish. The worker further testified that he was in charge of materials including paint and tools. He had a small storeroom in which he kept paint and tools for his crew. Workers do not have to sign documents when they receive material to use on the Company's property. When painting jobs are done he disposes of the empty paint pans. He does not have to account to anyone when he returns from outside his office, regarding the use of material and disposal of empty paint pans.

Balloon said he sent Kumar for the tractor to remove the sign and the rubbish and requested Maharaj, who was to accompany Kumar to put the "Chubby Soft Drink" bottle with the paint, in his car. His car was in the car park, where the workers were going to clean...Balloon also told Maharaj he will tell Kenneth Joseph when he comes to his office. Balloon said the next time he saw Kenneth was when he was summoned to the "Main Office". He testified that he was never warned or disciplined before for any transgression. Under cross-examination by Cezair, Consultant for the employer, Balloon admitted:-

a. He had no authority to ask Maharaj to take out the paint and put it in his car.

b. It was his Supervisor Kenneth Joseph who saw Maharaj outside in the car park with the paint.

c. It was Kenneth Joseph who seized the paint from Maharaj.

d. It was Kenneth Joseph who reported the matter of the paint to Security and the Human Resource Manager.

e. He knew that before anything is removed from the compound permission must first be obtained from security.

He said the paint he took was to be thrown away. He knew he had to speak to Kenneth Joseph about the paint but he "was not thinking" when he told Maharaj to put the paint in his car...The Union called its second witness Maharaj to testify. He testified inter alia that he did work on the 24th March, 1998. He arrived on the compound at 5.00 a.m. He accompanied Balloon, his Supervisor, to the warehouse. They saw the warehouse was in a "mess". There were old boxes, pieces of wood, saw dust and old paint. Balloon told him to clean up the warehouse. He had to throw away all the old empty paint pans and debris. He found a paint pan with hard paint on top. He pierced the hard surface of paint with a piece of wood and found there was soft paint underneath. He drew it to Balloon's attention. Balloon who told him to put it aside, and he will ask Kenneth Joseph for it. Maharaj said he put it aside.

Maharaj said he did not have to obtain approval from anyone before he throw away the empty paint pans or anything. He said when the workers need paint to paint outside the compound, Balloon would give them. The paint he found was black and it filled half a litre of a soft drink bottle. Balloon's instruction he put the said bottle with the paint into the trailer of the tractor on his way out to remove the sign and rubbish. Maharaj said Kenneth Joseph, also a Supervisor saw the bottle of paint on the trailer. It was not concealed. When Kenneth Joseph questioned him about the paint on the trailer, he told Joseph that Balloon had asked him to put it in his [Balloon's] car. Maharaj said he was not told by Balloon to inform Security about the paint. He said he knew that before taking anything outside the compound, security had to be informed.

We note the following:-

- Balloon was initially a cleaner. He cleaned inside and outside residential buildings. There was never a need to discipline him.
- He worked his way up from a labourer to a Supervisor.
- He had twenty years of unblemished service with the Company.
- He was forty-seven years of age when he was dismissed.
- The Employer did not find that he lied at any stage of the inquiry.
- He admitted that he took the paint for his personal use.
- He also admitted that the paint belonged to the Company.
- He said he knew there is a "procedure" whereby one must check with security for approval before leaving the compound with Company's property for one's personal use.

- He intended to obtain approval but inadvertently neglected to do so.
- In his own words he said he "was not thinking" at the time when he told Maharaj to put the item in his car, before seeking security's approval.

The small amount of black paint which amounted to half a Chubby soft drink bottle [which was put into exhibit in Court] was carded to be thrown away. So testified a Cleaner, Maharaj, who found the said paint in a discarded paint pan. Balloon, a Supervisor at the time of his dismissal had twenty years of unblemished service. Nowhere in the letter of dismissal of Balloon was it said by the employer that it gave due consideration to the worker's length of service and unblemished record. His upward mobility in the company is testimony of his dedication to work and loyalty to his Employer.

We believe that the worker particularly in his position as Supervisor, should not have been so complacent when handling such a situation. He is not without blame and his culpability should be reflected in our award. We are of the view that while looking at the breach of the "procedure" the employer should also have given serious consideration to the following factors:-

(1) Long service and unblemished record.

(2) Viewing each case on its own merits

(3) He admitted he failed to follow the existing procedure.

The dismissal of the worker has resulted in loss of:-

1. His twenty years of service.
2. The loss of his position of Estate Supervisor at a monthly salary of Five thousand three hundred and forty-five dollars and seventy-five cents [$5,345.75] and other financial benefits.

3. The loss of his full Pension/Provident Fund which he could have received anytime between 55-60 years, sixty years being the compulsory retirement age. He was forty-seven years of age when he was dismissed.

We note that the worker tried to mitigate his losses but was unable to find suitable employment. He testified that he has a shop which sells religious materials but it is not very profitable. However, we feel that the worker was also responsible for his demise.

The Union ask for reinstatement of the worker. We believe the justice of the case will be best served by reinstating the worker...Having considered the whole of the evidence, and for the reasons we have given herein, and in accordance with equity, good conscience, the substantial merits of the case, and having regard to the principles and practices of good industrial relations, the interests of the persons immediately concerned and the community as a whole, we find that the dismissal was harsh, oppressive, unreasonable and contrary to good industrial relations practices.

There were other options, which in our view, would have met the justice of this case such as a Warning Letter, Suspension, etc. The employer nevertheless chose the most severe punishment of summary dismissal. We order that the worker be reinstated into his former position or a suitable and comparable position with all his benefits applicable. Reinstatement to be effected not later than 31st July, 2002. We order damages of 40% of what he would have earned as salary for the period he was off the job which amounts to Eighty-three thousand, three hundred and eighty-two dollars [$83,382.00] to be paid not later than 31st July, 2002." [156]

156 TD No. 227 of 2001 National Union of Government and Federated Workers and Caribbean Development Company Limited.

This case was appealed in **CvA. No. 83 of 2002 between Caribbean Development Company Limited and National Union of Government and Federated Workers**. Sharma C.J. stated and held that:–

> "This appeal concerns the ambit of the Court of Appeal's jurisdiction to review decisions of the Industrial Court. The facts raise one critical issue – does the Court of Appeal have the jurisdiction to review an Industrial Court order of reinstatement in the absence of a specific statutory prohibition? This issue arose in the context of an order of reinstatement made in favour of Mr. Balloon.
>
> The company appealed against the Court's decision ordering Mr. Balloon to be reinstated to his former position or a suitable and comparable one with all the benefits applicable. The appeal is based essentially on the grounds that the court erred in law, rendering its decision perverse and exceeded its jurisdiction by considering the wrong principles. This appeal raises two fundamental questions of law:-
>
> 1. Does the Court of Appeal have jurisdiction to review the Industrial Court's decision to reinstate Mr. Balloon?
>
>   The determination of this issue is dependent on several preliminary issues:-
>
>   i. Is the decision to reinstate completely separate and apart from the decision that the employee's dismissal was harsh and oppressive?
>
>   ii. Is the discretion to reinstate conferred by section 10(4) of the Industrial Relations Act 1972 solely a question of law?
>
> 2. Did the Industrial Court err in law or act in excess of its jurisdiction? If the decision to reinstate is considered to be solely a question of law, is the Industrial Court's decision perverse, irrational and outside of its jurisdiction?

The preliminary issues that must be determined are:-

i. Is the court's decision perverse in the sense that no reasonable court properly directed would have reached such a conclusion?

ii. Did the Court apply wrong principles in ordering reinstatement in that:-

   a. it failed to consider the employer's right to dismiss the employee; and

   b. it failed to apply the principle that dishonesty goes to the root of the contract of employment and should result in a discharge except in extenuating circumstances.

   c. it erred it law in considering the employee's record of unblemished service, his admission of guilt and the fact that the stolen property was of nominal value as "exceptional circumstances" justifying the imposition of a lesser penalty.

   d. placed the wrong or no emphasis on the requirement of an assessment of whether the company had acted fairly or justly in determining the worker's guilt.

Issue 1 - The Court of Appeal's Jurisdiction

The jurisdiction of the Court of Appeal to review decisions of the Industrial Court is governed by the Industrial Relations Act Chapter 88:01 ("the Act"). The right of appeal against a decision of the Court and the limitations affecting it are found in sections 10(6) and 18 of the Act.

Section 10(6) provides: "The opinion of the Court as to whether a Court as to whether a worker has been dismissed in circumstances that are harsh and oppressive or not in accordance with the principles of good industrial relations practice and any order for compensation or damages including the assessment thereof made pursuant to subsection (5) shall not be challenged, appealed against, reviewed, quashed or called into question in any court on any account whatever.

Section 18(1) provides: Subject to subsection (2), the hearing and determination of any proceedings before the Court, and an order or award or any finding or decision of the Court in any matter (including an order or award)-

(a) shall not be challenged, appealed against, reviewed, quashed or called in question in any court on any account whatever; and

(b) shall not be subject to prohibition, mandamus or injunction in any court on any account whatever.

Section 18(2) provides: Subject to this Act any party to a matter before the Court is entitled as of right to appeal to the Court of Appeal on any of the following grounds, but no other:-

(a) that the court had no jurisdiction in the matter, but it shall not be competent for the Court of Appeal to entertain such ground of appeal, unless objection to the jurisdiction of the Court has been formally taken at some time during the progress of the matter before the making of the order or award;

(b) that the Court has exceeded its jurisdiction in the matter;

(c) that the order or award has been obtained by fraud;

(d) that any finding or decision of the Court in any matter is erroneous in point of law; or

(e) that some other specific illegality not mentioned above, and substantially affecting the merits of the matter, has been committed in the course of the proceedings.

The effect of these provisions has been the subject of much judicial debate but is concisely set out in the judgment of Sir Isaac Hyatali C.J. in Flavourite Foods Ltd. v. Oilfields Workers' Trade Union:-

> "It is of importance to note that the provisions of section 18(1) are made subject to the provisions of s.18(2) only, whereas the provisions of s.18(2) are made subject to the whole of the Act. The use of the expressions "subject to subsection (2)" occurring in s.18(1) and "subject to this Act' occurring in s.18(2) makes this abundantly clear. The consequences to which they lead are of utmost significance.
>
> In my judgment they are as follows:-
>
> (a) that the right of appeal conferred by s.18(2) on the statutory grounds therein set out and no other, overrides the summary commandments of s.18(1) that an order or decision of the Court shall not be inquired into, queried, appealed against or quashed or be subject to prohibition, mandamus or injunction in any court on any account whatever and
>
> (b) that the right of appeal aforesaid under s.18(2) being subject to the whole of the Act is subject in the result to section 10(6) thereof. It follows therefore that s.10(6) is to be read together with and given effect to as a proviso to s.18(2). In my opinion this conclusion is fortified by the fact that s.10(6) occupies a special place in the earlier part of the Act and to all appearances has been deliberately inserted there to put it beyond doubt that appeals will not be allowed against the Court's opinion in what is manifestly a highly specialised area of industrial relations, namely, whether or not a worker has been dismissed in circumstances that offend against the principles of good industrial relations practice or are otherwise harsh and oppressive. Consequently,

> if an appellant is unable to rely on any of the statutory grounds of appeal specified in s.18(2) then he is barred from appealing altogether since the Act prohibits him from relying on any other ground. If however, he is able to rely on one or other of those statutory grounds he will nevertheless be barred from appealing if the only ground of appeal on which he relies involves a challenge against an opinion of the Court given in pursuance of s.10(6)."

The Court of Appeal does not have jurisdiction to review orders for reinstatement even though such orders are not expressly ousted from the court's jurisdiction by s.10(6). To construe s.10(6) as conferring such jurisdiction would amount to a flagrant violation of the object and purpose of the provision. More significantly, the principles applicable to the decision to re-instate indicate that the discretion to re-instate depends in large measure on determinations of fact. For these reasons I consider the 2-stage distinction between questions of fact and law, proposed by counsel for the appellant, highly artificial.

The worker's length of service and unblemished record is an "exceptional circumstance" warranting reinstatement. The worker's length of service and unblemished record has been considered an exceptional circumstance warranting reinstatement in several cases. This reflects the principle that workers are perceived as having an equity in their employment relationship that increases with the length of service. However, the authorities establish that whilst seniority is one of the significant factors to be considered in mitigation of a penalty, it must be weighed with the seriousness of the incident. By itself, long service cannot be used as an excuse for serious misconduct.

In New Dominion Stores v. U.S.W.A. an employee with an unblemished record of 23 years of service was reinstated after the company discharged her for the theft of a pint of berries, a package of cheese and some other items. In Goodyear Tire Inc. v U.R.W. the worker was discharged for pilferage of a roll of film. He had an unblemished record of 19 years of service and the roll of film was worth $700. He was also a union steward for 11 years. Arbitrator Burkett ordered his reinstatement and reasoned as follows:-

> "I have weighed the competing interest in this case and I am not satisfied that in all the circumstances the company's interests in general deterrence should override all other considerations. I characterize the grievor's misconduct as an isolated transgression, which having regard to his prior unblemished long service, he is unlikely to repeat."

The nominal value of the stolen item is an exceptional circumstance warranting reinstatement: "Arbitrators have considered the nominal value of the stolen item as a factor justifying the imposition of a lesser penalty. This by itself may not be a sufficient basis for reinstating but when considered in conjunction with other factors it may justify reinstatement. This in no way suggests that "minor pilfering" may be overlooked."

The essential question remains whether or not the worker has acted in such a fashion as to undermine the employer's confidence that the employee is someone who can be trusted. That confidence may be undermined whether the stolen item is worth $10.00 or $100.00. However, the nominal value of the stolen item may mitigate the severity of the penalty.

In New Dominion Stores the Arbitrator considered the fact that the roll of film was only worth $7.00. Similarly, in Boise Cascade Canada Ltd. v. I.A.M...the grievor was dismissed for theft of company property in the form of scrap metal found in his lunch pail. The grievor was 61 years of age, with 17 years and no disciplinary record. While the arbitrator expressed doubts because the grievor continued to assert that he thought the material he had taken was scrap, he felt that the grievor could be trusted not to repeat the offence. He ordered his reinstatement with a 6-month suspension.

The Industrial Court did not fail to consider the company's right to dismiss Mr. Ballon and whether the company acted fairly in determining the worker's guilt...Counsel's argument that the Industrial Court did not balance the rights of the company with that of Mr. Ballon is clearly unfounded. It is implicit in the decision that the court recognised the company's right to dismiss Mr. Ballon but considered that the company acted harshly in exercising that right in the circumstances of the case. The rights of the company must have been considered if the Court was to reach the decision that it did. The fact that this was not expressly stated does not mean that it was not considered. In fact this is evident from the Court's decision at page 66 that the court considered the interests of both parties in deciding what the justice of the case required:-

> "We believe the justice of the case will best served by reinstating the worker. Having considered the whole of the evidence, and for the reasons we have given herein, and in accordance with equity, good conscience, the substantial merits of the case, and having regard to the principles and practice of good industrial relations, the interest of the persons immediately concerned and the community as a whole, we find that the dismissal was harsh, oppressive, unreasonable and contrary to good industrial relations practice. There were other options which in our view, would have met the justice of this case such as a warning letter, suspension etc. the employer nevertheless chose the most severe punishment of summary dismissal."

It is clear that the court considered all the circumstances of the case before ordering reinstatement. The court also balanced the interests of both parties before making the

> order. The fact that no express mention was made of the employer's rights and the exceptional circumstances on which the court relied, does not mean that the court exceeded its jurisdiction as it is clear that consideration was given to these matters. This appeal is dismissed. The appellant is ordered to pay costs." [157]

In **Caryle Anthony and BBR Sportive Ltd** the Hon. Philip A. Pilgrim, President of the Industrial Court of Antigua and Barbuda, examined the conduct of a worker to determine if such conduct warranted her dismissal. The Court gave consideration to the principles of natural justice and the right of a worker to a fair hearing. The facts briefly are as follows:-

> "Ms. Caryle Anthony was employed with BBR Sportive Limited from August 8, 1995 to June 12, 2004. BBR Sportive Limited owns a restaurant. She worked in it as an Accounts Manager. Apart from her main duties she also regularly performed other functions for the Employer. These included that of Receptionist, Payroll Clerk, Hostess, Bartender and Waitress. Her last position, however, was that of Dining Room Supervisor. An incident took place on the restaurant's premises on June 12, 2004. This incident involved the Employee and Peter Byers. He was a chef at the restaurant. He subsequently became deceased...The issues which require a determination are as follows:-
>
> 1. Whether Ms. Anthony's conduct on June 12, 2004 amounted to misconduct which was so serious that BBR Sportive Limited could not reasonably have been expected to take any course other than to summarily dismiss her.
> 2. Whether or not the Employer instituted a proper investigation of the incident which occurred on June 12, 2004.

157 CvA. No. 83 of 2002 Caribbean Development Company Limited and National Union of Government and Federated Workers.

3. In the event that Ms. Anthony is held to be unfairly dismissed what is the measure of damages due to her.[158]

Smith & Wood's Employment Law, Ninth Edition, Oxford thereof are of the following view:-

> "Misconduct in the modern statutory context fits into the overall pattern of unfair dismissal law in being essentially a matter of assessing the reasonableness of the employer's reaction to it in all the varied circumstances of the case,...it is a particularly wide category of dismissal, ranging from gross misconduct (still justifying summary dismissal) such as theft, violence, wilful refusal to obey an order and gross negligence."[159]

Faced with this wide diversity, there is sometimes an unfortunate tendency to attempt to over-classify, as if for example the many decided cases establish a "law on fighting at work;" while collecting together all the cases on one kind of misconduct may have some values, it must be stressed that that value is restricted to attempting to point out certain factors which may be important in certain of the more typical cases. Further than that, these matters remain clearly within the factual jurisdiction of the tribunals." "Conduct cases are very much based on their own facts"...The factors which the Courts have taken into consideration so as to determine whether the employer has acted reasonably or unreasonably include the following matters:-

(i) The degree of 'self-defence' and the type of business conducted by the employer.

(ii) The seriousness of the fight between the two (2) parties is of some useful value.

158 Reference No. 11 of 2005: Caryle Anthony and BBR Sportive Ltd.

159 Ian Smith and Gareth Thomas, Smith & Wood's Employment Law (Oxford Ninth Edition 2008), 509.

(iii) The length of service of the employees, any good conduct and whether the parties were subject to any prior serious disciplinary offences.

The precise reason for the employee's dismissal in this case was rendered by Mr. Bigler in answer to Mr. Fuller. The reason given by Mr. Bigler was that "she had the chance to walk away from the incident, but she did not walk away." The fact that Ms. Anthony did not walk away was insignificant in comparison to Mr. Byers' actions.

It is a basic principle of natural justice that an employee who is accused of committing an offence of misconduct is deserving of a fair hearing before that employee is dismissed. The principles of natural justice in the context of the requirement of an employer to institute a proper investigation were outlined by Rawlins J.A. (Ag) (as he then was) in The Epicurean Ltd v Medeline Taylor Civ. App. No. 4 of 2003. At page 10 paragraph [33] Rawlins J.A. stated inter alia as follows:-

> "Natural justice, the principles of natural justice are well known, trite and ancient. It is said that rules that required a fair hearing before impartial adjudicators can be traced to ancient times, were known in medieval precedents and reached a "high water-mark" in their development in Dr. Bonham's case (1610) 8 Co. Rep. 113b...It is imperative however that in a matter of this kind, natural justice does require not merely that a man shall have the chance to state his own case in detail; he must know in one way or another sufficiently what is being said against him. If he does not know sufficiently what is being said against him, he cannot properly put forward his own case."

See the observations of Slynn J. in Bentley Engineering Co. v Mistry [1979] I.C.R. 47 at page 51 letter D...In all the circumstances of this case I am satisfied that the Employer carried out a proper investigation of the facts and circumstances of the incident which took place on its premises on June 13, 2004.

The Decision

Was Ms. Anthony's action misconduct in accordance with C 58 (i) (a), (2) and C 59 (i) (a) of the Labour Code? There is an abundance of evidence in this case that Mr. Byers' behaviour towards Ms. Anthony was generally provocative in nature. Having regard to the actions of the Employee, and taking into consideration all of the facts of this case, I hold that her actions were reasonable. In all of the circumstances of this case this Court finds that Ms. Anthony's behaviour on June 12, 2004 did not amount to misconduct..." [160]

In this case the Employer was ordered by the Industrial Court of Antigua and Barbuda to pay compensation to the Employee.

In another decision of the Industrial Court of Antigua and Barbuda **Colet Acham and Caribbean Star Airlines Ltd** delivered by the Hon. Philip A. Pilgrim President, the Court stated as follows:-

"The Employee is an airline pilot by profession...On June 06, 2001 he obtained employment with Caribbean Star Airlines Limited in that capacity. He worked with the airline transporting its passengers and cargo to several Caribbean destinations...The Employee's employment with the Employer was terminated by letter dated October 18, 2004...the Employer contends in its Employer's Memorandum that the Employee was fairly dismissed due to his failure to pass a Base Check which rendered him incapable of flying pursuant to the Civil Aviation Act No.25 of 2003 and Regulation 2.1.4.11 and 8.10.1.20.

The First Issue: Does any evidence exist of an estoppel in the of a representation or conduct by the Employer to the Employee that Section 1.23 of its Operation Manual was

160 Reference No. 11 of 2005 Caryle Anthony and BBR Sportive Ltd.

inoperative and that there existed an agreement dated May 25, 2004 between the Employer and the Employee which the Employee relied upon?...The common law principle of estoppel by representation is stated at paragraph 957 of Halsbury.

The text states inter alia as follows:-

> "Where a person has by words or conduct made to another a clear and unequivocal representation of fact, either with knowledge of its falsehood or with the intention that it should be acted upon, or has so conducted himself that another would, as a reasonable person, understand that a certain representation of fact was intended to be acted upon, and the other person has acted upon such representation and thereby altered his position, an estoppel arises against the party who made the representation, and he is not allowed to aver that the fact is otherwise than he represented it to be."

Promissory estoppel paragraph 958 of Halsbury. The learned authors describe the doctrine as follows:-

> **"Promissory estoppel is an extension by equity of common law estoppel by representation. The principle of promissory estoppel is that, when one party has, by his words or conduct, made to the other a clear and unequivocal promise or assurance which was intended to affect the legal relations between them and to be acted on accordingly, then, once the other party has taken him at his word and acted on it, the one who gave the promise or assurance cannot afterwards be allowed to revert to their previous legal relations as if no such promise or assurance had been made by him, but must accept their legal relations subject to the qualification which he himself has so introduced. Promissory estoppel may prevent a party to a contract from going back on a concession he has made to the other party and so may modify**

> **contracts in the sense of suspending or even extinguishing contractual rights but cannot stand alone as giving a cause of action in itself and thus has not made any general inroads into the doctrine of consideration."**

The Second Issue: Whether the Employee's performance manifested any incapacity and if it did was the Employer required to give the Employee a written warning before he dismissed him. Were the requirements of C59 (5) of the Labour Code satisfied in this case? The Third Issue: Whether Caribbean Star honestly and reasonably believed that Mr. Acham was incapable and had not demonstrated at the time of his dismissal that he was able to perform his duties in a satisfactory manner?

Whether or not an Employee was capably performing his duties is to be determined by making use of a subjective test. That test was also applied in the case of Jewellers Warehouse v Cecile Norde Civil Appeal No. 29 of 2004. Mr. Justice Rawlins JA (as he then was) stated the test at page 13 of that judgment. He stated inter alia as follows: "That test was succinctly stated in David Lashley & Partners Inc. v Bayley as follows: 'If an employee is dismissed because of his incapability, the correct test to apply is whether the employer honestly and reasonably held the belief that the employee was not competent, and whether there are reasonable grounds for that belief. It is not necessary for the employer to prove that the employee was incompetent....In other words, the test....is a subjective one....it is sufficient if the employer honestly believes on reasonable grounds that the employee is incompetent...In Alidair Ltd. v Taylor Lord Denning also articulated the test at page 451 in the following manner. He stated inter alia as follows: "Whenever a man is dismissed for incapacity or incompetence it is sufficient that the employer honestly believes on reasonable grounds that the man is incapable or incompetent. It is not necessary for the employer to prove that he is in fact incapable or incompetent...having regard

> to all of the circumstances of this case, I hold that the airline as a reasonable Employer honestly believed on reasonable grounds that the Employee had not demonstrated at the time when his services were terminated that he was able to perform his duties satisfactorily. As a consequence of this finding I further hold that the Employer acted reasonably. Mr. Acham's employment was fairly terminated due to his inability to perform his duties as a consequence of his failure of a Base Check on October 15, 2004... The Fourth Issue: Whether any defect existed in the procedure to dismiss this employee and if so did it render the procedure intrinsically unfair?...In the circumstances of this case I find that there was no breach of procedure by the company. Having carefully examined all of the evidence led in this case, the submissions of both parties, the relevant provisions of the Labour Code and Section 10 (3) of the Industrial Court Act Cap. 214, I find that this Employee was not unfairly dismissed. The Reference is hereby dismissed. There shall be no order as to Costs." [161]

In the case of **Donna Christopher and Geotech Company Limited** the Hon. Philip A. Pilgrim, President of the Industrial Court of Antigua and Barbuda, upheld the decision by the Company to dismiss a worker:-

> "In this dispute Ms. Donna Christopher commenced employment with the Employer in March 1992 initially as a Secretary, she subsequently held the position of Accounts Clerk. She was responsible for a multiplicity of functions which included the ensuring of all transactions being recorded on a daily basis, a review of all vouchers and cheques which related to disbursements, the provision of financial statements to the General Manager and the Board of Directors on a monthly basis, and ensuring that accounting controls, internal and administrative controls were functioning efficiently and effectively.

161 Reference No. 9 of 2007 Colet Acham and Caribbean Star Airlines Ltd.

It is the Employer's case that several deficiencies arose in the accounting department of which the Employee was aware and took no proper steps to rectify them. Matters which concerned the Employer relative to the purchase of two LIAT (1974) Ltd. airlines tickets, the non-deduction of her staff loans and other loans, the findings of certain deficiencies and weaknesses in the company's accounting department, and her failure to maintain files and to accurately report on loan accounts to management caused the Employer to dismiss the Employee by letter dated November 16, 2007...In addition to the duty of the employee to discharge his responsibilities to his Employer with care, there also exists between the Employer and the Employee a fiduciary relationship of trust and confidence.

The First Issue: Whether in the circumstances of this case was the Employee's conduct of such a nature or kind which justified the Employer to summarily dismiss the Employee in accordance with Section C58 (1) (a) of the Labour Code...Ms. Christopher seems to have been prepared to use the company's resources for her own personal benefit. She has a duty to act responsibly. It is also her duty to use the company's financial resources in such a manner so as to benefit the company and not for her own personal use...The Second Issue: Did the Employer act reasonably to dismiss the Employee?...The Employer conducts a business which requires that its employees conduct their affairs in an honest manner. In the circumstances of this case I hold that the Employer acted reasonably in its dismissal of the Employee. It's dismissal of the Employee was fair."[162]

162 Reference No. 1 of 2009 Donna Christopher and Geotech Company Limited.

Constructive Dismissal

What Is Constructive Dismissal?

As a result of the jurisprudence which has emerged from the Industrial Court over the past 55 years, together with the jurisprudence for other jurisdictions, one can agree that constructive dismissal occurs when an employer has not directly and expressly fired the employee but has by his/her own act or inadvertence failed to comply with the contract of employment in some major respect or has unilaterally and substantially altered the terms of employment or expressed an intention to do so.

Halsbury's Laws of England, 5th Edition summarises the law related to constructive dismissal in the following terms:-

> "Constructive dismissal. An employee, who terminates the contract of employment, with or without notice, may still claim to have been dismissed if the circumstances are such that he is entitled to terminate it without notice by reason of the employer's conduct. The employee must leave in response to the breach of contract. While, as a matter of fact, the employee may usually be expected to indicate that he is treating the contract as repudiated, there is no rule of law that the employee must always inform the employer of the true reason for leaving. Delay in so doing may amount to waiver of the breach and affirmation of the contract, though this will depend on the facts of the case, and a realistic approach must be taken, so that it may be reasonable for the employee to work on for a period under protest, especially if trying to resolve matters without leaving or seeking other work before leaving. Whether there has been a repudiatory breach by the employer entitling the employee to leave is essentially a question of fact for a tribunal in the circumstances of the individual case." [163]

163 Halsbury's Laws (5th Edition, 2009) Vol. 40, para 720.

Additionally, 18th Edition of Selwyn's Law of Employment states:-

> "It follows, therefore, that only those cases where the employer's conduct amounts to a significant breach, going to the root of the contract, can be regarded as being authoritative. There must be a fundamental breach of contract by the employer, not merely a failure to act reasonably.[164] Thus, if the employer tries to impose a unilateral change in employment terms, such as a change in job, a significant change in hours,[165] a lowering of earnings,[166] a significant change in location of employment,[167] a demotion, then provided there is no contractual right to do so, such conduct will entitle an employee to resign." [168]

As we examine the cases of this type of dismissal, it is notable that the principles and practice of good industrial relations continue to be of critical importance to decision-making in the workplace.

In **Communication Workers' Union and Servisair Trinidad and Tobago Limited**, I examined several pertinent issues which relate to constructive dismissal and which I believe will give you, the reader, a better understanding of the Industrial Court's approach to the issue of constructive dismissal. Therefore I am presenting a large part of that decision herein:-

> "This is a dispute between Communication Workers' Union and Servisair Trinidad and Tobago Limited which concerns the Company's failure and or refusal to pay the wages to a worker for the period 16th December, 2009 to 7th January, 2010 and the alleged dismissal of the said worker. Due to the nature of the evidence and the extant criminal proceedings in the High Court, we will not name the worker in this dispute.

164 Wadham Stringer Commercials (London) Ltd v Brown [1983] IRLR 46 EAT.

165 Simmonds v Dowty Seals Ltd [1978] IRLR 211 EAT.

166 RF Hill Ltd v Mooney [1981] IRLR 258 EAT.

167 Courtlands Northern Spining Ltd v Sibson [1984] ICR 218, [1984] IRLR 43 EAT.

168 Astra Emir, Selwyn's Law of Employment (Oxford 18th Edition 2014) 407.

On 12th November 2015, the date of hearing, the Company had not complied with any of the orders of the Court and had not filed documents in this Trade Dispute, moreover the Company did not appear for the hearing. The Court proceeded to determine the matter by an ex-parte, some 18 months after the case was filed.

The undisputed facts as far as material are that the worker assumed duties with the Company on 18th January, 2008, as an Airline Agent. Her hours of work were based on a shift system.[169] She was initially rostered on the daylight shift, from 8:00am to 6:00pm. Sometime during the course of her employment her shift changed and she was rostered to work from 4:00am to 1:00pm.

On 19th August, 2008 when the worker was in a taxi on her way to work the 4:00am shift she was kidnapped and raped. (This matter is the subject of criminal proceedings in the High Court, and therefore we say no more about it). As a result of her kidnapping and rape the worker proceeded on two weeks' sick leave. The then Human Resource Manager, Mr. Anthony Wells, visited the worker while she was on sick leave, and assured her that on her return to work her hours of work would be adjusted and that she will no longer work on the 4:00am early morning shift, instead she will be rostered from 8:00am to 6:00pm daily.

As a result, when the worker returned to work her hours of work were adjusted accordingly. She worked from 8:00am to 6:00pm daily for nearly a year, until August, 2009 when Company's new Human Resource Manager, Mr. Jason Andrews, informed her that she had to revert to work the 4:00am to 1:00pm shift roster. No discussion was had with the worker and no explanation was given to her for this unilateral change in the terms and conditions

169 Shift system-5:00am to 2:00pm; 1:00pm to 10:00pm and 10:00pm to 7:00am, 4:00am to 1:00pm, 8:00am to 6:00pm.

of her employment...When she was informed of this change in her conditions of employment, the worker spoke to Mr. Andrews and also formally wrote to him on 18th December, 2009 reminding him of her past traumatic experience which still 1 5:00am to 2:00pm; 1:00pm to 10:00pm and 10:00pm to 7:00am, 4:00am to 1:00pm, 8:00am to 6:00pm haunted her and her fears of working the 4:00am shift. However, the Company's Human Resource Manager's response to her was that her past experience was "not his concern" and that the arrangements which were made to work 8:00 am to 6:00pm shift "was with Mr. Wells and not with him".

On 29th December, 2009, the worker again wrote to the Company informing it of the emotional hardships created by the change in the working hours. Without any form of discussion and giving no reasons, the Company refused to allow the worker to continue to work from 8:00am to 6:00pm and insisted that she works the 4:00am shift. As a result the worker submitted a letter to the Company dated 8th January, 2010 wherein she claimed that her health and safety was at risk and that she had been constructively dismissed.

The failure of the Company to file any documents and its non-appearance at the hearing does not supply this Court with any reason why this change was made. All the Court has before it is the uncontroverted evidence of the worker regarding the Company's Human Resource Manager's response to the worker's plight that this was not the Company's concern.

The Union also contends that the Company did not pay the worker for the period 16th December, 2009 to 7th January, 2010 and alleges that this failure to pay the worker also amounts to a repudiatory breach of the worker's contract of employment. The case before us highlights these issues. We find that the worker was constructively dismissed when the Company committed one or all of three repudiatory breaches of the fundamental terms of her employment contract. These breaches were (1) the unilateral alteration of the terms of her contract; (2) the breach of the implied duty of mutual trust and confidence; and (3) the failure to pay agreed wages.

Unilateral Change of Fundamental Contractual Term

While initially the worker was on a shift system, this term was altered by mutual agreement after the unfortunate incident which occurred on her way to perform duties at the 4:00am shift. She continued working with the Company after it was mutually agreed that she would no longer be asked to work on that shift (the early morning shift) but on the 8:00am to 6:00pm shift. It is hard to believe that given her traumatic experience that the worker would have chosen to continue to work with the Company on a shift that commenced at a time that placed her in the same extreme physical danger with its emotional traumatic fear that she would live with every day coming to work. We find that this new arrangement was the new term of the employment contract agreed by the parties. It is instructive that this arrangement continued for nearly a year and in the circumstances, we find that it constituted a fundamental term of her employment contract.

However, matters changed when a new Human Resource Manager assumed duty. Despite being informed of the terms of the contract, he sought to unilaterally vary that term of the Worker's contract by ordering her to return to working the 4:00am shift. This the Company could not do without the agreement of the Worker, as is noted in Derby City Council v Marshall [1979] IRLR 261 which discussed the legal effect of employer insisting upon working hours that a worker was not employed to do.

In Alleyne, Arthur and Hunte Ltd v Grifith (1992) WIR 53 the employer sought to unilaterally alter the terms of the employee's contract by requiring her to work on

Saturday, a situation grossly inconvenient to her because on Saturdays the employee was engaged in her own business. The Court of Appeal of Barbados held that this unilateral change was a repudiatory breach of the employee's contract entitling her to treat the contract at an end and claiming constructive dismissal.

We are aware that it is not every breach of contract which justifies an employee resigning and claiming that she has been constructively dismissed. For example, in Waithe v Caribbean Confection Co. (2004) 67 WIR 41, the unilateral change to require the employee to work half day on Christmas Eve, like all other employees of the company (18 months' notice of the change was given) was held not to be a fundamental change to the employee's terms and conditions to such a degree as to constitute constructive dismissal.

The critical point here is that the Court must view the importance of the term to each of the parties to the contract to determine whether it amounted to so significant an alteration as to amount to a fundamental breach. Reasonableness is the standard which is evaluated from the point of view of the importance of the term to the employee on the one hand and, on the other hand, whether it falls within the employer's managerial prerogative to maximise efficiency in the business for which the employee has an implied duty of obedience, co-operation and care. However, as was pointed out in Catamaran Cruisers Ltd v Williams [1994] IRLR 386, 389, in order to impose new terms unilaterally, an employer has to show "business reason so pressing that it was absolutely vital for the employer's business that the terms be accepted."

The court must balance the two interests involved in the employment contract. We adopt this standard as the correct balance in the employment relationship. Even if the alteration did not constitute a new term of the contract, we find that the second fundamental violation of the employment contract by the Company was the breach of the implied term of trust and confidence. It has been repeatedly held that without such a duty an employment contract cannot exist and therefore the implied duty of mutual trust and confidence is fundamental to the employment contract. It is the accepted duty of the employer as well as the employee to act in a manner so as to maintain the relationship of trust and confidence in the employment contract.

This includes situations in which one party has a discretion under the contract to make a particular decision or determination which may adversely affect the other party. The law is settled that, that party must exercise that discretion rationally and reasonably, and indeed in contracts generally. [170] Thus, even if there had been no contractual change in the shift system under which the worker had first worked, the Company was duty bound to exercise its discretion in rostering her after considering the reasonableness and fairness to the worker. This is good industrial relations practice. The Company as the employer is not entitled to behave in a wholly unreasonable manner.

The breach of the implied duty of Mutual Trust and Confidence

Indeed, the accepted definition of the implied term of mutual trust and confidence is that the employer shall not

> "without reasonable and proper cause, conduct itself in a manner calculated and likely to destroy or seriously damage the relationship of confidence and trust between employer and employee." [171]

170 Braganza v BP Shipping Ltd [2015] UKSC 17, [2015] IRLR 487.

171 Malik v Bank of Credit and Commerce International SA [1997] 3 All ER 1.

This definition has been repeatedly adopted by this Court. In this case, the change in hours was so significant to the worker that the Company bore a heavy burden to come forward with a reasonable explanation for restoring her to the early morning shift. There is no evidence of an explanation and from the response and lack of response to the worker, this Court can only conclude that the decision was arbitrary and unreasonable.

The Human Resource Manager's initial response to the arrangement with the worker can be deemed disrespectful, callous, uncaring, oppressive and inconsistent with the principles and practice of good industrial relations... Indeed, the new Human Resource Manager's initial response to the worker, that it was not his concern and that the arrangement was not with him, can only be described as being disrespectful, callous, uncaring, oppressive and inconsistent with the principles and practice of good industrial relations. This is contrary to the provision of the Industrial Relations Act, Chapter 88:01. Moreover, the Company ignored all the correspondence that the worker sent to it asking for a discussion, a reason or some accommodating consideration. There was no discussion, no further response. This went to the root of the contract and the worker was entitled to treat this behaviour as a constructive dismissal.

All of the aforementioned analysis reveals that the worker was constructively dismissed, as the elements of constructive dismissal synchronise with the Sharp case. This accords with Lord Denning's definition of constructive dismissal in Western Excavating (ECC) v Sharp [1968] QB 761, which has been accepted by this Court, in repeated decisions:-

> "If the Employer is guilty of conduct which is a significant breach going to the root of the contract of employment, or which shows that the employer no longer intends to be bound by one or more of the

> essential terms of the contract, then the employee is entitled to treat himself as discharged from any further performance. If he does so, then he terminates the contract by reason of the employer's conduct. He is constructively dismissed."

The conduct and the approach of the Company as it relates to the worker's safety to get to work in this dispute is unacceptable and demonstrates an alarming disregard of the worker's contractual right to work. This type of approach in the workplace destroys the degree of trust and confidence the worker is reasonably expected to have in the Company...The Company though aware of the recent incident in which their worker's physical safety was compromised and of the potential of possible harm and the mental trauma to the worker if she is rostered to begin work at 4:00am, still insisted on changing her hours of work without one scintilla of reason. This is clearly in breach of the duty of the Company as employer.

It goes without saying that the payment of agreed wages is a fundamental term of any employment contract and this failure to pay the agreed wages amounts to a repudiatory breach entitling the employee to terminate the contract and claim constructive dismissal. The case that is normally cited by this Court to support this proposition. The well-known case of Cantor Fitzgerald International v Callaghan and ORS, [1999] I.R.L.R. 234 supports this contention. Judge L.J., delivering the judgment of the Court, reviewed a number of relevant cases, including RF Hill Limited v. Mooney [1981] I.R.L.R. 258 where Browne-Wilkinson, J. observed: -

> "The obligation on an employer to pay remuneration is one of the fundamental terms of a contract. In our view, if an employer seeks to alter that contractual obligation in a fundamental way, such as he has sought to do in this case, such attempt is a breach going to the very root of the contract and is necessarily repudiation."

There may be occasions where the failure to pay is due to an error of calculation or technological glitches or a mere delay, which may make the situation not amount to a fundamental breach. However, where the failure is unexplained and persists over a long period, or there was deliberate non-payment, the Court can only be driven to conclude that the breach was indeed repudiatory.

In this case the only evidence before this Court is that the worker was not paid for the period 16th December, 2009 to 7th January, 2010 and no explanation was forthcoming from the Company, the only inference is that this is a fundamental breach of contract.

The worker has cited constructive dismissal as her reason for leaving her job with the Company. The question which this Court has to examine is whether the actions of the Company committed a repudiatory breach of the employment contract and acted in a manner that was arbitrary and oppressive and inconsistent with good industrial relations practice. We can do no better than to refer to the words of Lord Denning in Woods v W M Car Service (Peterborough) Ltd. endorsed the view of a parallel between the law of wrongful dismissal and constructive dismissal.

He stated as follows:-

> "Now under modern legislation we have the converse case. It is the duty of the employer to be good and considerate to his servants. Sometimes it is formulated as an implied term not to do anything likely to destroy the relationship of confidence between them...But I prefer to look at it in this way: the employer must be good and considerate to his servants."

Just as a servant must be good and faithful, so an employer must be good and considerate. Just as in the old days an employee could be guilty of misconduct justifying his dismissal, so in modern times an employer can be guilty of misconduct justifying the employee in leaving at once without notice. In each case it depends on whether the misconduct amounted to repudiatory breach as defined in Western Excavating (ECC) Limited v Sharp. [172]

In the instant case, there is no evidence that the Company had reasonable or proper cause to change the shift. As was stated before, the Company has filed no documents in this dispute.

In our view, it is clearly established as Arnold J said, that there is implied in a contract of employment a term that employers will not, without reasonable and proper cause, conduct themselves in a manner calculated or likely to destroy or seriously damage the relationship of confidence and trust between employer and employee.

> "It does seem to us that any conduct which is likely to destroy or seriously to damage that relationship must be something which goes to the root of the contract, which is really fundamental in its effect upon the contractual relationship." [173]

In Woods v W. M. Car Services (Peterborough) Ltd. Browne-Wilkinson J, after citing with approval the reasoning of Arnold J. went on to make the further point which the Court fully endorses that:-

> "To constitute a breach of this implied term it is not necessary to show that the employer intended any repudiation of the contract: the tribunal's function is to look at the employer's conduct as whole and to determine whether it is such that its effect, judged reasonably and sensibly is such that the employee cannot be expected to put up with it." [174]

---

172 Western Excavating (ECC) Limited v Sharp [1978] QB 761, [1978] IRLR 27.

173 Courtaulds Northern Textile Ltd. v Andrew [1979] IRLR 84.

174 Woods v W. M. Car Services (Peterborough) Ltd [1981] IRLR 347.

It is our findings that the change in the hours of work was fundamental in its effect on the contractual relationship between the worker and the Company.

We repeat what was said in Malik v BCCI by the House of Lords in defining the obligation of mutual trust and confidence. Lord Nicholls stated that this obligation requires the employer

> ".... not to engage in conduct likely to undermine the trust and confidence required if the employment relationship is to continue in the manner the employment contract implicitly envisages.... The conduct must, of course, impinge on the relationship in the sense that, looked at objectively, it is likely to destroy or seriously damage the degree of trust and confidence the employee is reasonably entitled to have in his employer..."

We find that the Company without reasonable and proper cause conducted itself in a manner which damaged and destroyed the relationship of trust and confidence between itself and the worker and in so doing repudiated the employment contract.

1. The evidence of the Union is uncontroverted.
2. The unilateral change in the modified terms of the worker's contract was a fundamental breach in the circumstances entitling the worker to accept the repudiation and claim constructive dismissal.
3. The Company committed a repudiatory breach of the fundamental implied term of mutual trust and confidence in its callous and disrespectful treatment of the worker that was arbitrary, oppressive and inconsistent with good industrial relations principles and practices.
4. The worker was constructively dismissed by the Company. We find pursuant to the principles that guide the exercise of our powers under the IRA section

10(3), that the Company did not act in accordance with good conscience but in a manner which was egregious, harsh, oppressive and contrary to the principles and practices of good industrial relations.

5. The Company committed a repudiatory breach of the worker's employment contract when it failed to pay wages to the worker for the period 16th December, 2009 to 7th January, 2010." [175]

In the dicta of **Transport and Industrial Workers' Union and Furness Employment Limited,** H H Seale stated inter alia:-

> "To sustain a claim of constructive dismissal when applying the contract test, an employee must show that the employer's conduct amounts to a breach of contract, not merely a failure to act reasonably. [176]
>
> However, our Court must ever be mindful that the English cases often address the doctrine of constructive dismissal from a statutory basis. Lord Denning in **Sharp** was addressing provisions in the **Trade Union and Labour Relations Act, 1974**. There are no statutory provisions in the IRA which entitle a worker to resign and claim constructive dismissal. In deliberating on an employer's conduct which gives rise to such a claim, the Court must, as in all cases of dismissal, have regard to section 10(5) to determine if the Worker has been **"dismissed in circumstances that are harsh and oppressive or not in in accordance with the principles of good industrial relations practice."**
>
> **Did the worker raise any other reasons for his resignation which resulted from the employer's conduct and if so was that conduct part of a course of conduct**

175 TD Nos. 345 and 346 of 2013 Communication Workers' Union and Servisair Trinidad and Tobago Limited. This case is pending decision from the Court of Appeal.

176 Wadham Stringer Commercials (London) Ltd. and Wadham Stringer Vehicles Ltd. v Brown [1983] IRLR 46 EAT.

which cumulatively amounted to a repudiatory breach of the implied contractual obligation of trust and confidence?

In addition to the letter of transfer which the Court accepts was the main reason for the worker's resignation, in his letter of resignation, he raised contemptuous and disrespectful treatment by members of management, his low level of pay which remained stagnant for a while and the Employer's statements to him that if he was dissatisfied he could leave the job. The Court accepts the Worker's evidence in this regard and finds the allegations against the employer to be consistent with its disregard for the principles of good industrial relations practice as evidenced by its failure to observe the provisions of the Minimum Wages Order as it related to hours of work and payment for overtime and its non – compliance with the Order of in Court in Trade Dispute No 228 of 1999.

Even if the worker had affirmed the contract after the letter of transfer, (although I have held he did not) in keeping with the principle in Lewis v Motorworld Garages[1986] I.C.R. 157, a series of minor incidents taken altogether could destroy mutual trust and confidence and thus amount to a fundamental breach. In that case the Court of Appeal held:-

> "...that where an employer had breached an express term of an employment contract but the employee had affirmed the contract, that breach could nevertheless be subsequently relied upon as part of a course of conduct which cumulatively amounted to a repudiatory breach of the implied contractual obligation of trust and confidence."

In the instant case the worker did not agree to the transfer. He raised the matter with his Union who in turn raised it Furness Group of Companies, of which the Employer is a member. It was a unilateral and fundamental change

> in his working hours which in effect would also have lowered his monthly rate. Additionally, the Employer had repeatedly and consistently failed to comply with the new rates of pay as ordered by the Court and up to the hearing of this dispute remained silent on its failure to comply.
>
> On the facts and the evidence, I find that on a balance of probabilities the Union has proved its case that the Worker was constructively dismissed by the Employer. I find the dismissal to be harsh, oppressive and contrary to good industrial relations practice." [177]

In **Oilfields Workers' Trade Union and Schlumberger (Trinidad) Incorporated,** H H Ramrekersingh examined the principle of constructive dismissal and noted that:-

> "Constructive dismissal occurs in circumstances where the behaviour of the employer is so unreasonable or intolerable that it amounts to a fundamental breach of the employment contract."
>
> "The foregoing should not be interpreted to mean that constructive dismissal only embraces a single breach going to the root of the contract. There may be a series of breaches over time culminating in the final straw at which point the employee leaves and may be considered to have been constructively dismissed. [178]
>
> "the judgment that an employer has an implied duty to act towards his employees in good faith. The House of Lords in **Mahmud v Bank of Credit and Commerce International SA (1997 IRLR 462) that "the employer shall not without reasonable and proper cause conduct itself in a manner calculated and likely to destroy or seriously damage the relationship of confidence**

177 TD No. 205 of 2007 Transport and Industrial Workers' Union and Furness Employment Limited.

178 Lewis v Motorworld Garages Ltd (1985) IRLR 465 and Omilaju v Waltham Forest London Borough Counsel (2004) EWCA Civ. 1493.

and trust between the employer and employee." (our emphasis)

One word of caution, though, not every breach is a fundamental breach; the breach must go to the root of the contract. **De minimis non curat lex** – the law is not concerned with trivial things. Moreover, there must be a direct causal relationship between the decision to leave and the repudiatory breach by the employer.

In Contracts of Employment 7th Edition Crump and Pugsley [179] summarise very succinctly the questions to be answered when deciding on constructive dismissal:-

1. Was there a contractual term?
2. If so, what were its provisions?
3. Was the term broken?
4. If so, was the breach repudiatory?
5. Was the employment terminated by the employee?
6. Was the termination of the employment contract by the employee an "acceptance" of the employer's breach by the employee?
7. Was the "acceptance" before the employee had affirmed the contract?" [180]

Unilateral Alteration/Variation of a Contract

As a principle of good industrial relations an employer ought not to unilaterally vary terms of the contract of an employee except if that employee has given the employer the right to do so by virtue of his/her agreement. The unilateral variation of the contract can be treated as a repudiation of the contract.

179 Douglas Crump and David Pugsley, Contracts of Employment (7th Edition Butterworths 1997).

180 TD 197 of 2002 Schlumberger (Trinidad) Incorporated and Oilfields Workers' Trade Union.

The issue of unilateral variation of contracts of employment was discussed in **Sheet Metal Components Ltd. v Plumridge & ors.** Sir John Donaldson, President in the judgment of the Court said:-

> "It is without doubt the law that there is no dismissal where both parties to a contract of employment freely and voluntarily agree to vary its terms. This happens whenever there is an increase in rates of pay or a promotion. However, the courts have rightly been slow to find that there has been a consensual variation where an employee has been faced with the alternative of dismissal and where the variation has been adverse to his interests, as Sir John Brightman said in Shield's Furniture Ltd. v. Goff [1973] ICR 187,190:-
>
> > "What is an employee expected to do in these circumstances? He does not want to be out of a job. Nor, if he is a conscientious workman, does he want to let his employer down if this can be avoided. In most cases, therefore, he goes to the new job. He goes with an open mind. There is a period when he is uncommitted. During that period he makes up his mind whether he will accept the new employment, in which case he is not entitled to a redundancy payment; or whether he will leave or, in legal language, accept the employer's repudiation.
> >
> > We respectfully agree that this is the right approach in cases which an employer has dealt informally with a change in the terms and conditions of employment."[181]

In **Walker v Josiah Wedgwood & Sons Ltd** where an employee resigned without giving any reason and when he was interviewed he referred to the fact that he 'had got a better job', the EAT upheld the tribunal's finding that the employer's repudiation had not been 'accepted' by the employee, instead the employee left for other reasons. Arnold J. stated that, whilst it was not necessary to make a formal assertion of the contractual position, it was necessary to

181 [1974] ICR 373.

indicate that the reason why a contract would not be continued was due to the conduct of the employer which was regarded as unjustified by the employee.

Arnold J. further stated that:-

> "...it is at least requisite that the employee should leave because of the breach of the employer's relevant duty to him, and that this should demonstrably be the case. It is not sufficient, we think, if he merely leaves...And secondly, we think it is not sufficient if he leaves in circumstances which indicate some ground for his leaving other than the breach of the employer's obligations to him." [182]

In **The Association of Technical, Administrative and Supervisory Staff and Grace Kennedy (Trinidad and Tobago) Limited**, H H Ramrekersingh examined the issue of the repudiation of a contract of a worker who was on probation:-

> "Was the Company's action of extending the worker's probationary period a breach of the principles and practices of good industrial relations?
>
> Was the worker constructively dismissed in April 2002?
>
> The issue is whether the Company can unilaterally vary the terms in the contract of employment. The Court concurs with the reasoning in Security Facilities Division Hayes (2001) IRLR 81 C.A. that the terms of the contract of employment may only be varied with the consent of both parties unless otherwise provided in the contract.
>
> A probationer may have less security than a permanent worker, but he/she is entitled to be treated fairly not and not to be the object of arbitrariness nor capricious or whimsical behaviour on the part of an employer.
>
> In view of the foregoing the Court has concluded that the Company did not show that it had taken the necessary steps to maintain appraisal of the worker during his initial

182 [1978] ICR 744 EAT.

> period of probation through guidance, assistance, advice, assessment and warning. The Court holds, therefore, that the action of the Company to extend the worker's probationary period was a unilateral variation of the employment contract and not in accordance with the principles and practices of good industrial relations.
>
> The vital ingredients of constructive dismissal – a fundamental breach by the Company and the worker's departure in direct response to the Company's actions – have been established by the Union. In the circumstances the Court holds that the worker was constructively dismissed. The Company's action was harsh and oppressive and not in accordance with the principles and practices of good industrial relations.
>
> In view of the foregoing as well as the impracticability of reinstatement, the Court acting *"in good conscience and the substantial merits of the case before it, having regard to the principles of and practices of good industrial relations"* orders that the Company pay damages to the worker". [183]

As can be seen by the cases so far, the repudiatory conduct by an employer can amount to constructive dismissal, however the Court has to determine whether or not the employee acted on the employer's repudiation. The decisions of the Courts are really based on a mixture of facts and law. There are two types of conduct by the employer which can be deemed repudiatory conduct:-

a. The employer may unilaterally alter the terms and conditions of an employee. For example, he/she can unilaterally remove a long established allowance or reduce the worker's salary.

b. The employer may insist that the employee agree to change the existing working arrangements like the hours of work, (as in the Servisair case mentioned before) or the employer may

183 TD No 47 of 2003 The Association of Technical, Administrative and Supervisory Staff and Grace Kennedy (Trinidad and Tobago) Limited.

transfer the employee to a new section and insists that he/she performs duties which are different from what he/she obliged to do.

Additionally, the employee may be forced to submit a resignation due to the threat of dismissal.

In **Banking, Insurance and General Workers Union and Cariflex Limited**, the Company redeployed the worker without consultation. I held that:-

> "The Company's evidence was that it considered whether or not a worker should be placed in another section where he will earn a lower wage, but the Court was given no good reason why such action was even contemplated. We accept the worker's evidence that he was sent to work in the Stripping Section of the Company by Mr. Sooknarine, When the Company informed the worker that he would be placed to work in another section at the lower rate of pay that was in fact an attempt on the Company's part to "demote" or "redeploy" the worker without the worker receiving any award and/or benefit.
>
> The worker protested very strongly against this arrangement. The worker's testimony that Mr. Keith James from the Ministry of Labour advised that this new arrangement can only be done if the worker has been paid all of his severance benefits, and an offer has been made to him to accept the new position in the Company at a lower rate of pay, was in fact very sound advice from the Ministry. Yet, Mr. Sooknarine assigned the worker to work in the Stripping Section at a lower rate after the Company received this advice.
>
> It is the view of this Court that an attempt to "redeploy" a worker without consultation and without an award of the necessary benefits can only be regarded as an attempt to dismiss a worker in unfair circumstances.[184] It appears that

184 Pillinger v Manchester Area Health Authority [1979] IRLR 430 EAT.

> when Mr. Sooknarine sent the worker to work in the new section at a lower rate of pay, he in fact ended the contract of employment which existed between the worker and the Company.
>
> The Worker complained about physical pains when he was "redeployed" and left work for home the same day. He then wrote to the Company letter dated 17th October, 2001. It is clear from the contents of this letter that the worker recognized that the transfer from one department to another at a much lower rate of pay was in fact an attempt by the Company to unilaterally and radically change his terms and conditions of employment to his disadvantage which, in fact amounted to the repudiation of his contract of employment." [185]

In **Government Industrial and General Workers Union and Island Club Casino Limited**, H H Seale considered whether the resignations of workers amounted to constructive dismissal:-

> "This Trade Dispute is in respect of the termination of the services on November 10, 2008, of seven workers, all Dealers employed by the Company for varying periods ranging from eight months to six years...The Court accepts the employees' evidence which in effect was that the Employer gave them an ultimatum to either resign or face an uncertain future with the company which would have likely ended in dismissal. While the Employer informed the Workers that it was downsizing its operations, their unchallenged evidence was that while they were being let go, workers were being trained to take their places. In the absence of evidence to contradict that of the Workers, the Court refutes any notion of termination on account of redundancy.

185 TD No. 303 of 2002 Banking, Insurance and General Workers Union and Cariflex Limited.

In a classic case of constructive dismissal, it is usually the employee who makes the decision to resign by virtue of the employer's conduct, but in this instance, it was at the urging of the Employer that the Workers resigned, the alternative being to face an uncertain future with the company. Moreover, a monetary inducement was made to entice the Workers. On the facts the Court must consider whether the Workers' resignation was voluntary or whether pressure was brought upon them such that they had no other course but to leave.

In one of Australia's authoritative cases, Allison v Bega Valley Council 1995 63 IR 68 in which the question of the true cause of dismissal was considered in circumstances where a worker resigned after being told that if he did not do so the police would have been called in, the Queensland Industrial Relations Commission stated: -

> "Where an employee initiates the termination of the contract it is necessary to consider whether that ostensible act of termination was given freely and without any undue pressure. If the ostensible resignation is, in effect, a response to and consistent with a desire by an employer that such resignation be forthcoming, then what has occurred may be that the termination has been brought about by the employer and that in this way the employee has been dismissed."

In the course of its judgment the Full Bench also stated that:- "The fact that the act of resignation subsumed the act of dismissal does not alter the essential transaction between the parties." In that case it was found that "in pith and substance" there was a dismissal.

The Court agrees with the reasoning of the Commission in the Allison case. I find that the enforced resignation by the employer with threats of uncertainty for continued employment was tantamount to a dismissal. In addition, in deliberating on an employer's conduct which gives rise to a claim of constructive dismissal, the Court must, as

> in all cases of dismissal, have regard to section 10(5) and make a determination whether the circumstances of the dismissal were **"harsh and oppressive or not in accordance with the principles of good industrial relations practice."**
>
> I find that on the facts of this case and having regard to all of the circumstances, the seven Workers were dismissed by the Employer. The circumstances of their dismissal were harsh and oppressive and not in keeping with good industrial relations practice. The fact that they were paid for their services did not negate the harsh nature of the dismissals which were without any good or sufficient reason. The Court is being required increasingly to address this type of conduct by employers especially in this industry. Such practices have the effect of depriving employees of tenure which impacts on employment opportunities for long-term benefits." [186]

In **National Union of Domestic Employees and Courts (Trinidad) Limited,** H H Seale addressed whether the resignation of a worker was consistent with good industrial relations:-

> "The question of resignation prompted by a threat of dismissal or resignation under "duress" has been considered by this Court[187]...from the cases it has emerged that "...the employer's conduct is also of importance in determining the voluntariness or otherwise of the worker's action"[188]... "In the Republic Bank Limited case, supra, the Court opined that the aspect of "duress" comes into play where the employer's conduct puts the worker in such a position that there is no other reasonably practical course to follow but to terminate the contract. Where the

186 TD No. 353 of 2009 Government Industrial and General Workers Union and Island Club Casino Limited.

187 TD No 5 of 1995 Bank Employees Union and Republic Bank Limited; TD No 92 of 2000 Bank Employees Union and Script J Printers Limited; TD No 187 of 2008 Banking, Insurance and General Workers Union and CLICO Investment Bank Limited.

188 Ibid. note 195.

resignation is brought about by a threat of dismissal and the employee resigns, "...the mechanics of the resignation do not cause it to be other than a dismissal." (Per Arnold, J. in Sheffield v. Oxford Controls Company Limited)...[189]

The evidence in this case also showed that the Worker was not informed before the meeting that he was attending a disciplinary meeting. One of the tenets of good industrial relations practice is that a Worker who is about to face disciplinary action should be informed of the allegations made against him and be afforded an opportunity to be heard on those allegations as well as on the proposed disciplinary action.[190]

This Court has accepted in a line of authorities that the test for constructive dismissal is the contract test involving conduct by the employer which goes to the root of the contract, resulting in the resignation of the employee... In the instant case the Court holds that the conduct of the Employer, which amounted to a threat of dismissal should the Worker fail to resign, was conduct likely to undermine the requisite "trust and confidence" in the employment relationship. This resulted in a fundamental breach of the employment contract by the Company and the Worker resigned immediately in response to the breach. In the opinion of this Court, this constitutes constructive dismissal.

The Court is not unmindful of the fact that by letter dated March 18, 2008, the Worker had received a letter of final warning concerning future stock variances which he was informed would be met with disciplinary action which "may include dismissal." However, there was no evidence to suggest that any further variances had occurred between the final warning and the Worker's

189 [1979] IRLR 133.

190 TD No. 2 of 2001 Banking, Insurance and General Workers Union and Hindu Credit Union Co-operative Society Limited.

> resignation. The Court finds that the threat of dismissal by the Company brought pressure to bear on the Worker and led him to sign the resignation letter. On the totality of the evidence the Court finds that the Worker did not resign voluntarily but was constructively dismissed on 26th March, 2008. The dismissal was not in keeping with good industrial relations practice." [191]

In contrast, in **Norwest Holst Group Administration Ltd. v Harrison,** the EAT found that an alternative ground for finding there was no constructive dismissal was the fact that the evidence strongly suggested that the threat of the loss of directorship was not the effective cause of resignation. Therefore, the test of acceptance of repudiation of a contract for a claim of constructive dismissal is ultimately one of whether the resignation was in fact caused by the employer's repudiation. [192]

In **Communication Workers' Union and Mega Brite Industries Limited**, I addressed the issue of unilateral alteration of the worker's terms and conditions without consultation with the Union:-

> "The worker was a very good worker, his performance at work was described by the Company as "excellent" and he was permanently employed with the Company from 1986 to 2003... The Company sought to unilaterally alter the worker's terms and conditions of employment without any form of consultation with the Union. See Trade Dispute 303 of 2002.[193]
>
> The Court is of the view that the Company ought to have afforded the worker the opportunity to receive advice from the Union and more importantly the Company ought to have had discussions with the Union on the matter.

191 TD No. 108 of 2009 National Union of Domestic Employees and Courts (Trinidad) Limited

192 [1984] IRLR 419 EAT.

193 TD No. 303 of 2002 Banking, Insurance and General Workers Union and Cariflex Limited.

The approach which was adopted by the Company, namely, that a worker can be suspended until he or she submits to the Company's directive is not only wrong but it is in flagrant violation of the principles of good industrial relations practices.

That the Company's decision to dismiss the worker a week before the actual date of the letter of dismissal even after it held discussions with the Union is of grave concern to us. This is not only unjust but it demonstrates a level of high handedness and arrogance on the part of the Company. In addition it is very baffling and totally repugnant to the spirit of good industrial relations practices that an employer would inform anyone of the dismissal of an employee before that employee is informed of the said dismissal.

The Company had constructively terminated the worker's services when it informed the worker in writing that he was suspended for an indefinite period. On the totality of the evidence we find that the suspension and dismissal of the worker was harsh oppressive and contrary to good industrial relations practices.

We order that the Company do pay to the worker exemplary damages and compensation." [194]

In **All Trinidad General Workers' Trade Union and Ace Contractors Limited**, H H George-Marcelle, examined whether or not the worker was constructively dismissed and made reference to TD No. 182 of 2007. The following is an excerpt of this judgment:-

"In analyzing the law on Constructive Dismissal it must be mentioned that there are three (3) critical ingredients of a constructive dismissal. The First being that there must be a fundamental breach of the terms and conditions of the worker's contract, that is to say, a breach which goes to the

194 TD No. 114 and 115 of 2004 Communication Workers' Union and Mega Brite Industries Limited.

root of the employment contract. The Second ingredient is that the worker must acknowledge the breach by bringing it to the attention of his employer. Finally, the worker must leave his place of employment on account of the breach whether or not he gives notice. [195]

The Worker whose evidence, the Court accepted indicated that on his return from his vacation on the 15th January, 2013 he was not given any work for approximately two (2) weeks. He then received a call on the 23rd January, 2013 from his Supervisor Mr. Jagroop instructing him to report for duties on 28th January, 2013 at the Mechanical Workshop of the CNCL Plant to sort tools, to which the Worker had complied. However, on the 30th January around 11:00 he received another call from Mr. Jagroop instructing him that he was responsible for the collection and disposal of garbage and that his pay would have been consequently reduced to $35.00 per hour.

The Worker, then vehemently complained to his Supervisor about the Company's unilateral decision to alter his terms and conditions of service. Needless to say, this decision was a fundamental breach going to the root of the Worker's contract of employment. Furthermore, the Worker, obtaining no satisfactory response from the Company then took a decision to leave the employ of the Company. Clearly, the Worker by his response to the Company's fundamental breach of his contract of employment fulfilled all the elements of a constructive dismissal.

1) The Court found that the Company's witnesses were unreliable and did not represent the truth;
2) The worker was honest and truthful;

195 TD No. 182 of 2007 National Union of Domestic Employees and Columbia Marketing and Contracting Company (Caribbean) Ltd.

3) The Company breached the Worker's contract of employment, which the Worker resented and left the Company's employ;

4) As a result the Worker was constructively dismissed;

5) The Worker's services were thereby terminated in circumstances which were harsh and oppressive and contrary to good industrial relations practices.

The Court now orders the Company to pay the Worker damages." [196]

In summary, a dismissal severs the employment contract between the parties and it is regarded as the 'ultimate' punishment. Consideration such as employee's misconduct; the reasonableness of the employer's reaction to the alleged misconduct; the length of the employee's service; and whether the employee had an unblemished record must factor in decision making. As Sharma C.J. stated in his dicta:-

> "The worker's length of service and unblemished record is an "exceptional circumstance" warranting reinstatement. The worker's length of service and unblemished record has been considered an exceptional circumstance warranting reinstatement in several cases. This reflects the principle that workers are perceived as having an equity in their employment relationship that increases with the length of service. However, the authorities establish that whilst seniority is one of the significant factors to be considered in mitigation of a penalty, it must be weighed with the seriousness of the incident. By itself, long service cannot be used as an excuse for serious misconduct". [197]

196 TD No. 106 of 2014(S) All Trinidad General Workers' Trade Union and Ace Contractors Limited.

197 CvA No. 83 of 2002 Caribbean Development Company Limited and National Union of Government and Federated Workers.

It follows that the principles of equity, natural justice, fairness and the right to be heard, together with the practice of good industrial relations, are fundamental pillars of decision making, especially when a dismissal is contemplated by an employer. Courts insist that these pillars are entwined in the deliberations of Management before a decision is taken to dismiss any employee.

Chapter VII

REINSTATEMENT

When a determination is made by the Industrial Court of the Trinidad and Tobago that a worker has been dismissed in circumstances which are harsh and oppressive and contrary to the principles and practice of good industrial relations, the Court must then consider the appropriate remedy.

The remedies which are available to the Court are,

(1) an award of compensation and damages

(2) an order of reinstatement or

(3) an order of re-employment.

Although awards for compensation and damages are the most common reliefs and remedies used by the Court, the Court also makes orders for reinstatement and re-employment with or without awards for damages.

Reinstatement at the Industrial Court of Trinidad and Tobago

As mentioned before, the Industrial Court of Trinidad and Tobago was established in 1965 as part of a system of compulsory arbitration for unresolved disputes. Initially the Court did not have the jurisdiction to make orders for the reinstatement of workers, this was noted by the Court of Appeal in Civil Appeal No. 53 of 1966 between Trinidad Bakeries Limited and Union of Foods, Hotels, Beverages and Allied Workers. In that case the Court of Appeal, ruled that the Industrial Court has no jurisdiction to make a non-consensual order or award for the reinstatement of dismissed workers and that accordingly it acted ultra vires in making such an order.

As a result, there were amendments to the ISA which conferred on the Industrial Court jurisdiction to order the reinstatement or the re-employment of workers and also to award damages in lieu of reinstatement or re-employment. The Industrial Stabilisation Act No. 8 of 1965 was eventually ,repealed and replaced by the IRA.[198] The Industrial Court continues to have the power to order the reinstatement of workers pursuant to section 10(4) of the IRA. By virtue of this section, the Court is empowered in any dispute which relates to the dismissal of a worker, to order the re-employment or re-instatement (in the former or a similar position) of that worker. The Court may also make an award for the payment of compensation or damages.

In **Bank and General Workers' Union and Trinidad Express Newspaper Limited** H H Elcock held that:-

> "An order for reinstatement is both a vindication of the rights of a worker who has been harshly and oppressively dismissed and a form of rebuke to the employer concerned....the Act has granted a statutory exception to the common law principle of non-reinstatement for the express purpose of benefitting the Worker." [199]

198 Industrial Relations Act Chapter 88:01 of the Laws of Trinidad and Tobago.

199 TD No. 74 of 1997 Bank and General Workers' Union and Trinidad Express Newspaper Limited.

I discussed in **Trinidad and Tobago National Petroleum Marketing Company Limited and Oilfields Workers' Trade Union** the role and jurisdiction of the Industrial Court and the Orders of the Court. In that case I held that:-

> "This guardianship role of the Court has been reiterated by the Court of Appeal on several occasions. In Caroni (1975) Limited v Association of Technical Administrative Supervisory Staff, de la Bastide CJ made clear the breadth of the jurisdiction of the Court:-
>
> > "The Industrial Court is a comparatively recent creation of statute, and so is the right given to appeal from it to the Court of Appeal. The intention of Parliament, clearly expressed in s 10(6), is that the question whether the dismissal of a worker is in any case harsh and oppressive and contrary to the principles of good industrial relations practice, should be reserved to the Industrial Court. What distinguishes a dismissal that is harsh and oppressive from one that is not, is a matter which the Act clearly regards as grounded not in law, but in industrial relations practice. The practice, which is not codified in our jurisdiction, is to be determined and applied to the facts of each case by the Industrial Court. The policy of the statute is obviously to entrust that function only to judges of the Industrial Court who come equipped with experience of, and familiarity with, industrial relations practice. This is a qualification which judges of the Supreme Court do not necessarily or even ordinarily have. It is considerations like these which presumably underlie the prohibition in s 10(6) against the Court of Appeal reviewing the decision of the Industrial Court that the dismissal of a particular worker does, or does not, have the quality which triggers the grant of the remedies of compensation and reinstatement."

FAIR HEARING

Natural justice, in a case such as this requires not merely that the 68 workers have the opportunity to state their case in detail; they must know sufficiently what they are accused of so that they can put forward a proper answer to their respective cases.

There is no evidence that the workers were informed that among the charges they had to answer were charges of illegal industrial action. There is also no evidence that they were given the opportunity to respond to the employer's allegations which was that they were involved in illegal industrial action, which from the Company's evidence was the main reason for the dismissal.

When an employer is considering disciplinary action against workers, the procedure which is adopted by the employer must be fair, and that to do otherwise will be contrary to the principles of good industrial relations.

> "This is indeed the case with the Industrial Court of Trinidad and Tobago, industrial common sense causes us to examine the extent to which Management's own action or omission call into question the reasonableness of the decision to suspend the workers and then to dismiss them."

We remind parties of the provisions of s 10(3) of the Act and the principles which were expressed by Sir Isaac Hyatali, CJ earlier in this judgment, these principles are essential to the smooth operations of an organisation. Fairness and good industrial relations are the overarching principles which should guide policies and practices of industrial relations in the workplace: to do anything to the contrary tantamount to conduct which is harsh, oppressive and contrary to the principles and practice of good industrial relations.

Pursuant to the provisions of section 10(3) to 10(6) of the Act. We hereby order that:-

(1) the sixty-eight (68) workers who are named in the list attached to this judgment be reinstated immediately to their respective position without any loss of seniority and benefits.

(2) the Company computes the salary and pecuniary benefits of each of the sixty-eight (68) workers from the date of their dismissal namely 21st October, 2013 to 19th November, 2014 and pays to each worker the sum of the said computation on or before 30th January, 2015. [200]

This decision was upheld by the Court of Appeal in **Civil Appeal No. P 306 of 2014 between Trinidad and Tobago National Petroleum Marketing Co. Ltd. and Oilfields Workers' Trade Union,** Bereaux J.A delivered the majority judgment and made several salient points, namely:-

> "The Industrial Court was entirely correct to find that the disciplinary hearings did not meet the minimum requirements of natural justice and that they were not conducted in accordance with the principles of good industrial relations. It would follow that the Court's finding that the worker's dismissals were harsh, oppressive and contrary to good industrial relations practice, was also correct. There was a proper evidential basis upon which it could have made its findings of fact. The section 10(6) prohibition applies and the Court of Appeal cannot interfere. In any event I agree with the findings.
>
> Mr. Jairam sought to make a distinction between labour law and public law, contending that a public law approach in so far at [sic] natural justice is concerned has no place in industrial relations practice. But the issue of fairness which is at the heart of the natural justice concept is a universal concept. Indeed, the resurgence of

200 TD No. 717 of 2013 and IRO 23 of 2013 (consolidated) Trinidad and Tobago National Petroleum Marketing Company Limited and Oilfields Workers' Trade Union.

the concept can be traced to the decision of the House of Lords in Ridge v. Baldwin, a case which has no little connection with labour law principles. The submission is without merit.

REINSTATEMENT

The reinstatement of the workers, the payment of wages forgone during the period of dismissal and the payment of damages or compensation were all live issues which flow from any finding by, the Industrial Court that the termination of the workers' services was harsh, oppressive and contrary to the principles of good industrial relations practice. The court has the power under sections 10(4) and (5) to order reinstatement or the payment of compensation upon any finding of harshness and oppression. The important question in this case is whether it ought to have heard evidence and arguments from the parties before making the orders in respect of reinstatement, payment of salary and other lost benefits and compensation.

The decision of this Court in Caribbean Development Company Limited v. National Union of Government and Federated Workers, Civil No. 83 of 2002, holds that the Court of Appeal has no jurisdiction to review a decision of the Industrial Court ordering reinstatement. See Sharma CJ at paragraph 23 page 12:-

> "The Court of Appeal does not have jurisdiction to review orders for re-instatement even though such orders are not expressly ousted from the court's jurisdiction by s. 10(6). To construe s. 10(6) as conferring such jurisdiction would amount to a flagrant violation of the object and purpose of the provision. More significantly, the principles applicable to the decision to reinstate indicate that the discretion to re-instate depends in large measure on determinations of fact...

> The overriding consideration in construing the ambit of s. 10(6) must be the purpose of the provision. The Industrial Relations Act 1972 repealed and replaced the Industrial Stabilisation Act 1965 and is designed to make better provision for the stabilisation, improvement and promotion of industrial relations. Its object is the maintenance of sound industrial relations practices and the preservation of stable industrial peace. The Legislature conferred jurisdiction on the Industrial Court to ensure that these objects were achieved in employment relationships in this country. What is of critical importance is the fact that in addition to conferring this jurisdiction on the Industrial Court, the Legislature expressly ousted the Court of Appeal's jurisdiction in certain matters considered essential to determining good industrial relations practice. These matters are ones considered to be questions of fact and determinations based on the evidence which the members of the Industrial Court are best qualified to answer. This is consistent with the fact that the Legislature vested the Industrial Court with the responsibility of ensuring that good Industrial relations practices are maintained in employment relationships. S. 10(6) lists these matters as: The circumstances of a workers' dismissal - whether it was harsh, oppressive or contrary to good industrial relations practice. The orders of the court consequent on the finding that the dismissal was harsh and oppressive - orders of compensation and damages."

It would follow that the order of compensation and damages made in this case in the normal course would be precluded from review subject of course to the Schlumberger exception.

The dicta of three Chief Justices speak to the supremacy of the section 10 provisions. The dictum of Sharma CJ in Caribbean Development Company Limited v National Union of Government and Federated

> Workers (supra) is to the effect that a reinstatement order cannot be reviewed even though not expressly prohibited by section 10(6). While the union did not specifically ask for compensation, it did seek an order that the dismissals were harsh, oppressive and a breach of industrial relations practice (which itself would have invoked the Court's section 10(4) powers) reinstatement without loss of earnings and "any further relief which the Court may deem it". The orders for reinstatement without loss of salary and other benefits thus fell within the claim made by the union. So too the order for compensation, as being such "further relief" as the Court considered appropriate." [201]

In **The Amalgamated Workers Union and the Chief Personnel Officer** H H Mahabir adjudicated upon the issue of the lengthy suspension of a worker. Not only was this suspension very lengthy, an equally lengthy period of time was taken for the internal tribunal to complete its hearing and to present a report of its findings. The decision of this case was appealed to the Court of Appeal and then to the Judicial Committee of the Privy Council which delivered its judgment on 13th July, 2020.

A digest of the pertinent facts of this Trade Dispute and the findings of the Industrial Court is as follows:-

> "Daniel Riley was employed in 1983 as a daily-rated Medium Chauffeur with the Transport and Cleansing Department of the Corporation. On May 8, 1999, the worker was charged by an officer of the Corporation's City Police on an allegation that on May 7, 1999, he stole property of the Corporation. On May 8, 1999, the worker reported for duty and, the foreman, Mr. Holder, told him not to work as he was suspended. The Superintendent's letter, dated May 13, 1999 addressed to the City Clerk, Mr. Christopher Samuel, (Samuel the City Clerk) confirmed

201 Civil Appeal No. P 306 of 2014 Trinidad and Tobago National Petroleum Marketing Co. Ltd. and Oilfields Workers' Trade Union delivered by Bereaux, J.A. 24 March 2016.

the worker's verbal suspension from duties effective Monday, May 10, 1999, pending investigations into the matter. The worker was suspended without pay.

Eventually the case of theft was heard and dismissed in the Magistrates' Court on Januarv 17, 2002. The dismissal caused the Union to write to the City Clerk, indicating that because of this fact, the worker was to be reinstated as a matter of procedure. The City Clerk thought otherwise and, consistent with advice received, he instructed the relevant officer to fix a hearing for March 22, 2002, into the disciplinary charge of "The unauthorized removal of gasoline from the Port-of-Spain Corporation, Transport and Cleansing Department on the night of May 7th, 1999". The charge was laid 2.75 years since the imposition of suspension on the worker on May 7, 1999.

The Union retained the services of an Attorney-at-Law and discovered through correspondence that the Corporation had considered the worker as having voluntarily resigned his position. In this regard, Samuel relied on the worker's purported lack of interest in his employment status, having not reported for duty since the charge of theft was preferred against him. For the avoidance of doubt, this was the first official contact the Union had made with the Corporation since the suspension of the worker. Samuel's position on the disciplinary charge though, baffled the Union because it was difficult to understand why the City Clerk would pursue disciplinary action against a person who was no longer its employee. To this end, Murray cynically questioned "...whether he (Samuel) would have done similarly if he understood the worker had passed away."

Suffice it to say that Murray assumed conduct of the Union's case. Hearings of the Tribunal chaired by Mrs. Laraine Alexander (Alexander/Ag. Deputy City Clerk) started on March 22, 2002, and ended on January

23, 2007. By way of explanation as to the cause(s) of this significant delay, Alexander accused the Union, specifically Murray, of stultifying the progress of the Tribunal and, pointed, inter alia, to his scurrilous attacks on her impartiality and his (and the worker's) frequent unavailability.

SUSPENSIONS

Suspensions are temporary by definition. Accordingly, an indefinite suspension is unlawful and may also give rise to a personal grievance for an unjustifiable dismissal. Moreover, it is impossible as a matter of good industrial relations practice for an employer to indefinitely suspend an employee merely because the employer seeks to investigate the claim against the employee.

Here, the Corporation did not investigate the claim, supra, but waited erroneously for almost three (3) years on a decision in the criminal court as a condition of the worker's continuing employment status. Upon receipt of the decision, the Union wrote to the City Clerk, drew the information to his attention and also called for the worker's reinstatement.

TRIBUNAL HEARING

It is an uncontroverted fact that the Tribunal took five (5) years to complete hearings of the charge and a further fourteen (14) months to submit a Report on its findings to the C.P.O. We acknowledge as factual some of the challenges Alexander encountered in chairing the proceedings. But, it was her responsibility as chairperson to determine the correct procedures to adopt after considering such issues as fairness, practicality, the economic use of time, paying due regard to the G.P., the principles of good industrial relations practice and the worker's circumstance. This case should have been prioritized; clearly, it was not.

Further, in the absence of any credible evidence, we reject the Employer's conclusion that the worker had abandoned his job! In order for an employer to be justified in terminating an employee for abandonment, there must be an unequivocal indication of an employee's intention to abandon a position. There is no evidence of this fact nor is there any notification or separation paperwork from the Corporation to the worker to corroborate its claim

ANALYSIS OF EVIDENCE

Having considered all of the evidence in the dispute, balancing the impact of the delay on the worker with the causes of the delay proffered by the Employer, we find that the delay to process an ordinary matter in accordance with the G.P. and/or the principles of good industrial relations practice was excessive and, in the absence of good cause, unreasonable. We, therefore, uphold the Union's claim and find that the Employer's action, or shall we say inaction, resulted in substantial unfairness to the worker. Consequently, the Employer has waived the right to impose discipline on the worker.

ORDER

Based on our findings, the Court hereby orders that:-

The worker, Daniel Riley be immediately reinstated in his former position without loss of seniority emoluments and other benefits whatsoever;

The Employer computes the worker's salary and pecuniary benefits from the date of his alleged dismissal namely, May 10, 1999 to November 9, 2012, and pays to the worker the sum of that computation on or before December 17, 2012." [202]

202 TD No. 25 of 2008 The Amalgamated Workers Union and the Chief Personnel Officer.

In **Civil Appeal No. P 285 of 2012 between Chief Personnel Officer and the National Union of Government and Federated Workers** dated the 25th June, 2014 before the Honourable Mr. Justice P. Jamadar, J.A., Madam Justice M. Rajnauth – Lee, J.A. and Mr. Justice M. Mohammed, J.A. it is ordered that:-

1. The Appeal is dismissed.
2. There be no Order to Costs.
3. Stay granted on the 17th day of June 2013 is discharged forthwith.
4. The Order of the Court made on 9th November, 2012 is reinstated.

As stated before, the decision was further appealed to the Judicial Committee of the Privy Council. Here is an abridged version of that judgment.

In **Privy Council Appeal No. 0081 of 2015 between Chief Personnel Officer (Appellant) v Amalgamated Workers Union (Respondent) (Trinidad and Tobago)** before Lord Kerr, Lord Wilson, Lord Carnwath, Lady Arden and Lord Kitchin the judgment was delivered on 13th July, 2020 by Lord Kitchin:-

> "The Board readily accepts that the Industrial Court has been established as a new superior court of record with its own broad jurisdiction to deal with disputes between employers and their workers and between employers and unions which represent those workers. The court's procedures are flexible and may be informal, and wide powers are conferred on the court to make orders which are fair and just having regard to all the circumstances including the interests of the parties, others who are immediately concerned in the dispute and the community as a whole. The judges of the court are no doubt appointed on the basis of, among other things, their knowledge and expertise and their understanding of local communities and labour relations, and so they are well equipped to achieve the objective of resolving disputes speedily and, in most cases, finally.

It is therefore no surprise that the 1972 Act limits the right of any party to a dispute before the Industrial Court to appeal against its decisions. These limitations are contained in, among other provisions, sections 10(6) and 18(1). They render it very difficult for any party to appeal against findings of fact or to challenge evaluative decisions that necessarily involve the assessment of a number of different matters which the Industrial Court is, in light of its experience and expertise, particularly well placed to make. But these provisions are, implicitly in the case of section 10(6) and expressly in the case of section 18(1), subject to section 18(2) which provides a right of appeal to the Court of Appeal on any one of the five specified grounds. These grounds, including as they do such matters as want of jurisdiction, or that the order was obtained by fraud or error of law, provide a valuable safeguard and are eminently suitable for consideration by the Court of Appeal.

The Board has no doubt that proceedings before the Industrial Court are civil proceedings within the meaning of section 82(1)(a) and that a final decision of the Court of Appeal on an appeal from a decision of the Industrial Court is a final decision in civil proceedings. So too a decision of the Court of Appeal on such an appeal is a decision on an appeal in a civil matter within the meaning of section 82(3). If there were ever any doubt about this, it was resolved by the decision of the Board in Sundry Workers (represented by Antigua Workers Union) v Antigua Hotel and Tourist Association [1993] 1 WLR 1250; (1993) 42 WIR 145. There the Board was required to consider whether an appeal lay to the Board from a decision of the Court of Appeal of Antigua and Barbuda on an appeal from a decision of the Industrial Court in that jurisdiction. In considering the very similar wording of section 105 of the Constitution of Antigua as established by the Antigua Constitution Order 1967 (SI

1967/225), the Board could see no ground for excluding such a decision of the Court of Appeal from the ambit of the phrase "any civil or criminal matter" in section 105(3). Nor could the Board justify excluding from the ambit of the phrase "civil proceedings" in section 105(1)(a) proceedings which were civil in character and which had come to the Court of Appeal from the Industrial Court.

It is also important to have in mind that the grounds on which an appeal to the Court of Appeal is permitted by subsection (2) of section 18, including as they do matters such as want of jurisdiction, may well raise issues of considerable general importance and it would be surprising indeed if the 1972 Act had, essentially by a process of implication and without any express reference, removed or materially limited an avenue of appeal afforded by the Independence Constitution (and now the Republican Constitution) to the Board.

The Board therefore concludes that the CPO has properly exercised the right of appeal conferred by section 109(1)(a) of the Republican Constitution and that the Board has jurisdiction to hear the appeal. The Union's submissions to the contrary are rejected.

DID THE INDUSTRIAL COURT HAVE THE POWER TO MAKE THE ORDER THAT IT DID?

The particular event which triggered the reporting of the dispute was the failure by Ms Alexander to produce her report in ten working days as the procedure required. But this was only one element of the overall failure by the Corporation to deal with its disciplinary action against Mr Riley in a timely and proper way. The failure began in May 1999 when it suspended Mr Riley without pay for alleged theft and without taking formal disciplinary action against him. That suspension ran for nearly three years while the criminal proceedings took their course. Then, instead of abiding by the outcome of those proceedings and accepting Mr Riley's acquittal as dispositive of the allegation of theft, it chose to pursue that allegation for itself by initiating internal disciplinary proceedings.

Having regard to the time that had already elapsed and Mr Riley's continuing suspension without pay, the Corporation, through Ms Alexander, as chairperson, ought to have ensured the expeditious progress of the proceedings. Instead they took some five years, an astonishing period of time having regard to the nature of the charge and the very small value of the goods allegedly stolen. Following the adjournment of the proceedings on 23 January 2007, Ms Alexander ought to have produced her decision within ten working days, which she failed to do. A yet further unacceptable delay ensued. By the time the decision was produced, on 6 March 2008, a period of a just under nine years had elapsed from the date of the alleged offence, and for the whole of this time Mr. Riley had been suspended without pay.

The Industrial Court considered all of these matters. It assessed the extent of the delay and whether and to what extent the Corporation was responsible for it. It concluded that the delay to process an ordinary matter such as this in accordance with the grievance procedure and good industrial relations was unreasonable and resulted in substantial unfairness, and that the Corporation was substantially responsible. The Board has no doubt that these findings fell squarely within the scope of the first trade dispute and had an ample basis in the evidence. The only cause for concern, as the Court of Appeal correctly recognised, is whether the Industrial Court was then entitled to conclude, as it did, that the Corporation had waived its right to impose discipline on Mr Riley and whether it was entitled to order Mr Riley's immediate reinstatement and that he should be paid his salary and other benefits from the date of his suspension to the date of the order.

The Board has reached the conclusion that the Industrial Court did have the power to make these orders. Section 10(1)(b) confers on the court a power to make an order relating to any of the matters in dispute and section 10(3) confers on the court a power to make such order or award in relation to a dispute before it as it considers fair and just, having regard to the interests of the persons immediately concerned and the community as a whole. These powers are deliberately broad and allow the court to frame its order in such a way as to achieve a result that it believes to be fair and just having regard to the dispute before it and the findings it has made. Here the orders made by the Industrial Court plainly did relate to the matters in dispute in that they arose from and sought to remedy the failure by the Corporation to abide by the grievance procedure over a prolonged period of time. The failures by the Corporation were so substantial that, in the Industrial Court's view, the legality of the disciplinary process had been fatally undermined, necessarily rendering any subsequent dismissal for the alleged offence unfair.

Moreover, the Board does not accept that there had to be a dispute about reinstatement for an order for reinstatement to be made. That is to confuse the dispute with the order the court may make in relation to it. Here the dispute arose from and concerned the Corporation's failures to comply with the grievance procedure and an important aspect of those failures was its decision to suspend Mr Riley for so long without pay. The dispute having been resolved in Mr Riley's favour, and the court having found that the disciplinary proceedings had been fundamentally compromised, an order for his reinstatement was a perfectly appropriate order for the court to consider making. Indeed, that is what the Union sought in its letter of 23 January 2002. What is more, and as the Board has explained, the issue of reinstatement, though not substantially developed during the course of the hearing before the Industrial Court, was raised at its outset.

The Board therefore concludes that the Industrial Court did not exceed its jurisdiction in making its order. The Court of Appeal made no error in rejecting this aspect of the CPO's appeal.

UNFAIRNESS, BREACH OF NATURAL JUSTICE, IRRATIONALITY AND ERROR OF LAW

The Board does not accept that the Industrial Court committed any breach of natural justice or that its decision or order involved any unfairness of the kind alleged, and that is so for the reasons we have given in addressing the immediately preceding ground of appeal. The parties must at all times have been well aware of the scope of the powers conferred on the court by the 1972 Act including, under section 10(3), the power to make such order or award as the court considered fair and just and to act in accordance with the substantial merits of the case before it, having regard to the principles and practices of good industrial relations. Moreover, the issues before the court included the question whether Mr Riley had voluntarily resigned or had voluntarily accepted that his status as an employee of the Corporation had come to an end. It was or ought to have been plain that, if the court were to find in favour of the Union on this issue and more generally in relation to the first trade dispute, it would or might make an order for Mr Riley's reinstatement.

HAS THERE BEEN ANY SUBSTANTIAL MISCARRIAGE OF JUSTICE?

In the Board's view, this pithy metaphor is entirely apt. It would be most unjust for the Board to attach any weight to the CPO's arguments that the scope of the first trade dispute did not extend to questions concerning Mr Riley's reinstatement or the payment to him of his salary and benefits from the date of his suspension. This is a clear

> case for the application of section 18(4) of the 1972 Act. The Board is satisfied that there has been no substantial miscarriage of justice.
>
> DAMAGES
>
> In light of the foregoing, this issue does not arise.
>
> CONCLUSION
>
> For the reasons given above, this appeal must be dismissed."[203]

As stated before, the Industrial Court, from time to time, makes orders for the reinstatement of workers. The following are among the factors the Court considers when determining whether an order of reinstatement is the appropriate remedy:-

1. Whether the employee wishes to return to that job;
2. Whether it is practicable for the employer to comply with the order;
3. The harsh and oppressive nature of the dismissal.

It is useful to note that an order for reinstatement, unlike that of re-employment, is an order to the employer to restore the worker to his/her former position treating him/her in all respect as if he/she had never been dismissed. Therefore, all rights, including all arrears of pay, seniority, wage increases and pension rights are restored on reinstatement.

203 Privy Council Appeal No. 0081 of 2015 Chief Personnel Officer v Amalgamated Workers Union [2020] UKPC 17.

Chapter VIII

Labour Supply Contracts/Labour Only Contracts

Labour supply Contracts/Labour only Contracts are commonplace in the energy sector in Trinidad and Tobago.

The term "Labour only Contract" is the broad expression which used to describe an agreement to provide the supply of workers by a service provider to a receiving company in need of those services.

In ruling on a preliminary point in 2006, I noted that

> "more and more we are witnessing new trends in contracts of employment and in the employment relationships between parties. The emergence of these new forms of employment have been evident in Trinidad and Tobago by the procurement of the services of workers by companies on terms and conditions which very often differ from terms within an employment relationship. The pertinent question

therefore is whether these types of contracts fall within the framework of the employment relationship in industrial Relations. It is therefore the duty of the Court to determine this issue".[204]

Indeed, what has been emerging as described by H H Rabathaly is "a triangular relationship between worker, employer and a third party". This has been so for the past two decades or more in the energy sector in Trinidad and Tobago.

The lead authority on Labour only Contracts is the case of **Steel Workers' Union of Trinidad and Tobago and ArcelorMittal Point Lisas Limited (formerly Caribbean Ispat Limited)**. The judgment of this case was delivered by H H Rabathaly at the Industrial Court. This decision was challenged by the Company at the Court of Appeal of Trinidad and Tobago then at the Privy Council in England. The following are the rulings by the three Courts on this issue.

Steel Workers' Union of Trinidad and Tobago and Caribbean Ispat Limited:-

"The Union stated, inter alia, that there exists at ISPAT's plant a parallel workforce employed by contractors for the purpose of providing their services to ISPAT. These workers perform work normally done by workers in the bargaining unit, and have been doing so on a continuous basis for a number of years...Mr. Phillip Sancho, a Supervisor with the Casting Department of ISPAT testified on behalf of the Union that in the Casting Department there were three (3) 8-hour shifts with (13) thirteen persons each in operation daily over a 24-hour period, with another shift alternating with the other three (3), so that one (1) shift was always off duty during any given 24-hour period... On his shift, where they cast liquid steel into solid steel, the personnel included two (2) senior casters, four (4) casters, two (2) ladle operators, two (2) panel operators,

204 TD No. 277 of 2004 National Union of Government and Federated Workers and N.P. Service Station.

one (1) cooling bed operator and two (2) attendants. Of the four (4) casters, three (3) were employed by ISPAT and the other, Phillip St. Clair, by a firm called Management Technical Services Limited (MTS). He stated further that if a worker (from MTS) did not attend work, a call would be placed to Mr. Randy Rampersad at the MTS office and another worker would be sent to ISPAT. This practice had been going on all the years he had been employed by the Company...Mr. Randolph Rampersad who testified on behalf of the Company, is the Managing Director of both Management Technical Services Limited (MTS) and System Maintenance Services Limited (SMS). MTS, he stated, supplied skilled labour to ISPAT, whilst SMS bid for jobs (at ISPAT) along with other contractors, and when successful on a bid SMS is issued with a purchase order...He said that on Thursdays of every week he sits with the ISPAT supervisor and make up the roster for the following week and workers are sometimes moved around by him, sometimes by ISPAT, so that although a worker may be in the same department he may be doing different jobs from time to time. MTS, he stated, disciplined the workers, paid them, paid NIS, PAYE and was also involved in Workman's Compensation (re: Elton Pearl). Indra, he said was Supervisor and Timekeeper and "her first job was to ensure that the time was recorded for the workers coming in on the shifts. Then she would go to the ISPAT Supervisor's office, and ensure that the MTS workers were, in fact on the Plant and on their job..." The Union stated that the outcome of this application turned entirely on the proper interpretation of section (2)(4)(b) of the Industrial Relations Act Chapter. 88:01('the Act') which provides that:-

> *"For the purposes of this Act –*
>
> *where a person engages the services of a worker for the purpose of providing those services to another, then, such other person shall be deemed*

to be employer of the worker under a labour only contract."

It is apparent from that section that Caribbean Ispat (now Mittal) will be deemed to be the employer of the workers concerned in this case where two conditions are satisfied:-

i) the services of the workers are engaged by SMS & MTS;

ii) for the purposes of providing those services to Caribbean Ispat.

The Union felt that evidence in this case demonstrated that SMS and MTS are engaged in the employment agency business, that is to say, the business of providing the services of workers to others. SMS and MTS provide labour to Caribbean Ispat in several of its departments, probably even the entire gamut of functions required to produce steel. But by no stretch of the imagination can it be said that SMS and MTS are engaged in the steel business. The labour they provide to Caribbean Ispat merely supplements ISPAT's supervisory staff when carrying out their functions. Moreover, they work alongside ISPAT permanent staff performing identical functions...In other words, **the industrial relations reality is that they are part and parcel of ISPAT's permanent and casual workforce.** (my emphasis) If the workers provided by SMS and MTS are integrated into ISPAT's business as a matter of practical industrial relations reality, it must follow that SMS and MTS have engaged the workers solely for the purpose of providing their services to ISPAT, which would make ISPAT the deemed employer under Section 2 (4) (b)...The Union felt that It is instructive to compare the position in Trinidad and Tobago, where Parliament has deliberately sought to deal with the problem of triangular employment relationships through section 2(4) (b) with other jurisdictions where no such attempt has been made.

As recorded in Teamsters Local 419 v K Mart Canada Limited 1983: CLLC 14, 311, in determining who the real employer is Labour Relations Boards have regard to the following criteria:-

a. the party exercising direction and control over the employees;

b. the party bearing the burden of remuneration;

c. the party imposing discipline;

d. the party hiring employees;

e. the party with authority to dismiss employees;

f. the party who is perceived to be the employer of the employees; and

g. the existence of an intention to create the relationship of employer and employee.

More interestingly, in Dacas v Brooks Street Bureau [2004] ICR 1437, common law courts have shown themselves prepared to use existing common law principles to find the existence of implied contracts of employment between workers and the end-users in a triangular relationship. The typical triangular relationship is one where the worker concerned is employed and paid by an employment agency but works for the employment agency's client or end-user who exercises direct control over the functions performed by the workers...The Court of Appeal found in Dacas that it was this element of control which was pivotal in determining the existence of a contractual relationship between the worker and the end-user and it made little difference that the worker was paid by the employment agency since the end-user paid for the workers services, albeit indirectly...Also in that Dacas case, the common law courts revised, what is referred to as, *"an implied contract of employment in order to provide protection for workers in this triangular relationship"*. So that the Courts are now prepared to say, depending on what the circumstances are, that there is an implied contract between the workers and the end-user. And therefore, the worker will be able to lay claim to any benefits provided for under the employment legislation. Under that employment legislation you will have to establish that you have a contract of employment in order to lay claim to the benefits.

In this case, ISPAT is in the position of the end-user and SMS and MTS are in the position of the employment agency. And, of course, the contract workers complete the other point in the triangle. The Court has been asked to determine in this case whether those workers, either all of them or some of them, are employed under, labour only contracts.

The question is whether MTS and SMS are engaging the services of the workers concerned for the purpose of providing those services to ISPAT? That is the question that the Court will have to ask and answer and that question only by the Court look at the evidence to see exactly what was the purpose for which SMS and MTS engaged the services of the workers.

The Union concluded by submitting that Section 2(4)(b) of the Industrial Relations Act has done directly what courts in other jurisdictions have tried to achieve by employing established legal principles. The test in Trinidad and Tobago is whether the employment agency has engaged the services of the workers for the purposes of providing those services to the end-user. Indeed, if ISPAT is not deemed to be the employer of the workers employed by SMS and MTS, there is nothing in theory which would prevent an arrangement whereby all ISPAT labour is provided by SMS and MTS with the remarkable result that ISPAT would be carrying on a multi-million dollar steel business without any employees of its own capable of being protected under the Industrial Relations Act.

Mr. Martineau S.C. began his submissions by highlighting certain aspects of the evidence as it pertained to departments/sections of the Company in an effort to show that it was difficult to determine the purpose for which workers were hired by MTS/SMS.

There is no dispute that the people being considered are workers. And the critical words are, "for the purpose". So one has to find the purpose "for which their services are engaged." It has nothing to do with control or any other factor for that matter.

"The purpose for which their services are engaged." And the purpose must be *"the purpose of providing those services to another"*. And that is also an important fact - providing the services to another.

"...then such other person shall be deemed to be employer."

The test is not whether one is engaged in any other business or is the supplier of labour, but the purpose for which the workers were employed.

The evidence in this dispute has demonstrated that there are at least five (5) categories of persons who SMS/MTS send to ISPAT to fulfill certain work obligations.

What has emerged in this case is that generally in all of the above categories where possible, the same persons are sent to ISPAT daily, weekly or otherwise.

In essence, however, the Union is saying that regardless of the manner of distribution of their labour, those persons for the most part work exclusively for ISPAT, although paid by SMS, and as such fall within the ambit of Section 2(4)(b) of the Act (p. 14 supra).

In fact, the Union was adamant that such a situation as presented by this dispute is exactly why that Section was inserted into the Act, to ensure that workers are not, unwittingly perhaps, manipulated by both Agency and end-user in a triangular working relationship resulting in them having no rights of representation, and maybe no employer at all.

The Company on the other hand has insisted that the Court must look at the Act to ascertain whether it could decide the "purpose" for which the said workers were contracted by SMS/MTS.

Whilst the full meaning of the relevant section of the Act must be employed to resolve this dispute, this developing "trend" of triangular working relationships has been observed in Trade Disputes No. 278 and 280 of 2007 where the Court stated at page 7 (Lines 10-27):-

> "Over the years a trend has emerged in employment contracts which appear to be steadily redefining employer/employee relationship from the traditional contractual relationship as we know it, particularly in the energy sector. In this sector, several large companies are no longer directly recruiting skilled workers instead these workers are mainly recruited by what can loosely be called Labour Service Providers. These Labour Service Providers operate very similar to employment agencies.
>
> What is emerging more and more is a triangular relationship between a worker, an employer and a third party who is usually a service provider. The question for the Court to determine, is the nature of the employment relationship which the worker shares with the Labour Service Provider.
>
> Also whether there is a merging or overlap of the contractual relationship between the employer and the Labour Service Provider on the one hand and the employee on the other.
>
> These issues are becoming more relevant as the employment contract continues to evolve."

In the K. Mart case the evidence showed that following certification of its distribution centre, K. Mart increased its use of part-time workers hired through employment agencies.

The Board found that the move to increase the use of contracted in part-time workers was motivated at least in part by anti-union animus, and that, but for the contracting in, the work would have been performed by bargaining unit employees.

With respect to determining who was the actual employer the Board examined the following criteria:-

1. the party exercising direction and control over the employees;
2. the party bearing the burden of remuneration;
3. the party imposing discipline;
4. the party hiring the workers;
5. the party with authority to dismiss the workers;
6. the party perceived to be the employer by the worker; and,
7. the existence of an intention to create the relationship of employer and employee.

The Board also determined that while no order of priority exists, the factor of who exercises "overriding control" is of considerable significance.

The Dacas case was unanimously decided by the Court of Appeal of the United Kingdom in 2004.

The Appeal Court noted, however, per curiam, that the absence of an express contract between an agency worker and the end-user does not preclude the implication of a contract of service between them.

This issue was further considered by the EAT in 2006- Ms. M. James (appellant) v Greenwich Council (respondent) ULEAT 0006 06 2112, where the appellant was supplied by an agency to carry out work for Greenwich Council.

She had no express contract with the Council, but she contended that there was an implied contract following the guidance given by the Court of Appeal in Dacas (supra). The Employment Tribunal had concluded that there was no **mutuality of obligation** (my emphasis), and therefore no contract with the Council at all. The appellant submitted that the Tribunal had erred in law, and reached a perverse conclusion but the EAT rejected the appeal, holding that the Tribunal had properly assessed the evidence, and was entitled to conclude that there was no mutuality of obligations.

The EAT examined, inter alia the case of Cable and Wireless plc v Muscat (2006) IRLR 354 where the Court of Appeal had to give further consideration to Dacas, although the facts of both cases were very different. In the former, the Employment Tribunal held that the "worker" had an implied contract with Cable and Wireless, which was upheld by the EAT on appeal.

The EAT felt the relevant question for a Tribunal faced with this type of issue to pose is whether there exists **an irreducible minimum of mutual obligations** (my emphasis) between the worker and the end user.

The EAT concluded by stating that:-

> "if any such contract is to be inferred, there must be subsequent to the relationship commencing some words or conduct which entitle the Tribunal to conclude that the agency arrangements no longer dictate or adequately reflect how the work is actually being performed, and that the reality of the relationship is only consistent with the implication of the contract. It will be necessary to show that the worker is working not pursuant to the agency arrangements but because of mutual obligations binding worker and end user which are incompatible with those arrangements."

It is therefore the finding of the Court:-

That the workers who were recruited by Mr. Rampersad and his companies (SMS/MTS) and were sent to ISPAT to perform jobs/tasks – whether daily or otherwise – are caught within the framework of the Act and are operating as workers under labour only contracts with ISPAT.

That being the case it is consequently right and proper that good industrial relations principles and practices be observed, and in accordance with Section 10(3)(b) of the Act the Company (ISPAT) is hereby ordered to apply the appropriate collective agreement(s) to these workers. Any monies due and payable to the workers concerned shall attract interest at the rate of 8% from the due date to the date of payment, which should not be later then 30th September, 2009." [205]

In **Civil Appeal No. 211 of 2009 ArcelorMittal Point Lisas Limited (formerly Caribbean Ispat Limited) and Steel Workers' Union of Trinidad and Tobago** delivered by Narine J.A.:-

"The Appellant has not appealed the finding of the Court that ISPAT was deemed to be the employer of the workers under labour only contracts. The appeal concerns the consequential order made by the court pursuant to Section 10(3)(b) of the Act, and the award of interest..."

ISSUES

The issues that arise for decision are:-

1. Whether the Court of Appeal has jurisdiction to entertain this appeal.
2. Whether the Industrial Court had the jurisdiction to make the orders for the application and enforcement of the appropriate collective agreements.

205 Application No. 2 of 1998 Steel Workers' Union of Trinidad and Tobago and Caribbean Ispat Limited.

3. Whether the Industrial Court erred in law in ordering the Appellant to apply collective agreement(s) which, though current at the time of the Respondent's application to the Industrial Court, had expired by the time the Court gave its decision.
4. Whether the Industrial Court had the power to order the payment of interest on sums found to be due and payable by the Appellant.
5. Whether the orders of the Industrial Court were made in contravention of the rules of natural justice in that the Appellant was not provided with an opportunity to adduce evidence and arguments on the issue of the application and enforcement of the appropriate collective agreements to the workers.

JURISDICTION

The Respondent contends that the Appellant is not entitled to appeal on the ground that the Industrial Court had no jurisdiction to make the order for the application of the collective agreement(s) to the workers, since this jurisdiction had not been invoked by the Respondent's application before the Court. In making this objection, the Respondent relies on section 18(2)(a) of the Act.

It is clear from Section 18(2)(a), that an Appellant is not entitled to raise lack of jurisdiction in the Court of Appeal unless objection to jurisdiction was taken in the proceedings before the Industrial Court. However, the condition does not apply to appeals grounded on excess of jurisdiction.

However, the Appellant contends that the Industrial Court had no jurisdiction to make an order in accordance with section 10(3)(b), since there was no trade dispute before it.

In its submission, the court should have granted the declaration pursuant to Section 2(4)(b) and should have left it up to the parties to apply the appropriate collective agreement to the workers. If the Appellant failed or refused to apply the collective agreement, then a trade dispute would have arisen, which the parties would first address outside of the court process.

This submission of the Appellant does not bear scrutiny. It contemplates that the parties would abide by the decision of the Industrial Court in relation to the status of the workers and act in accordance with good industrial relations practice. It follows that the parties would then sit and decide which collective agreement should apply and calculate the amounts due to the workers under the terms and conditions of the agreements, and acting in good faith, would pay to the workers all such sums that are found to be due and payable.

The order of the Industrial Court did not deprive the parties of the opportunity of going through that process. The Court ordered that the Appellant should apply "the appropriate collective agreements" to the workers.

The application under Section 2(4)(b) was brought precisely because the Appellant had refused and continued to refuse to apply the collective agreement to the workers.

The procedure to access the Industrial Court and the rules regarding proceedings before it, were designed for the use and benefit of workers and persons acting on behalf of workers, who are not required to be legal practitioners. The intention of the framers of the Act was clearly to ensure that the process of the Court would not be defeated or frustrated by technical legal arguments. This is made clear by section 9(1) of the Industrial Relations Act, which provides:-

> "9(1) In the hearing and determination of any matter before it, **the Court may act without regard to technicalities and legal form** and shall not be

> bound to follow the rules of evidence stipulated in the Evidence Act, but the Court may inform itself on any matter in such manner as it thinks just and may take into account opinion evidence and such facts as it considers relevant and material, but in any such case the parties to the proceedings shall be given the opportunity, if they so desire, of adducing evidence in regard thereto". (Emphasis added)

In addition, the court is given wide powers in order to achieve a just result in relation to any matter before it in accordance with Section 10 of the act.

Accordingly, in our view the Industrial Court did not exceed its jurisdiction in making the order for the application of the collective agreement(s) to the workers in the matter before it having regard to the issues that were placed before it. The mere fact that section 16(2) was not expressly invoked cannot detract from the fact that what the Respondent was seeking was an application of the registered collective agreement, which the court has the express jurisdiction to deal with under section 16(2) of the Act.

ILLEGALITY

The essence of the complaint of the Appellant is that the Industrial Court erred in law when it ordered the Appellant to apply expired collective agreements retroactively in favour of the workers. It is to be noted at the onset that the Industrial Court did not expressly order the company to apply expired collective agreements. The court in fact ordered the company to apply "the appropriate collective agreement(s) to these workers".

Since the making of the application in December 1997, there would have been several agreements, which would have expired by the date that the court made the order in July 2009. The Appellant contends that this is illegal, and the only collective agreement that could be applied was that which was existing at the date of the order, that is, 31st July 2009.

In support of this submission the Appellant relies on sections 43, 47 and 48 of the Industrial Relations Act, and the decision of this court in Bank Employees Union v. Republic Bank Ltd Civil Appeal No. 9 of 1995.

The meaning and effect of these provisions were explained by Jones J.A. in the Bank Employees Union case (supra.) at page 11, where he stated:-

> "What Parliament has done specifically by section 48(2) is to permit the parties to use the dispute resolution procedures contained in the agreement after the agreement has expired. The specific reference to section 43(1) is significant since it is that subsection which determines the life span of a collective agreement. When the prescribed period expires what is left of the collective agreement are the provisions relating to the procedure for the resolution of disputes.
>
> The remainder of the collective agreement qua collective agreement dies, but the terms and conditions of the individual contracts of the workers do not die with the expiration of the collective agreement. They continue on until those terms are replaced, amended or confirmed by the new collective agreement. They survive, not as terms of a registered collective agreement but as the terms and conditions of the individual contract of employment of the workers. The dispute resolution procedures are preserved by section 48(2) and these may be invoked in dealing with any dispute that may arise."

In this case, it is not in dispute that since the filing of the application in December 1997, the collective agreement then in existence, and subsequent collective agreements would have expired, before the Industrial Court gave its decision in July 2009.

By virtue of the legislation, the terms and conditions of the expired collective agreements would have survived as terms and conditions of their individual contracts of employment, and the workers would have been entitled to be compensated accordingly.

By ordering the employer to apply "the appropriate collective agreement(s)", the court was clearly seeking to devise a formula by which the compensation due to each worker could be calculated by reference to the terms and conditions of workers in the same bargaining unit, as contained in the collective agreement then current at the time the workers provided their services to the company.

Clearly, the most sensible interpretation of the order of the court, was that it was ordering the employer to apply the terms and conditions contained in the collective agreement existing at the time the services of each worker were provided, which would have become terms and conditions of his individual contract at the time that the statutory life of the collective agreement expired. In making this order, the court was not ordering the application of the collective agreement qua collective agreement, but as an agreement containing the terms and conditions of the worker's individual contract of employment pursuant to section 47(2) of the Act.

INTEREST

The Appellant also appealed the award of interest on sums payable to the workers. The power to award interest is given by section 25 of the Supreme Court of Judicature Act Chap. 4:01, which provides:-

> "25. In any proceedings tried in any Court of record for recovery of any debt or damages, the Court may, if it thinks fit, order that there shall be included in the sum for which judgment is given interest at such rate as it thinks fit on the whole or any part of the debt or damages for the whole or any part of the period

between the date when the cause of action arose and the date of the judgment, but nothing in this section-

(a) shall authorise the giving of interest upon interest;

(b) shall apply in relation to any debt upon which interest is payable as of right whether by virtue of any agreement or otherwise; or

(c) shall affect the damages recoverable for the dishonour of a bill of exchange."

By virtue of section 4(1) of the Act, the Industrial Court is a superior court of record. Further, by virtue of section 10(7) of the Act, the sums awarded to the workers under the order, are deemed to be damages. Accordingly, the Industrial Court had the power to make the order for the payment of interest on monies due to the workers under the award it made.

NATURAL JUSTICE

The Appellant further complained that the orders of the Industrial Court were made in contravention of the rules of natural justice, that is to say, without first affording the Appellant an opportunity to adduce evidence and/or arguments in relation to an award to the workers.

The underlying purpose of the application under section (2)(4)(b) of the Act was to ensure that the employer accorded to the workers the same terms and conditions contained in the collective agreement in relation to workers providing the same services in bargaining Unit I. To make the position even clearer, in its Evidence and Arguments filed on 18th December, 1998 the union expressly asked the court for an order that the employer be bound to apply the collective agreement in relation to the workers on whose behalf the application was made. This relief was never expressly or impliedly withdrawn.

> Accordingly, the Appellant had every opportunity to deal with the issue, in a Reply or in submissions before the Industrial Court. It failed to avail itself of this opportunity and cannot now complain as it does, that the court made the order without giving it an opportunity to address the issue.
>
> For these reasons we dismissed this appeal and made no order as to costs." [206]

In the judicial committee of the **Privy Council Appeal No 0087 of 2013 ArcelorMittal Point Lisas Limited (formerly Caribbean Ispat Limited) (Appellant) v Steel Workers' Union of Trinidad and Tobago (Respondent) (Trinidad and Tobago)** delivered on 6th August, 2015 the Board held as follows:-

> "This appeal comes from Trinidad and Tobago and concerns the applicability of collective agreements to persons employed under 'labour only' contracts...In his decision given on 31 July 2009, nearly 12 years after the application was issued, H H Rabathaly ("the judge") held that the persons recruited by two contractors (Systems Maintenance Services Limited ("SMS") and Management Technical Services Limited ("MTS")) were operating under labour only contracts with the employer and were therefore deemed to be workers employed by the employer. Further, the court ordered the employer to apply "the appropriate collective agreement(s)" to those persons and that any moneys due to the workers should attract interest thereon at the rate of 8% per annum from the "due date to the date of payment". The employer appealed to the Court of Appeal but the appeal failed. The order of the judge was upheld by the Court of Appeal on 9 December 2011.
>
> The employer now appeals to the Board.

206 Civil Appeal No. 211 of 2009 ArcelorMittal Point Lisas Limited (formerly Caribbean Ispat Limited) and Steel Workers' Union of Trinidad and Tobago.

The employer says that the Court of Appeal was wrong to uphold the decision of the Industrial Court, both (a) because on a true construction of the Act it was wrong in law and made in excess of the court's jurisdiction and (b) because in making it, the court acted in violation of the rules of natural justice.

The principal issues which the employer raises in this appeal are as follows:-

i. Did the Industrial Court commit an error of law or exceed its jurisdiction by applying or enforcing (expired) collective agreements in relation to the deemed workers in considering the application before it?

ii. In all of the circumstances, was the employer afforded a fair opportunity to deal with the issue of the Industrial Court's reliance on section 10(3)(b) of the Act in ordering the application or enforcement of expired collective agreements to the deemed workers?

Where a trade union is certified by the Registration Recognition and Certification Board ("the Board") as the recognised majority union, by section 35(a), it "shall have exclusive authority to bargain collectively on behalf of workers in the bargaining unit and to bind them by a collective agreement registered under Part IV so long as the certification remains in force" and, by section 40, "the employer shall recognise that trade union as the recognised majority union; and the recognised majority union and employer shall ... in good faith, treat and enter into negotiations with each other for the purposes of collective bargaining". A collective agreement may be made in various ways but such an agreement must be registered with the court to be effective. By section 47(1), the terms and conditions of a collective agreement registered under section 46, namely a "registered agreement", shall be binding on the parties and shall be directly enforceable, but only in the court. Section 47(2) provides:-

> *"(2) The terms and conditions of a registered agreement shall, where applicable, be deemed to be terms and conditions of the individual contract of employment of the workers comprised from time to time in the bargaining unit to which the registered agreement relates."*

It appears to the Board that the effect of section 47(2) is that a registered agreement applies, not only to workers in the bargaining unit to which the agreement relates who were employed when the agreement was registered, but also to workers who are employed in the bargaining unit at any time thereafter. This is the effect of the provision that deems the terms and conditions of a registered collective agreement to be the terms and conditions of the individual contracts of employment of the workers comprised "from time to time" in the bargaining unit.

A registered collective agreement only applies to workers who are employed by the employer who is a party to the agreement. It appears to the Board (and does not appear to be in dispute) that a registered collective agreement applies to (and its terms and conditions are deemed to be the terms and conditions of the contracts of employment of) workers comprised from time to time in the bargaining unit who are deemed by section 2(4)(b) to be employed by the employer under labour only contracts.

In its judgment the Industrial Court found that the contract workers were engaged by the employment agencies for the purpose of providing their services to the appellant. The consequence of that finding, which has not been appealed, is that the appellant is deemed by section 2(4)(b) of the Act to be the employer of the contract workers under labour only contracts.

The union has summarised the issues in the appeal under three heads which it has called the pleading point, the natural justice point and the defunct collective agreement point. It is convenient to do the same in this judgment. In doing so the Board considers the various issues identified on behalf of the employer.

The pleading point

First, as stated above, from the time it received the Statement of Evidence and Arguments of 18 December 1998 the employer can have been in no doubt that the union was seeking an order applying the appropriate collective agreement or agreements to the contract workers. Second, there is no ground for saying either that there was some basis for seeking to negotiate different terms of employment on behalf of the contract workers or that the union was interested in pursuing that course....The contract workers were accordingly part of the workforce comprised in the bargaining unit and, in accordance with section 47(2) of the Act, the terms and conditions of the collective agreement were deemed to be the terms and conditions of their individual contracts of employment. There was accordingly no room to negotiate different terms for them as long as those agreements were current. In any event, given that they were doing the same work as others in the bargaining unit, there was no basis for separating them out for different treatment, and the employer has pointed to no reason which would have justified such treatment.

Furthermore, far from there being any suggestion that the union was making the application so as to negotiate "acceptable but different terms for them", in para 5 of its Statement of Evidence and Arguments it alleged specifically that the employer did not apply the collective agreement to the contract workers and accordingly sought an order in para 6 that the employer was bound to apply the collective agreement to them.

The Board prefers the submissions of the union to those of the employer on this point. In short, as the Court of Appeal expressly held, the position was made clear in the union's Statement of Evidence and Arguments of 18 December 1998.

As to the second reason, which overlaps with the defunct collective agreement point, it is true that the Statement of Evidence and Arguments expressly referred only to "the registered collective agreement", which was presumably a reference to the one in force at the time....the Board accepts the union's submission that it could not have anticipated when it filed its Evidence and Arguments how long the proceedings would take and cannot therefore be blamed for not pleading then that an order should be made that all future agreements be applied to the contract workers. In any event, as submitted on behalf of the union, it appears to the Board that, subject perhaps to any particular contract, it would have followed automatically that all future agreements would apply to them.

The Board accepts the submission that the witnesses, whether for the union or the employer, gave evidence long after the proceedings had commenced and spoke of what was currently happening at the plant and of what was happening during the course of the subsequent agreements. The Board accepts the submission made on behalf of the union that, having found that the contract workers were deemed to be employed by the employer, it would have made no sense for the Industrial Court to restrict the consequential relief to an agreement in the past and not also order that more recent agreements be applied as well.

Moreover, by section 10(1)(b) of the Act (quoted in para 22 above) the court is empowered *"in relation to any matter before it"* to *"make an order or award ... relating to any or all of the matters in dispute"*;

and, by section 10(3)(b) (also quoted), it is empowered, "*notwithstanding anything in this Act or in any other rule of law to the contrary*", to "*act in accordance with equity, good conscience and the substantial merits of the case before it, having regard to the principles and practices of good industrial relations*".

In all the circumstances the Board accepts the submission that it was unreasonable to expect the union to lodge a separate application for the contract workers to be deemed to be employed under labour only contracts and for an order that the then current collective agreement applied to them, whenever a new collective agreement came into force.

That said, it is important to note that the order made by the court and upheld by the Court of Appeal was in broad terms. It merely obliges the employer to apply "the appropriate collective agreement(s)". How they apply will depend on the facts of the particular case.

As to the third reason, it is true that a claim for interest was not made by the union. However, there is no doubt that the court has power to award interest. Although there is no provision in the Act expressly empowering the court to award interest on damages, section 25 of the Supreme Court of Judicature Act, Chapter 4:01, provides, so far as relevant:-

> *"25. In any proceedings tried in any court of record for recovery of any debt or damages, the court may, if it thinks fit, order that there shall be included in the sum for which judgment is given interest at such rate as it thinks fit on the whole or any part of the debt or damages for the whole or any part of the period between the date when the cause of action arose and the date of the judgment, ..."*

There are a number of English cases which have held that it is not necessary to plead a claim for interest, notably Riches v Westminster Bank Ltd [1943] 2 All ER 725 (CA). In De Souza v Trinidad Transport Enterprises Ltd and Nanan (No 2) (1971) 18 WIR 150, at 152 Hassanali J (relying on Riches) rejected a submission that the court ought not to exercise its power under section 25 of the Supreme Court of Judicature Act because the claim for interest was not pleaded.

The Board accepts those submissions, essentially for the reasons given on behalf of the union. In the opinion of the Board the union did not abandon the claim it made in para 6 of the Statement of Evidence and Arguments, not only for an order "declaring ISPAT to be the employer of the said contract workers under labour only contracts" but also, critically, for an order declaring "that ISPAT is bound to apply the collective agreement in relation to them".

The Board further rejects the submission made on behalf of the appellant, for substantially the same reasons, that the court had no jurisdiction under section 10(3)(b) of the Act (quoted at para 22 above). To the extent that the Industrial Court relied on section 10(3) (b), the appellant submits that "as is apparent from its opening ('the court in the exercise of its powers shall') this does not found any self-standing jurisdiction or power to make orders which it cannot otherwise make: it is merely a direction as to how its powers arising under other provisions are to be exercised. There must be some trade dispute or "any other matter brought before it, pursuant to the provisions of the Act" [see section 7(1) (a) and (e) quoted at para 22 above] for its jurisdiction to arise. ... As there was none, there was no jurisdiction to make the award it purported to make in relation to collective agreements."

The union alleged in its Statement of Evidence and Arguments that the contract workers were performing bargaining unit work but that the collective agreement was not being applied to them, and asked for an order that it be so applied. The appellant's response was that the contract workers were not its employees and it does not now dispute that the collective agreement was not being applied to them.

Section 16(2) of the Act specifically permits any trade union or employer to apply to the court for the determination of a "difference as to the ... application of the provisions of a registered collective agreement"...The union did not expressly invoke the Industrial Court's jurisdiction under section 16(2). But the court is mandated by section 9(1) of the Act (quoted in para 22 above) to act without regard to legal technicalities.

The Court of Appeal was therefore right to find (at p 11):-

> "The mere fact that section 16(2) was not expressly invoked cannot detract from the fact that what the respondent was seeking was an application of the registered collective agreement, which the court has the express jurisdiction to deal with under section 16(2) of the Act."

It is submitted on behalf of the union that in both instances there was, therefore, clearly a "matter" which could properly be brought before the court for its determination. The Board accepts that submission.

The natural justice point

The appellant puts the point in this way. It submits that at the very least it was not unreasonable for it to assume from the way the case unfolded, as described above, that the case was limited simply to the section 2(4) (b) issue. As a result, it is submitted, if the court was thinking of making an order going beyond that issue, which would have important financial consequences, both by reason of the application of "appropriate" collective agreements, and the provision for interest, it was essential that it should give the appellant the opportunity to comment on these points; and the Court of Appeal should have so held. Any other approach was fundamentally unfair.

The appellant's case under this heading assumes that the case had become limited to the issue of the applicability of section 2(4) (b), either because the union had abandoned its claim to have the collective agreement applied or that there was an agreement between counsel to this effect. The Board has already given its reasons for rejecting this submission. The Board is not persuaded that there has been any breach of natural justice here.

The defunct collective agreements point

It is submitted on behalf of the employer that to the extent that the order of the Industrial Court required the appellant to apply collective agreements which, at the date when the judgment was delivered on 31 July 2009, had already expired or, as it says, were defunct, the Industrial Court lacked jurisdiction to do so since the collective agreements had become unenforceable upon expiry.

The provisions of an expired or defunct collective agreement can only be enforced by way of the trade dispute procedure in Part V and that procedure was not invoked in this case.

By way of response, it is submitted on behalf of the union that it was open to the appellant to object to the jurisdiction of the court in respect of expired agreements.

Throughout the many years of the proceedings no objection was taken to the jurisdiction of the court, notwithstanding the fact that, as the Board has held, the union did not withdraw its claim for a declaration that the appellant was bound to apply "the collective agreement" in relation to the contract workers. Moreover, as explained above, the debate extended over the events of many years without any objection to its jurisdiction to do so. In these circumstances the Board concludes that the Court of Appeal was not (or would not have been) competent to entertain an appeal on the ground of want of jurisdiction by reason of the express terms of section 18(2) (a), which is quoted at para 23 above.

In these circumstances it is not necessary to resolve the issue of jurisdiction. However, as at present advised, the Board is of the opinion that, where an alleged breach of a registered collective agreement occurred within the currency of the agreement, the court has jurisdiction to determine an issue under section 16(2) of the Act after the agreement had expired. So far as the Board is aware, there is no decided case to the contrary.

Conclusion

For these reasons the Board concludes that the appeal must be dismissed.

However, it is important to note that this conclusion does not preclude all future negotiations arising out of the order of the Industrial Court. The union correctly accepts in para 58 of its case, that, in any event, the order which the court has made must, necessarily, ultimately involve discussions between the parties concerning the ways in which the collective agreements are to be applied to the contract workers. There will be negotiations as to the sums due. Moreover there may be scope for debate as to what is meant by the expression "the appropriate collective agreement(s)" in the order. For example, it might be said that the employer was entitled to set off benefits which the employees' contractors gave them, which differed from and were better than their employees' collective terms, against sums due under the collective contracts. Any difference or dispute between the parties would thereafter be resolved through the normal channels available for such resolution under the Act. They include the case where any question arises as to the interpretation

> of any order of the court, in which case express provision is made for an application to the court under section 16(1) of the Act quoted in para 23 above." [207]

The main take away from this case is the ruling of H H Rabathaly that:-

> "What is emerging more and more is a triangular relationship between a worker, an employer and a third party who is usually a service provider. The question really is what is the nature of the contractual relationship which the worker has with the Labour Service Provider.
>
> Also whether there is a merging or overlap of the contractual relationship between the employer and the Labour Service Provider on the one hand and the employee on the other.
>
> These issues are becoming more relevant as the employment contract continues to evolve:-
>
> That being the case it is consequently right and proper that good industrial relations principles and practices be observed, and in accordance with Section 10 (3) (b) of the Act the Company (ISPAT) is hereby ordered to apply the appropriate collective agreement(s) to these workers. Any monies due and payable to the workers concerned shall attract interest at the rate of 8% from the due date to the date of payment, which should not be later than 30th September, 2009." [208]

207 Privy Council Appeal No. 0087 of 2013 Arcelormittal Point Lisas Limited (formerly Caribbean Ispat Limited) v Steel Workers' Union of Trinidad and Tobago [2015] UKPC 36.

208 Application No. 2 of 1998 Steel Workers' Union of Trinidad and Tobago and Caribbean Ispat Limited.

CONCLUSION

> "The world of work is undergoing transformative change that is unprecedented in its pace and scope, as a result of technological innovations, demographic shifts and climate change. Jobs will be lost in some sectors, but others will be created. It is up to us all to meet those challenges and to seize the opportunities. And we need to do so with the conviction that the future of work is not predetermined.
>
> We have a compass to guide us the very principles of the ILO that tell us there can be no peace without social justice, that labour is not a commodity, that freedom of expression and association are essential to sustained progress and that poverty anywhere is to threat to prosperity everywhere."[209]

It is reasonable to conclude that Labour Courts insist on equity and fairness in the workplace and on practices which promote the just and fair resolution of disputes. This can only be achieved by the robust application and enforcement of the laws, policies and the adherence to the principles and practice of good industrial relations in the labour market.

As stated before, labour is at the heart of a society's human and socioeconomic development. Economic policies which engender social and economic development and social peace can only be achieved and sustained with the promotion of inclusiveness, equity, equality and decent work in the labour market. Therefore, the application of international labour standards and the principles and practice of good industrial relations must be the linchpin of all workplace policies including those which are related to fixed-

209 Working for Peace and Social Justice; An ILO Publication.

term contracts, collective bargaining, management prerogatives, retrenchment, layoffs and dismissal.

Since 1919, the ILO has assisted its 187 Member States to build just and fair societies by promoting and encouraging the adoption of International Labour Standards to guide laws and policies in the world of work. These standards have also been adopted by Labour Courts and Tribunals globally as international best practice and they are integral to the practice of good industrial relations. Indeed, they go a long way in the achievement of the sustainable developmental goals, the creation of quality jobs with decent wages, good working conditions in an environment of *"freedom, security and dignity"*.

BIBLIOGRAPHY

<u>**Books:-**</u>

An Introduction to Legal Reasoning, Edward Levi, University of Chicago Press, 1949

Commonwealth Caribbean Employment and Labour Law, Natalie Corthesy and Carla-Anne Harris-Roper

Contracts of Employment Seventh Edition, Butterworth, London, Edinburgh, Dublin, 1997

Employment Law, Sixth Edition (6th), Gwyneth Pitt, Sweet & Maxwell Ltd. 2000

Halsbury's Laws of England, Fourth Edition

Halsbury's Laws of England, Fifth Edition

Labour Law, Sixth Edition, S Deakin & G Morris, Hart Publishing

Legislative Drafting for Democratic Social Change, A Seidman, R Seidman & N Abeysekere, 2001

Selwyn's Law of Employment, 18th Edition, Oxford University Press, 2014

Smith & Wood's Employment Law, Ninth Edition, Oxford University Press, London, 2008

The Evolution of Labour Relations Legislation in Trinidad and Tobago, C. Okpaluba, 1980

What's Right with Rights, M. Freeman, Int. J.L.C., 2006

Publications:-

E Goveia Slave Society in the British Leeward Islands at the End of the Eighteenth Century, Westport, Connecticut: Greenwood Press, 1980

Human Resources Management - Implications for Teaching, Theory, Research and Practice in Industrial Relations, John Purcell (Paper presented at the Ninth World Congress of the International Industrial Relations Association, August–September, 1992, Sydney, Australia)

ILO: General Survey concerning labour relations and collective bargaining in the public service (Third item on the agenda: Information and reports on the application of Conventions and Recommendations Report of the Committee of Experts on the Application of Conventions and Recommendations (articles 19, 22 and 35 of the Constitution) Report III (Part 1B), 2013)

M G Smith Culture, Class and Race in the Commonwealth Caribbean, Mona, Jamaica: Department of Extra-Mural Studies, UWI 1984

Working for Peace and Social Justice; an ILO Publication

Speeches:-

Local Judicial Perspective: Management Prerogative: Concept Or Reality? 16th October, 2013 delivered by Her Honour Mrs. Deborah Thomas-Felix President of the Industrial Court of Trinidad and Tobago at the ECA/ESC Conference.

Special Sitting Opening of the Industrial Court for the 2020/2021 Law Term Address by Her Honour Mrs. Deborah Thomas-Felix President Industrial Court of Trinidad and Tobago, 17th September, 2020

The Industrial Court's Meet with the Court Symposium, Dr. Leighton M. Jackson, 16th May, 2015.

Websites:-

COVID-19 leads to massive labour income losses worldwide (last visited on 16th December, 2021) https://www.ilo.org/global/about-the-ilo/newsroom/news/WCMS_755875/lang--en/index.htm

International Labour Office: Decent Work and the 2030 Agenda for Sustainable Development, (undated), 19 pp. (last visited on 7th December, 2020)
https://www.ilo.org/wcmsp5/groups/public/—europe/—ro-geneva/—ilo-lisbon/documents/event/wcms_667247.pdf

United Nations: Transforming our world: the 2030 Agenda for Sustainable Development (Resolution A/RES/70/1 adopted by the General Assembly on 25th September, 2015), 35 pp. (last visited on 7th December, 2020)
https://www.un.org/ga/search/view_doc.asp?symbol=A/RES/70/1&Lang=E

United Nations: The Sustainable Development Goals (last visited on 7th December, 2020)
https://www.un.org/sustainabledevelopment/development-agenda/

Made in the USA
Middletown, DE
04 November 2026

36552536R00195